Fathers Matter

Celia Conrad

The **Essential** guide to contact on separation and divorce

Fathers Matter

3rd Edition (Fully Revised and Expanded)

Celia Conrad

Creative Communications

Dedication
In memory of my beloved father
And for loving fathers everywhere

Published by Creative Communications
Suite 327, 28 Old Brompton Road, London SW7 3SS
ISBN 978 0 9546233 57

Further copies of this publication are obtainable from **www.fathersmatter.co.uk** and www.creativecom.co.uk

Designed by Andrew Dorman   www.andrewdorman.co.uk

Printed and bound by CPI Group (UK) Ltd, Croydon, CR0 4YY

Acknowledgments

Once again I would like to thank all the people, who, in speaking to me about their problems, have both encouraged and enabled me to write this book, but who perforce must remain nameless – they know who they are. I would also like to thank everyone who has written to me and/or contacted me with their positive comments about the first and second editions.

Thanks to Andrew Dorman for his cover design and layout and to CPI for their speed of production; and to my family for their unstinting encouragement and support. Finally, special thanks to Sir Bob Geldof for his comments on the first edition of this book and to the Rt. Hon. Iain Duncan Smith MP, while in Opposition, for his positive comments on the second edition and for asking me to be a Consultee and to give my comments on 'Contact & Conflict' for the Policy Report by the Family Law Review *Every Family Matters* produced by the Centre for Social Justice in July 2009.

Contents

Table of Abbreviations 22

Comments on the First Edition by Sir Bob Geldof 23

Preface to the Third Edition 24

Preface to the Second Edition 26

Preface to the First Edition 27

Introduction – Revised January 2013 29

Part I   Family matters 32

Chapter 1   **The importance of fathers** 32
A father's role 32
How the family unit has changed 32
The contribution a father has to make 33

Maintaining a role 34
Benefits for the children 34
What about cases where the father does not maintain a role? 34

Fathers have feelings too 35
The emotional roller coaster 35
A father's predicament: 36
   How fathers can help themselves 36
   What about when matters become really bad? 37

Chapter 2   **Resolving issues amicably** 38
Reducing conflict 38
The cycle of conflict 38
   How the cycle of conflict is compounded 38
   Why fathers get caught up in this cycle of conflict 38
   Breaking the cycle 39

Alternative Dispute Resolution (ADR) 39
Forms of Dispute Resolution Services (DRS) formerly ADR 40
Counselling 40
   Purpose 40
   Forms of counselling 40
Mediation 41
   Definition 41
   What the process involves 41
   Can a mediator really help with children issues? 41

Not a substitute for legal advice 42
How much does mediation cost and how long does it take? 42
How to find a good mediator 42
Will the children have to attend mediation sessions? 43
Positive benefits of mediation 43
What is a Mediation Assessment Information Meeting (MIAM)? 44
The debate on compulsory mediation 46
Current developments and reform 46
Collaborative Law 47
Family Group Conferences (FGCs) 47
Current developments and reform 48
Parenting Plans & Agreements 48
Current developments and reform 48
Avoiding the legal process but using legal advice 49
Clarification of legal position 49
Using the advice constructively 49

Chapter 3   **What about the children?** 50
Telling the children 50
When, where and how 50

How the children might react 50
Relevant factors 50
General reactions 51
General symptoms for children of all ages 51
Reactions at different ages 52
How the parents' relationship impacts on the children's reaction 52

What a father can do to help 53
Put them first 53
Be alert to signs of distress 53

Things a father should *not* do 54

The children's wishes 54
A child's perspective 54
What are the children thinking? 54
Needs and requirements in light of age and understanding 55

Stepchildren 55
The significance for them of the breakdown of the second relationship 55

Recent developments and reform: the child's voice 55

Chapter 4   **Post-separation fatherhood** 57
The post split father/child relationship 57
What is going to happen? 57

Carving out a new role   57

Choices for fathers   58
Giving up   58
Hanging in there   58
Reinventing a role for father   58

Making the most of contact: pointers for fathers   59
Make contact as normal as possible   59
   Keeping the children entertained   59
   Disciplining the children   59
   Avoid making any negative comments about their mother   59
   Be prepared to give a little   60
   Do not pressurize the children   60
Dealing with problems   60
   Reasons for resisting contact   60
   What to do if the children won't see their father   60

External influences: dealing with new partners   61
Adjustments to be made   61
Introducing the children to a new girlfriend   61
The mother's new partner and its relevance to the father/children
   relationship   62
And another thing…   62
Mother moving away   63

Chapter 5   **Friend or foe: dealing with your ex**   64
Working together   64
Acting in the children's best interests   64
Facilitating contact   64
   Contact schedules   64

The parental relationship   65

Parental interaction   65

What type of relationship do the parties have?   65
Friends   65
Formal acquaintances   66
Warring parties   66
Sworn enemies   66
Disconnected partnerships   67

Communicate to negotiate   67
It takes two…   67
Communicating effectively   67

Maternal gatekeeping 68
Sabotaging the father/child relationship 68
  What do fathers consider to be sabotage? 68
  Sabotage by mother or justifiable position? 69
  Examples of reasons for maternal sabotage provided by fathers 69
  A mother's justifiable concerns 70
  A final word... 71

Part II   **The law** 72

Chapter 6   **In brief: the law and legal system** 72
                 The law in outline 72
                 The Children Act 1989 72
                   Private law orders 72
                   Public law orders 73
                   Two further orders of significance for fathers... 73
                   Recent developments and reform: the child arrangements order 73
                   Underlying principles under the Children Act 74
                 How the court decides 74

                 The courts and court protocol 74
                 The courts 74
                   Jurisdiction 74
                   Which courts deal with children matters? 75
                   Which is the right court for my case? 75
                   Transferring cases between courts 77
                   Court layout and dress 77
                   Relevant court personnel 77
                   Court address 78
                 Recent developments and reform 78
                   Establishing a single Family Court for England and Wales 78
                   Family Procedure Rules (FPR) 2010 79
                   Consequences of failure to comply with FPR 2010 80
                   Court forms 80

                 The role of solicitors and barristers 81

                 The court process 82
                 General procedure 82
                 What is CAFCASS? 83
                 Current developments and reform 85

Chapter 7   **Your solicitor** 86
                 How do I find a good family solicitor? 86
                 Personal recommendation 86

Reputation 86
Law Society 86
The Solicitors Regulation Authority (SRA) 87
   The Solicitors' Code of Conduct 87
Resolution (formerly the Solicitors Family Law Association 'SFLA') 88
Memberships 88
   Collaborative lawyers 88

Other considerations which may affect the choice of solicitor 89
How much they cost 89
Case management 89
Personal qualities to look out for 90
   Affability 90
   Availability 90
   Ability 91
Characteristics to avoid 91
   Arrogance 91
   Aggression 91
   Antagonism 91

The solicitor/client relationship 92
Client Care under the SRA Code 2011 92
Giving and receiving advice 92
   Instructing the solicitor 92
   Seeking clarification 92
   Help to keep the costs down 92
Terms of business and costs 92
   The terms of business letter 92
   Complaints 93
   Payment of costs 93
   Costs queries 94
Orders for costs 94
   Costs assessments 95
   Wasted costs orders 95
Public funding of legal costs 96
   Family help 96
   Legal representation 97
   Legal Aid reform and the implications of the Legal Aid, Sentencing &
      Punishment of Offenders Act 2012 98

Chapter 8   **Paternity & Parentage** 99
            Paternity 99
            Starting point 99
               Presumption of legitimacy 99
               Where there is no presumption of legitimacy 99

Establishing Paternity   100
   A right to establish paternity?   100
   Application for a declaration of parentage under the Family Law Act
     1986   100
   Obtaining a declaration of parentage unde the Child Support Act s 27   100
Proving Paternity by scientific means   101
   Blood samples and DNA Testing   101
   Can I just apply for the court to order a DNA test?   101
   How will the court approach the case?   102
   My ex won't give a sample for DNA testing. What can the court do?   102
   The child's right to know who the biological father is   102
   Does a man have a right to know he's the biological father?   103
   Can a paternity case be re-opened now that DNA is available?   103

Parentage   104
Who's the father now? Altering the legal status   104
The Human Fertilisation & Embryology Act (HFEA) 2008   104
   Fathers and HFEA 2008   104
   Surrogacy   106
   Mothers, female parents and HFEA 2008   106
The Adoption & Children Act 2002   106
Does biological parentage matter?   106
   HFEA 2008 again...   106
   Biological and psychological parents   107
   When the sperm donor is known to the parties   107
   Legal implications   108

Chapter 9   **Parental responsibility**   109
   What is parental responsibility?   109
Married fathers and parental responsibility   109
Unmarried fathers and parental responsibility   109
   Registering the child's birth   109
   Reform of the birth registration process   110
   Other ways to acquire parental responsibility   110
The married stepfather and parental responsibility   111
   What are the ways a stepfather can acquire parental responsibility?   112
   Limitations   112
The unmarried stepfather and parental responsibility   112
Civil Partners and parental responsibility   112
Same-sex male cohabitees and parental responsibility   113
Sperm donors and parental responsibility   113
Current developments and reform in relation to fathers acquiring parental
   responsibility   113
Is parental responsibility really necessary?   114

Exercising parental responsibility 114

Can a father apply for parental responsibility where his child was not born in the UK and does not reside here? 115

Can a father lose parental responsibility? 115

What happens if the father entrusts his children to the care of someone else? 116

When does parental responsibility come to an end? 116

Further developments and reform 117

Chapter 10 **Formalizing arrangements** 118

Child arrangements for divorcing fathers 118

What is meant by the term 'relevant children'? 118

How does the court know if the arrangements proposed are adequate? 118

How will the father find out what arrangements are being proposed? 119

If the judge does not approve the arrangements what will he do? 119

Child arrangements for unmarried fathers 120

Child arrangements for married stepfathers 120

Child arrangements for unmarried stepfathers 120

Child arrangements for Civil Partners 120

Child arrangements for same-sex male cohabitees 120

Current developments and reform 120

Deciding whether to make an application to the court 121

Considering the options 121

What are the objectives? 121

Chapter 11 **Key principles under the Children Act** 124

What factors will the court consider if an application for a s 8 order is made? 124

The welfare principle 124

How many legal presumptions are there under the Children Act 1989? 124

The difference between a legal presumption and judicial guidance 125

The welfare factors 125

The no-order principle 128

Where an order would definitely be made 128

Avoidance of delay 129

Chapter 12 **Preparing your case for court** 130

Automatic right to make an application or not? 130

Those with an automatic right to apply for any s 8 order   130
Those with an automatic right to apply for a residence or
    contact order   130
Those who need leave of the court to apply for a s 8 order   131
    Applying for leave to make a s 8 application   131

Commencing proceedings   132
Making an application   132
    Completing the application form   132
    What is form C1A?   132
    Parenting Plans   133
    Form FM1   134
    Issuing and serving the application   134
Tell me about the proceedings   135
What is the purpose of the First Hearing Dispute Resolution Appointment
    'FHDRA'?   136
The approach of the court at the First Hearing Dispute Resolution
    Appointment 'FHDRA'   136
    Conciliation and dispute resolution   136
    Safeguarding   137
    Consent orders   138
    Identification of issues and case management   138
    Welfare reports   139
    S 37 reports   140
    Expert evidence   140
    Witness statements   144
    Disclosure   144
    Wishes and feelings of the child   145
    The order   145
Further hearings and hearing dates   146
    Court bundles   147
    Time estimates   147
    The final hearing   147
    Judgment   148
    Post-judgment   148
How long will the order last for?   148

Other procedural concerns...   149
Applying to be joined as a party   149
What does it mean to make an application without notice?   149
Controlling further applications being made   150
Withdrawing the application   151
Recent developments and reform of the court process   151
    Safeguarding checks and a track system   151
    What about the FHDRA and judicial continuity at further hearings?   152

Chapter 13 **Public law** 153
  Implications for fathers with children taken into care 153
   Care Order 153
   Emergency Protection Order 153
   Supervision Orders 153
  Removing a child from its parent 153
  The local authority has taken the child into care but the father wants
   contact. Is he entitled? 154
  The Public law Protocol and Public law Outlines 155
  The Munro Review 155
  The Family Justice Review 2011 and Government Reform 155
   Delay, case management, timetabling and expert reports 155
   The role of the court and the local authority 156
   Alternatives to court 156
  Rights of children in care 157

Chapter 14 **Special consideration for the children** 158
  Children and s 8 proceedings 158
  A right to be heard 158
  The children's ascertainable wishes and feelings 158
  The child witness 160
   Competency of the child to give evidence 160
   Benefit v Burden 160
   Supporting and protecting children giving evidence 161
   Attending court 162
  Meeting the Judge 162
  Joining the child as a party 163
  Guardians and Next Friends 164
   The child as a party with a guardian or next friend 164
   The child as a party without a guardian/next friend 165
  Reform in this area 166

Chapter 15 **Litigants in person** 167
  Self-representation 167

  What is a McKenzie Friend? 167
  McKenzie Friends and court proceedings 168
  The documents which may be disclosed to a McKenzie Friend 169
  Other considerations 170
  Recent developments 171

Chapter 16 **Disclosure, Confidentiality, Publicity & Media Access** 172
  Disclosure & Confidentiality 172
  When disclosure must be made 172

Rules about what may be disclosed   172
Changes to the rules of disclosure in proceedings held in private   173
  Where Chapter 7 of Part 12 of the FPR 2010 and Practice Direction 12G
    applies   173

Publicity & Media Access   175
Background   175
Why all this secrecy in the family courts anyway when the starting point
  is open justice?   176
Access to family court proceedings: the general public and the media   176
  Access to court documents by the media   178
  Should the judgment be given in public?   178
  Publication of the judgment   179
  Reporting the proceedings   179
  The benefits of open justice...   181
Part II of the Children, Schools and Families Act 2010   182

Chapter 17   **Residence**   183
The question of residence   183
The primary carer   183
The non-resident father   184
  Current developments and reform   185
Applying for residence   185
  Considerations for the court   185
Shared residence   186
  The current legal position   186
  Proposed legislative change   188
  What fathers want   189
  Attitude of the courts   189

What are the implications of a residence order?   190
Name changes   191
  Child arrangements order and name changes   192
Removing a child from the jurisdiction   193
  Holidays or short periods   193
  Leaving the country permanently   194
  Relocation and shared residence   196
Recent developments and reform   197
  The Washington Declaration on International Family
    Relocation 2010   197
  Child arrangements order and relocation   197
  Moving within the jurisdiction   197

Chapter 18   **Contact**   199
             Reasonable contact   199
             What is reasonable contact?   199
             Existing approach   200
             The form of contract   200
                  Direct contact   201
                  Supported and supervised contact and Child Contact Centres   201
                  Indirect contract   202
                  Attaching conditions to contact   203
                  Interim contact   203
                  No contact at all   204

             Making contact work   204
             Applying to court to make or vary a contact order   205
                  Warning Notices   205
             Applying to the court to enforce the contact order   205
                  Children & Adoption Act 2006   206
                  • Measures to facilitate contact   206
                       Contact Activity Direction   206
                       Contact Activity Condition   207
                  • Measures to promote contact   207
                       Monitoring by CAFCASS   207
                       Family Assistance Order   207
                  • Measures to enforce contact   208
                       Enforcement Orders   208
                       Financial Compensation   209
                  Other enforcement powers of the court   209
                  • Enforcement by an Officer of the court   209
                  • Imprisonment, committal and fines   210
                  • Sequestration of assets   211
                  • Transfer of residence   211
             Current developments & proposed reform   211
                  Changes to contact – child arrangements order   213

Chapter 19   **Domestic violence and contact**   214
             What happens where there has been domestic violence?   214

             Background to domestic violence   215

             Family Procedure Rules (FPR) 2010 Practice Direction 12J   216
             Investigating Allegations of domestic violence and abuse   216
                  When should there be a fact-finding hearing?   217
                  What is a split hearing?   217
                  What happens if allegations are withdrawn before the hearing?   218
                  The fact-finding hearing   218

Orders to be made   218
Deciding issues of residence and contact where there has been domestic violence   218

Recent developments and reform   219

Chapter 20   **Emergency procedures**   221
Prohibited steps order   221
Where a prohibited steps order would be appropriate   221

Specific issue order   222
Where a specific issue order would be appropriate   222

Making an application for a prohibited steps order or specific issue order   222

Child abduction   223
Basics   223
Authorized removal or abduction?   223
Isn't child abduction kidnapping?   224
Preventative measures   224
   Port alert procedures   224
   Passports   225
Remedies   225
   Convention countries   225
   Non-convention countries   226
Information on child abduction   226
My child has been abducted to England from another country. What do I do?   226
Mediation in cases of international child abduction   227
Other procedures   227
   Missing children – Family Law Reform Act s 33   227
   Application for recovery of a child – Family Law Reform Act s 34   228
Recent developments and reform   228

Chapter 21   **Two further orders of relevance to fathers...**   229
Special guardianship order   229
What is the difference between guardianship and special guardianship?   229
When would special guardianship be suitable?   229
How does special guardianship work?   230
Who may apply to be a special guardian?   230
   Those entitled to apply   230
   Those not entitled to apply   230
   By order of the court   231
Making the application   231
   Notice to the local authority   231

The application itself 231
Who are the Respondents? 231
Which other interested parties must be notified? 232
How does the court decide? 232
What are special guardianship support services? 233
How long does an SGO last for? 233
    Varying or discharging an SGO without leave 233
    Varying or discharging and SGO with leave 233
    Varying or discharge of an SGO without an application 234
Special guardianship orders and Family assistance orders 234

Family assistance orders 234
What is a family assistance order? 234
Who may be named in the order? 234
Where a s 8 order is in force… 235
Is an FAO suitable for the case? 235
What happens when the FAO comes to an end? 235

Chapter 22   **Grandparents and the extended family** 236
    Contact scenarios 236
Contact subject to parental control 236
Post-separation contact 236
Is promotion of contact generally dependent upon the mother or not? 236
Other family members 237

**The current legal position for grandparents and members of the
    extended family** 237
Special Guardianship Orders (SGOs) 238
Is there a case for changing the law to accommodate grandparents and the
    extended family? 239
Recent developments & reform 240
    Leave to apply 240
    Child arrangements orders and grandparents 241
    Family Group Conferences 241

Chapter 23   **Appeals under the Children Act 1989** 242
    Making an appeal 242
Family Proceedings Court 242
County Court 242
High Court 243
Appeals to the Court of Appeal 243

The appeals procedure 243
Filing a notice of appeal 243
Grounds of appeal 244

Permission to appeal   244
Serving the notice of appeal   245
The appeal bundle   245
Skeleton argument   246
Transcripts & notes of judgment   246
Respondent's notice   246
Orders which may be made on appeal   246
   When an appeal will be allowed   247

Chapter 24   **Child Support**   248
   The Child Support Act 1991 and the Child Support Agency   248

   **The Child Maintenance and Other Payments Act 2008 (CMOPA) and
     C-MEC**   248

   Child maintenance and the DWP   249
   A new child maintenance system   249
   The existing child maintenance system   252
     Family Based Arrangement   252
     Payments through the CSA   253
     • The rates of pay   253
     • Calculation of net income   253
     • Shared care   254
     Payments through the court   254

   Contact & Child Support   255

   Maintenance and relocation   255
   Enforcing maintenance when the paying parent moves abroad   255

Chapter 25   **The Human Rights Act 1998 & The Children Act 1989**   257
   Implications of the Human Rights Act for fathers   257
   If a father makes an application under the Children Act what effect does
     the Human Rights Act have on the court's decision?   257
   Bringing a claim   258
     Can a father bring a claim?   258
     Who are victims and how does a victim bring a claim?   258
     Who can a claim be brought against?   258

   Which convention rights affect Family law and fathers' rights?   258
   Article 6: the right to a fair trial   258
   Article 8: the right to respect for private and family life   259
     Respect for private life   259
     Respect for family life   259
     What would be a justifiable interference into family life?   260
   Article 9: freedom of thought, conscience and religion   261

Article 14: prohibition of discrimination   261
Remedies for breach of rights   261
   Changing a decision   261
   Compensation   261
   Declarations of incompatibility   262

Contact & The Human Rights Act   262

Part III   **Reform**   263

Chapter 26   **Pressure for change**   263
          **The Final Report of the Family Justice Review and the Government's
            Response**   263

          Judicial proposals for modernization of family justice   264

          **Proposed legislation on the involvement of both parents in a
            child's life**   264
          Introduction   264
          Background to the current reforms   264
          The current reforms   267

Chapter 27   **A way forward**   269
          Shared care for 'fit' parents   269

          A look at what happens in another jurisdiction…   270

          Final thoughts   271

Appendix   **Some useful contacts and addresses**   274

Table of Abbreviations

ADR	Alternative Dispute Resolution
ATPO 2008	Allocation and Transfer of Proceedings Order 2008
CAFCASS	Children & Family Court Advisory Support Service
CAO	Child Arrangements Order
CFR	Court & Family Reporter
DRS	Dispute Resolution Services
FAO	Family Assistance Order
FHDRA	First Hearing Dispute Resolution Appointment
FGC	Family Group Conference
FPR 2010	Family Procedure Rules 2010
HFEA 2008	Human Fertilisation & Embryology Act 2008
MIAM	Mediation Assessment Information Meeting
PIP	Parents Information Programme
SGO	Special Guardianship Order

Comments on the First Edition by Bob Geldof KBE

'I wish this book had been around when I went through my contemptible experiences at the hands of the Family Courts. It would have helped explain what was happening to me. It could have been the clear, cool voice of knowledge, experience, understanding and sympathy that is necessary to take men through the grief and pain and loss of having their children taken from them simply on the basis of their being male – a very suspect condition if you're a father, at least in the blinkered, myopic, outdated and reactionary view of our legal hierarchy.

This book is a timely, invaluable guide around the many hurdles and obstructions the Courts will put in a man's way to stop him being a dad to his kids. Read it and learn. Then try and change things so that children may know their dad loves them even if the law does not.'

Bob Geldof KBE
July 2004

Preface to the Third Edition

Family law must constantly evolve and develop to meet the needs and requirements of our ever-changing society. The term 'family unit' has taken on a whole new meaning with all the different familial relationships and arrangements that now exist in our modern society – it is an unenviable task attempting to meet the needs and requirements of all those families and a constant challenge to anyone working within the family justice system, particularly as the system is much in need of reformation. Recognizing that reform to family law is critical, recent Governments have undertaken a series of in-depth consultations and reviews with the firm intention of introducing changes to alter completely the face of family law in England & Wales for the better.

The Final Report of the Family Justice Review Panel, chaired by David Norgrove, was published in November 2011. As part of its review, the Panel called for views on how the family justice system might be improved to create a more accessible and child focused system, and which enables families to settle their disputes without resorting to court proceedings. We consider the recommendations of the Family Justice Review Panel, and the Government's response to those recommendations throughout the course of this book.

We also consider recent developments affecting private law children proceedings, including the Family Procedure Rules (FPR) 2010 which came into force on 6 April 2011 and which now govern the practice and procedure to be followed in family proceedings in the High Court, County Courts and the Magistrates Court in England & Wales. The FPR 2010 has had an enormous impact on procedure. The Government has placed great emphasis on resolving disputes without resorting to court through alternative dispute resolution (ADR) and we look at the various forms of ADR including mediation in depth in Chapter 2. But the fact is that for there to be effective reform there must be sufficient resources and funding, and with the family justice system already hugely under-resourced where is this additional money to come from bearing in mind the enormous cuts to public funding, and the radical reform in the Legal Aid, Sentencing & Punishment of Offenders Act 2012 which will affect recipients of family legal aid? With cuts meaning that there will be next to no public funding for private law applications under the Children Act 1989 and therefore no access to legal representation for many, there will be significantly increased numbers of litigants in person who must receive due consideration from the Court. We consider the whole future of Legal Aid and the reduction in Public Funding for private Children Act matters in Chapter 7.

Since the second edition was published in March 2007 there have been a number of other developments. In May that year a new Ministry of Justice (MoJ) was established replacing the Department of Constitutional Affairs (DCA) with responsibility for policy on civil, criminal, family and the administrative justice system as well as the courts, tribunals, legal aid and constitutional reform. Family Court Hearings were opened to accredited media from 1 April 2009. The Supreme Court opened its doors on 1 October 2009. The Department for Children, Schools & Families became the Department for Education in 2010.

It is to be hoped that with a greater emphasis on out of court settlements more cases will settle. However, it is likely that the cases that do not settle will be the most intractable ones where there are high levels of conflict between the parties and which have little chance of resolution without court intervention. These parties will still be within the court system and they will need 'in court' resources and access to specialist legal advice but again that comes down to available resources. The whole area of enforcement of contact orders continues to be beset with difficulties and we look at the methods of promoting, facilitating and enforcing those orders in light of the implementation, in December 2008, of the provisions of the Children & Adoption Act relating to enforcement measures and the Government's latest proposals for reform. The heated debate on shared parenting grows ever hotter and we consider the recommendations of the Family Justice Review Panel, the Government's Response, the latest Government Consultation and proposals for legislative reform in Chapter 17 and Part III.

With more families where there is one parent who comes from overseas, applications to relocate, that is, for leave to remove a child from the jurisdiction, have increased. We look at developments in this area and what the future holds for fathers. We also consider child abduction and recent developments. In terms of paternity and parentage, The Human Fertilization & Embryology Act 2008 removed the law that required Doctors to consider a child's need for a father before referring a woman for IVF treatment. We look at the implications for biological fatherhood in Chapter 8.

As well as completing revising the second edition, this third edition includes separate chapters on paternity and parentage to take account of the Human Fertilization & Embryology Act 2008 and the development of new family relationships, parental responsibility, children (including a section on children giving evidence); grandparents and the extended family; litigants in person; Human Rights & the family; child support, disclosure, confidentiality, publicity and media access; and appeals, and expanded sections on alternative dispute resolution (ADR); contact and enforcement, domestic violence, shared residence, relocation and legal funding. Once again, mindful that there has been important case law over recent years I have included the case reference details for cases which might be of further assistance and finally, there is an appendix of some useful 'resources' and addresses at the back of this book.

Celia Conrad
January 2013

Preface to the Second Edition

Since the first edition was published in October 2003 there have been a number of developments in this area of family law. The law is increasingly having to expand and adapt to the different circumstances which may arise when parties separate and/or divorce to take account of the variety of 'family' relationships within our changing society. This is reflected by the introduction of both the Adoption & Children Act 2002 and the Civil Partnership Act 2004. A civil partner in a registered partnership is now able to acquire parental responsibility of his/her partner's child in the same way as a step-parent giving rights to single sex-partners. Gay and lesbian parents may adopt under the Adoption & Children Act 2002. Lesbian couples may have a child by donor insemination.

Of course relationships where one or either party already has children from one or more previous relationships are hardly new, but there is an increasing number of cases where the party applying for an order under the Children Act 1989 has no biological connection with the child or children who happen to be the subject of that application.

The difficulties of promoting, facilitating and enforcing contact between children and parents who do not live with them are ongoing. The Children & Adoption Act 2006 includes new measures to deal with this and we consider them in Part II. Over the past few years the Department of Constitutional Affairs (DCA), which replaced the Lord Chancellor's Department in June 2003, has produced a number of consultation papers to address key reforms in this area in response to direct criticisms of the family court system and mounting pressure for change from campaigners both within and outside the legal system.

In 2004 the DCA produced a Green Paper Parental Separation: Children's Needs & Responsibilities setting out its agenda for reform, following which the Constitutional Affairs Committee carried out an inquiry Family Justice: the operation of the Family Courts to consider the Government's proposals and to seek submissions from interested parties on the proposals. I myself submitted written evidence and attended one of the oral evidence sessions in January 2005 together with Tony Coe, the President of Equal Parenting Council and John Baker of Families need Fathers.

Following the enquiry the Government produced its report Next Steps setting out its agenda. We look at the reforms and proposed changes where appropriate throughout the course of this book. In Part III we review the whole issue of reform and contentious matters such as compulsory mediation and a statutory presumption of shared care.

As well as completely revising the first edition, this second edition has been expanded to include additional sections on paternity; civil partnerships; grandparents; the separate representation of children; litigants in person; disclosure, confidentiality and publicity; and appeals. Mindful that there has been important case law over recent years, I have included the case reference details for cases which might be of further interest. Finally, as before there is an appendix of some useful contacts and addresses at the back of the book.

Celia Conrad
February 2007

Preface to the First Edition

The idea for this book was conceived as long ago as 1999, while I was still working full time in private practice. One father, for whom my then firm was acting, asked me if I had considered writing a book to help address fathers' issues. After a chance encounter with a father in my local gym – my firm had ironically represented the mother – and to whom I subsequently spoke at length about his own predicament, I felt compelled to write this book.

The first draft was completed over two years ago at a time when, unfortunately, the whole issue of fathers' rights was still regarded by many as only a passing phase and I was told that there would be no interest in a book solely directed at fathers, as it would be too narrow and too controversial. This perception has persisted despite the fact that during this period of time there has been ever increasing media interest in the plight of fathers. Rarely a week has gone by without us reading or hearing about harrowing cases of fathers who have fought for but lost contact with their children, some of whom have been financially crippled in the process.

Frustrated by the lack of cohesion in this area and progress on their behalf, fathers' rights groups have been driven to take on the campaign for change themselves. This is no more evident than in the activities of Fathers4Justice, a civil rights group launched in December 2002 to support estranged fathers, which has gained enormous media coverage and aims to raise the public's awareness of the injustices fathers suffer and is pressing for change within the law.

The recent criticisms by fathers' rights groups of the judiciary, has sparked considerable debate. Are the courts biased towards fathers? Certainly, the majority of fathers who have been through the court process have no faith in it to produce an unbiased result. Their confidence in the legal system has already been undermined. A father is not interested in hearing his lawyer say to him at the end of a case, after he has expended thousands and thousands of pounds, that the result is very unfair and the legislation needs to be changed but there is nothing he can do about it because that is the law. This is not going to resolve the problem for the father and is regarded by many as 'a cop out' and does none other than to inflame an already heated situation.

Celia Conrad
October 2003

Fathers Matter: The essential guide to contact on separation and divorce

Introduction – Revised January 2013

The content of this book stemmed from a number of conversations I had with male clients during the course of their relationship break-up and in relation to their respective roles as fathers. Several clients told me that, on separating from their wives/partners, they searched the bookshelves in their public library and all the major bookstores in order to find some information for fathers going through a divorce, or who were 'splitting up' with their partner. The only guides they could find were for mothers.

Essentially what they were looking for was a user-friendly guide, which provided a thorough overview of the issues they now faced and addressed ways of dealing with those issues constructively. They indicated to me that they needed a comprehensive guide dealing with both the emotional impact on and legal implications of separation and divorce for fathers and their children. Although there were DIY divorce guides and books on child law, there were no specific guides relating to fathers' problems from a father's perspective. That is, to assist fathers with any queries, worries, and emotions – as well as the general confusion surrounding a divorce/relationship breakdown. Additionally, they wanted to have a better understanding of their legal position and the legal process as applicable to them. In short they wanted a practical handbook for fathers.

I have written this book for all loving fathers who wish to build and/or maintain healthy relationships with their children after separation and divorce. I hope that by reading this book they will be able to cope better with the breakdown of their relationship and the adjustments that have to be made by them and their children upon separation. The breakdown of any relationship is traumatic and a degree of anger and conflict between parties is likely at this time. But when a relationship comes to an end, and especially in the early stages when emotions are riding high, understandably the parties often cannot see the bigger picture and the bearing that the actions of today will have upon their relations tomorrow, and the impact this will have upon their children because it is clouded by an emotional haze. It is evident that how parties interact, and what steps they take to reduce conflict and to resolve the issues between them, not only has a major bearing on their future relationship but also on their children and in turn that relationship. Both parents need to work together for the benefit of their children and to act in their children's best interests. This is crucial.

A father who has been able to reach an amicable agreement with the mother probably does *not* need to read this book. This book is directed at fathers who want to reach an agreement with the mother of their children but for one reason or another cannot do so. Clearly it is preferable, and ultimately in the interests of all parties concerned, to avoid court proceedings; but the reality is that for many a father the possibility of ever reaching an agreement with the mother seems a totally unattainable goal. There is more and more emphasis now on directing parties away from the court process and proceedings and to make arrangements themselves, and there are cases where all that is required is intervention from an independent third party to guide, direct and assist the parents, to enable them to work through the issues so as to enable them to forge an agreement acceptable to them. But, both parents have to be fully committed to resolving the problem, and to finding a workable solution. Unfortunately, this is where the problems arise, as a lack of cohesion and compromise between the parties is one of the major stumbling blocks to reaching an agreement. Cases where there is high conflict between the parties generally will not be resolved between the parties themselves.

Independent third parties include counsellors, doctors, mediators and lawyers. Counsellors may be able to help with the emotional aspects; doctors with the symptoms of trauma and stress; mediators with clarification of the issues and assistance in putting them into perspective. A family lawyer has many hats. To a client on an emotional roller coaster, in the initial stages of a divorce or potentially heavily contested child application, a client may use their lawyer as a confidante, counsellor, emotional prop, punch bag, sounding board, listening post, psychologist as well as advisor. Many lawyers are also qualified mediators and some are also collaborative lawyers.

Seeking the advice of a lawyer over a child issue does not mean proceedings *must* be commenced or at least not immediately – unless there is an imminent threat of danger to the child or the possibility that he/she might be abducted. In this situation court proceedings will be the first resort, on the basis that urgent action is required, since delay could be detrimental to the child. But if a father is in any doubt as to his legal position he should seek legal advice because knowledge of the legalities of a particular situation may assist in dealings with the mother. The role of a lawyer, as advisor, is to advise clearly and constructively so that rash decisions – which a party might later come to regret when the consequences of those decisions come full circle – are avoided. Unfortunately, a complaint by many clients, male or female, is that it is the lawyers who all too often inflame the situation and are confrontational, aggressive, and litigious and add fuel to the flames. This in turn creates more conflict and is destructive.

Many of the fathers I have spoken to, who have taken legal action, told me that they did so reluctantly. The crux of the matter was that, although ideally they wanted to resolve questions relating to their children and avoid conflict, court applications and costs, they felt they had no other alternative as the contact arrangements proposed by the mother, or already in existence, were totally unacceptable to them. In some cases communication had broken down completely between the parties, or if they were still talking to each other they could not do so without arguing, and/or they were entrenched in their respective positions.

Compared with the number of children involved, the number of cases that reach a final court hearing is small because the majority of cases are compromised along the way. However, this does not mean that fathers are satisfied with the compromise reached and that they are 'getting a fair deal' from the legal system. In fact most of the fathers I have dealt with did not think they had been well served and had been 'squeezed' by it. A case might be compromised, for example, where a father wishes to protect his children from the 'fall out' of the proceedings and the adverse affect a court case may have on them, or where he gives up after receiving legal advice that his chances of success are next to nothing. Therefore, the fact that a matter is compromised is definitely not an indication of a positive outcome for either the father or his children.

The Children Act 1989 assumes that the parties will do their best to resolve differences by negotiation and cooperation. It introduced a non-intervention and no-order policy. This means that the court will only intervene and make an order where it would be better to make an order than no order at all. This is ironic. The fact is the law *only* works for parents who are able to act in the best interests of their children and reach an amicable agreement, because in that situation the law does not need to intervene at all. The problem arises when parents cannot agree and the law is used to try to resolve what they cannot. Reliance upon the legal system to deliver what fathers want often leaves them bitterly disappointed and totally disillusioned with the family justice system.

I did not write this book because I am pro fathers and anti mothers, but to highlight the areas of concern fathers expressly requested I address, to provide the information they need and to help raise their profile. In fact much of the material in this book is of relevance to both parents and anyone connected to a party in this situation, not just fathers. It has been my intention to set out the material in the book succinctly and coherently for those reading it; it is *not* intended to be a legal textbook.

I do not advocate (no pun intended) the use of solicitors in this book, but merely point out situations where it might be necessary to take legal advice. Having worked as a specialist family lawyer in private practice and, having listened to my clients and fathers in the course of my research, I have taken on board the concerns and criticisms raised against the legal profession, particularly solicitors, which is why there is a section dedicated to choosing one in the book. Mindful that there are an increasing number of fathers acting in person either through choice or out of necessity, due to cuts in legal aid, I have expanded the chapter on litigants in person and given helpful pointers throughout the text to assist those who may be representing themselves. Although this is not a legal textbook, this third edition is heavily footnoted as I feel it is very important that fathers, whether they are represented or not, have necessary reference material to hand when dealing with the legal profession and the judiciary.

Chapter 1
The importance of fathers

A father's role

The concept of the family, and the role of a father within it, has been defined and redefined over the centuries. Traditionally it was expected and accepted that the male's role, as husband and father, was to go out to work and to provide financially for the family. The female's role, as wife and mother, was to run the home and care for the children and to be the emotional crutch of the family. By virtue of the fact that fathers were the breadwinners, and not at home with their children, their financial contribution was regarded as more important than their emotional one. A mother's relationship is 'seen' to be closer and it has been assumed that women, by nature, are better suited to love and care for the children.

However, more women now have their own careers and therefore contribute financially to the family, sometimes equally or even more. The number of situations where fathers share the parenting duties with the mother has steadily increased. Where the father is self-employed and able to work around any child care arrangements he may even be the primary carer. This social change has been recognized; shared residence orders are made far more frequently by the courts than they were a decade ago when they were rare and only made in unusual circumstances. We examine this shift towards shared residence orders in detail in Chapter 17.

How the family unit has changed

That 'traditional' concept of the family has completely changed. The stereotypical division of a mother and father's roles does not match the reality of the modern family. In today's society many parties do not marry, almost 50% of children are born to cohabiting couples and there are more single mothers where no father is present at all. Data from National Statistics[1] reveals that in 2011 there were 17.9 million families in the UK and of these 12 million consisted of a family with or without children. The number of opposite sex cohabiting couple families increased from 2.1 million in 2001 to 2.9 million in 2011 and the number of dependent children living in opposite sex cohabiting couple families increased significantly from 1.3 million to 1.8 million over that same time period. Interestingly enough, 38% of cohabiting couple families had dependent children, the same percentage as married couple families. There were 2.0 million lone parents with dependent children in the UK in 2011. This figure stood at 1.7 million in 2001.

---

[1] Office for National Statistics. *Release: Families and Households, 2011 (Released: 19 January 2012).*

Of course with the advent of Civil Partnerships there are more families where both parents or one parent and his/her partner are of the same-sex and, with the introduction of the Human Fertilization & Embryology Act (HFEA) 2008 there are other ways in which parenthood may be conferred like surrogacy for example and this will have a bearing on family dynamics. We consider the whole issue of parentage in Chapter 8. What constitutes family life must be examined in light of the Human Rights Act 1998.

The definition of what makes up a family unit is now very wide but what is clear from the statistics is that some children will live in more than one family unit during their childhood without a father figure at all. We have a higher proportion of reconstituted families than ever where one family unit has been broken up on separation and divorce and then another one re-established, for example, on re-marriage or cohabitation with a new partner of the opposite sex or same-sex.

The contribution a father has to make

What is a father's contribution to contemporary family life supposed to be? There has been a shift on the financial front so you might expect that this would mean a shift on the emotional front in favour of fathers. The reality is that from an emotional point of view mothers are regarded differently from fathers and there is definitely a lack of agreement about a father's potential role in child-rearing. Mother Nature is a major factor and the maternal bond is a very strong and special one, but this does not mean that a father loves his child any less than a mother does or is incapable of loving his child as much.

There is no question that a father plays a pivotal role in his children's lives, and they in his. In fact, in 1998 the Government produced a consultation paper *Supporting Families* in which it was stated that fathers do have a crucial role to play in their children's upbringing. Fathers have a very positive contribution to make to their families both emotionally and financially. This role is no less important than the one mothers play, albeit the role is played out differently. A mother and father each have a significant contribution to make. They have different styles of parenting and different attributes and should complement one another. Parenthood should be a partnership. In the case of Re G[2] which we examine in detail in Chapter 8 when we look at parentage and the role of the biological as opposed to the psychological parent, Baroness Hale of Richmond referred to the various meanings of parent: the genetic parent – both the mother and the father; the gestational parent – the mother who conceives and bears the child; and the psychological parent – both the mother and father and any other party who provides 'for the child's needs, initially at the most basic level of feeding, nurturing, comforting and loving, and later at the more sophisticated level of guiding, socialising, educating and protecting.'

---

[2]   Re G (Children 2006 UKHL 43)

As she put it, in the majority of cases the natural mother combines all three and the natural father combines genetic and psychological parenthood but the contribution each parent makes is unique. Furthermore, in relation to the father, she stated that, 'In these days when more parents share the tasks of child rearing and breadwinning, his contribution is often much closer to that of the mother than it used to be; but there are still families which divide their tasks on more traditional lines, in which case his contribution will be different and its importance will often increase with the age of the child.'

So to what extent does all of this impact on a father's role with his child after a relationship split? How does this affect his role?

Maintaining a role

Benefits for the children

The fact that a loving father no longer lives with his children does not make him any less significant, nor does it mean he wishes to be uninvolved with them. In the majority of cases this could not be further from the truth. A devoted father strives to have contact with his children and to retain a strong and positive presence in their lives. It is only circumstances that have dictated that he no longer lives with them. A father who does not live with his children is known as the 'non-resident' parent, a term which in itself is a bone of contention for fathers.

These fathers feel they provide the important function of 'being there' for their children. Many do this by helping with homework, attending parents' evenings at school and taking children to and from school. They can offer an alternative home when the need arises. They usually provide an important base for their children and relish taking responsibility for them, which they may not have had until they have sole care of them.

Certainly it is easier for a father to build a strong relationship with his children where there is a harmonious relationship between the parents, but that does not mean that a father who has to overcome obstacles cannot maintain a role although it is considerably harder.

What about cases where the father does not maintain a role?

Where does this leave the children of one parent families or where fathers do not wish to be involved? Are we to believe that these children will not be as well-adjusted because they are denied that relationship? Many single parents will argue that this is not the case, and their children go on to do well at school and to form healthy relationships. Most of these children will have never known a father's presence. That may not be detrimental but it certainly does not mean that they would not have benefited from it.

It is of course a sad fact that not all fathers wish to have contact with their children. We hear complaints from fathers about mothers who do their best to frustrate contact but equally there are fathers who do not behave in a responsible manner. There are cases where a father, who despite repeated pleadings from the mother for him to visit, or even applications by the mother to the court for an order for him to have contact, still neglects his children.

The father may have left his partner for someone else or just disappeared at the end of the relationship and ceased to have contact with his children and then, after several years, decides he wishes to re-establish contact and wonders why the mother does not play ball. It is no surprise that in these circumstances a mother protests and is hostile if a father turns up demanding extensive contact and threatening her with court applications if she does not comply. On the other hand, for fathers who are consistent in their intentions and behave in a responsible manner towards their children there is no reason why contact should be denied. Cases of errant fathers must not be allowed to prejudice the cases of those fathers who are genuine.

We look in detail at fathers' post-separation relationship with their children in Chapter 4.

Fathers have feelings too

The emotional roller coaster

Fathers say that being separated from their children has a devastating effect on them. When they no longer see their children every day and/or their contact is limited or even prevented, they suffer a terrible sense of 'loss' and can feel helpless. Anyone who has lost someone very close to them only has to put themselves into a father's position and imagine his feelings in such circumstances. Men of course are not meant to be emotional – big men never cry. But they are and they do. Fathers are not immune to the emotional roller coaster. The emotions that emerge can come and go unpredictably, and they can feel up and then down and as if everything is out of control. They may experience feelings of grief, sadness, misery, desperation, desolation, isolation, rage, resentment, bitterness and hostility too. Sometimes the emotions are so overwhelming that fathers have suicidal thoughts. Sometimes they act on them.

I have seen fathers in a terrible emotional state and who have broken down in tears on the telephone, trying to come to terms with their situation. Numerous fathers have told me how heartbroken they were because they could not see their children every day. For fathers who are devoted to their children being separated from them is unbearable. A client who was a successful businessman said that the toughest decision he had ever had to make was in relation to his children. He felt emotional constantly but he was afraid of showing his true feelings because he believed it would be seen as a sign of weakness in the negotiations. It was not surprising he was feeling emotional because he genuinely loved his children and was upset about the effect the divorce was having on them. The point is fathers have feelings too.

A father's predicament

Fathers find themselves in a no-win situation. They do not think the legal system addresses these points and that it has little regard for how they feel when decisions are made relating to their children and that it is biased against them. Right or wrong that is the perception. Unable to reach an agreement with the mother and faced with battling against the establishment it is understandable why these fathers are under emotional stress. One father told me there were times when he felt like walking off the roof because he was so desperate about his situation, but the one thing which would always stop him taking that step was his love for his daughter.

A father often feels pushed right to the limit; desperate times may mean desperate measures. Some fathers take drastic action. Some fathers are so terrified of losing their children that they abduct them. While such action can never be condoned, there is a world of difference between a desperate father who just wants to spend time with his children and is driven to snatching them because he has not had any meaningful contact for months, and a father who abducts with malicious motive, who wants to punish the mother by taking her children away from her permanently and/or who poses a serious danger to the children.

There are some terrible cases where children have been abducted to a country with which the United Kingdom does not have a reciprocal agreement in respect of the abduction and return of children. These are known as non-convention countries as they do not comply with the Hague Convention which provides procedures for tracing children and their return. In any event, the consequences for a father who abducts are dire, because, if he is caught, he will have ruined any chances of meaningful contact with his child. This will be the case whatever the reason and ultimately it is the children who suffer the most. The issue of child abduction is addressed more fully in Chapter 20.

How fathers can help themselves

As matters progress, feelings change and the issues or challenges faced are also different. There are things a father can do to make it through:

- Look after himself. It helps to cope with the changes going on around him. Eating and sleeping are important. At times of stress people do not/cannot/forget to eat and have difficulty sleeping.
- Keep focused on what the objectives are but be realistic.
- Take a step back and think about the implications of any actions taken and avoid making decisions that he will later regret. Revenge tactics may seem a good idea at the time but often backfire and do not bring about desired results.
- Talk about his problems to someone he can trust if he can. It does not change things but it may make him feel better because holding emotions inside can exacerbate stress and illness.

- Take time out for himself. With so many changes going on in his life at this time he is likely to feel overloaded.
- Consider writing down his feelings. Some fathers keep diaries to vent their frustrations.

One of the questions fathers ask is how they are meant to feel. There probably is no right answer. We are all individuals and one father may react differently from another. It also depends upon the particular circumstances. However, the range of emotions referred to above is indicative of a father's reaction in the majority of cases.

What about when matters become really bad?
It is common for people going through emotional trauma to feel depressed and have problems concentrating on work and focusing on anything else, because nothing else matters. Many fathers who run their own businesses report a major downward turn in productivity, as they cannot focus due to the surrounding uncertainty. They are unable to commit time to the business because they are devoting so much time to personal matters. Many fathers in employment find it difficult to hold down their jobs when their emotional life is in chaos. On the other hand, some fathers bury themselves in their work as a means of dealing with the fact that their family has fallen apart.

One father told me that he found it very difficult to cope when he could not see his children. He became an emotional wreck. He had been taking sleeping tablets and anti-depressants and became dependent on them. He developed severe depression and was withdrawn. Fortunately, his family saw the warning signs and encouraged him to seek professional help. The support of his family and the qualified professionals helped him through. Others are not so lucky. They do not have that emotional support. Alone and depressed they become dependent on medications, other drugs or alcohol and unable to function without them. Sometimes it is all too much and the dreadful reality is that there are cases where fathers have committed suicide because they have not been allowed to see their children. The tragedy is that, on the face of it, these were fathers who appeared to be 'coping'. I was contacted by a grandmother whose son set fire to himself because he had been refused contact for nearly two years with his not yet three year old daughter. We rarely hear of these terrible cases though and this is an issue that must be addressed.

Chapter 2
Resolving issues amicably

Reducing conflict

How can parents resolve issues in relation to their children when they are at loggerheads? In the Introduction we looked briefly at how they deal with conflict and handle their relationship and why this has a major bearing on the way they resolve issues generally, including matters relating to their children. We now examine this more closely. We consider the on-going parental relationship in Chapter 4.

The cycle of conflict

In any relationship each person is constantly reacting to the other. We may not think about this consciously but this is what happens. If someone is judgmental and critical towards a person how he/she reacts will be very different from how he/she reacts if someone is pleasant and full of praise for him/her. In the first instance he/she is more likely to respond well to the person, unless he/she has reason to suspect that there is a hidden agenda behind the display of warmth. Either way what is happening is that each person is determining the other's reaction. Put this in the divorce/relationship breakdown/contact context where there is an explosion of emotions, when parties are most likely to be feeling anger, hurt, guilt, regret, hate, fear and lash out at the other party. What happens then? It creates conflict.

How the cycle of conflict is compounded
Sometimes we feel that the only way to resolve something in our favour is to fight for it. If we fight enough we will achieve the desired result, so we believe, and the other party will back down. That may happen sometimes but generally what happens is the opposite. The more we fight someone the more of a threat we become to them and they fight back harder, and this in turn comes back on to us; there is a cycle of conflict. This is all too apparent in the father versus mother context.

Why fathers get caught up in this cycle of conflict
I asked a number of fathers why they fought so hard for contact. The answer was unequivocal: fear of losing their children. The problem that many fathers have is that on separation they are invariably the ones to leave the family home so they immediately lose continuity of contact with their children. A father does not start on an equal footing with a mother. He is on the back foot.

If the child is an infant then the contact is more likely to be limited, as he/she will stay with the mother unless the mother has a particularly good arrangement with the father and allows the child to stay with him. If the father moves into rented accommodation, it may be unsuitable for the children to stay there and other less satisfactory arrangements may have to be made.

Sometimes this means that a father will be unable to have as much contact as he would like with his children and, with relations in the family already strained as a result of the breakup, contact may be difficult. Fathers also fear about precedents for contact being set at these early stages. An agreement may not be possible and many fathers complain that they find it extremely difficult, next to impossible, to establish any regular pattern of contact with their children, so naturally they fight for it.

If fathers were guaranteed satisfactory contact then the fear of losing the children would evaporate and so would the need to fight for it. We look at the current legal position in Chapter 18. We know that court proceedings should be seen as a method of last resort and that parties should look for an amicable solution. If court proceedings are issued they are generally resolved in some sort of compromise which nobody finds satisfactory; the final solution ordered by a court could even be less satisfactory. But what are the alternatives for a father who has not seen his children for months or even years due to the recalcitrance of the mother?

Breaking the cycle

In order to agree, parties need to communicate, but if communication breaks down and barriers go up that becomes a remote possibility, particularly when every attempt to communicate turns into an argument. The ideal scenario would be to take a step back from the other person and let matters calm down, not to enter into tit-for-tat arguments and focus on ending the conflict for the sake of the children. In reality, in such an emotionally charged situation where both parties are entrenched in their positions, the likelihood of achieving this is minimal.

Alternative Dispute Resolution (ADR)

In many a case third party intervention can help parties resolve any 'dispute' between them and assist them in making workable arrangements post-separation for their children. In the past the emphasis has been on the parties deciding on whether to seek third party assistance for themselves, as it is more likely that parties will come to an agreement if it is one entered into voluntarily and where both parties are truly committed to the welfare of their children.

The policy now is actively to encourage parents to make their own parenting arrangements without court intervention and to steer them away from the court process where this is possible and appropriate – cases of child abduction, abuse and domestic violence have different criteria and we deal with these later. Assisting parties has a two pronged approach. First, to keep parties out of court, resources need to be available and the parties need to be aware of those resources so they can avail themselves of them to help them come to an agreement. Second, if parties do reach the stage of court proceedings, at the very beginning of the court process the judge needs to direct the parties to attempt ADR and away from court with a view to encouraging them to settle. It is worth noting that at any stage in the proceedings the court must consider whether ADR is appropriate and direct parties to attempt ADR.

The Final Report of the Family Justice Review made a number of recommendations 'to enable parties to resolve their disputes safely outside of court, where possible'[3] and the Government has accepted most of them. One of the recommendations that was accepted was to rebrand 'Alternative Dispute Resolution' as 'Dispute Resolution Services' and the term is now being used instead of ADR. We deal with this and all the recommendations in detail under current developments and reform below.

Forms of Dispute Resolution Services (DRS) formerly ADR

Counselling

Purpose
The purpose of counselling is to help the parties deal with the emotional side of their relationship. A party might attend counselling sessions for a number of reasons and those reasons vary from individual to individual.

Forms of counselling
There are different forms of counselling and different purposes for it. A father might want to find out if he can salvage his relationship and how he might do that. If his relationship cannot be saved then counselling may help him cope with his feelings, and to come to terms with the situation. After separation he may seek counselling to enable him to deal with all the changes that are happening in his personal life. This includes the adjustments that have been enforced upon him in terms of his relationships with his ex, his children and any new partners on both sides. He may also want help in dealing with issues raised by other members of his family.

When people think of marriage guidance they think of Relate. Relate does not just provide Marriage Guidance Services but an extensive range of counselling services. It has offices in most areas. Organizations such as the Institute of Family Therapy, Jewish Marriage Council and Catholic Marriage Advisory Council provide counselling to name but a few.

---

[3] Family Justice Review Final Report – November 2011, pp.35, 150-172.

Mediation

Definition

If parties feel they cannot negotiate themselves but still wish to, then they can attend mediation sessions. Mediation is not Marriage Guidance. It is not counselling. Originally the mediation process in the UK was called conciliation but the word mediation is now universally used (probably because conciliation could be confused with reconciliation, and that is not what mediation is for). In mediation it is assumed the marriage/relationship has broken down and the focus is on helping the parties resolve the issues between them arising out of separation and this includes their children.

What the process involves

Mediation is a process open to a couple, married or unmarried, and the aim of it is to assist the parties to work though the issues between them with a view to reaching a compromise. It does not matter whether they are legally represented or not, nor whether they have started any legal proceedings. In mediation both parties agree to the appointment of a neutral third party who is impartial and who has no 'authority' to make any decisions in respect of their issues. In other words, unlike a court that will make a decision binding upon them, the mediator as a neutral individual is there to help them work through their problems. This is the case whether it is in relation to separation, divorce, children issues, property and finances or any other issues that may be raised. The mediator's role is to help the parties to reach their own informed decisions by negotiation and without adjudication.

In mediation the parties control the decision-making. The mediator cannot bind them to any decision, but is there to manage and control the process, guide them through the issues and will chair the meetings.

Can a mediator really help with children issues?

As well as dealing with 'all issues' mediation, there is also child-focused mediation. Mediation is a popular way to try and sort out contact problems. The mediators who work in this area may have experience as counsellors, social workers, family therapists or family solicitors. If the mediation is child-focused the parties will concentrate on the children issues. The mediation tries to encourage co-operative parenting. They can discuss arrangements for the children, with whom they are to live, and how much time they should be spending with each parent, or whether they are to be looked after by another relative. A mediator can look at schooling and religion and encourage the parents to come to an agreement in relation to these points as well. It may be that the parents are poles apart on these issues, and in particular on the 'living' arrangements for the children, but if nothing else a mediator might be able to help with interim arrangements.

Not a substitute for legal advice

Mediation may be a way of avoiding litigation but it is not a substitute for taking independent legal advice. Parties may want to take advice about what they discussed at the mediation. At the same time, there is no point in going along to mediation sessions if they do not go there with an open mind and are not prepared to tackle the issues between them. They will be wasting everybody's time including their own. If parties have legal advisors they should keep them fully informed of any progress made, as any legal action to be taken may depend upon the outcome of the mediation.

How much does mediation cost and how long does it take?

Mediation sessions are normally one and a half hours each. When giving advice solicitors generally charge by the hour, so if they are mediators they will generally charge their hourly rate. Some mediators operate a sliding scale of fees and the amount paid depends upon how much a party can afford, depending upon his/her income. There are some voluntary organizations as well. If a party has virtually no money at all he/she may be entitled to public funding and can obtain assistance on this through the Community Legal Service (CLS). (We look at the cost of funding legal costs in Chapter 7.) The number of sessions will depend on the issues, but five or six sessions are not uncommon.

How to find a good mediator

If parties are going to proceed with mediation then they need to find a properly qualified mediator otherwise they cannot hope to derive any benefit from it. This is essential as only a properly trained and accredited mediator can provide a quality and meaningful service for them.

To find a mediator a party could contact, among other organizations:

- The College of Mediators, formerly the UK College of Family Mediators. It established and monitors best practice standards for family mediators and promotes practice guidance on a range of professional issues. It became the College of Mediators in September 2007. The idea was to open and broaden the membership to mediators from other fields.
- National Family Mediation, NFM, is a registered charity and offers 'not for profit' family mediation services to couples in England and Wales. NFM is a Founder Body of the the Family Mediation Council.
- Family Mediation Association (FMA). This is also a registered charity.
- The ADR Group. This is nationally and internationally renowned for offering mediation and other dispute resolution techniques.
- Resolution's (formerly The Solicitors Family Law Association) mediators are solicitors specializing in family law who have trained to be mediators. As solicitors they have an in depth knowledge of the legal process and may be able to assist the parties to make fair and sensible arrangements both in relation to their finances and children. Alternatively, they may prefer an independent mediator totally removed from the legal process. At the end of the day it is up to the parties.

- The Law Society represents solicitors in England and Wales. It has a Family Mediation Accreditation Scheme which means that all the solicitors who have been accredited by the Law Society will have had to meet stringent professional standards before being able to offer mediation services.
- Family Mediation Council. This is Ministry of Justice (MoJ) and Legal Services Commission (LSC) backed. It was launched in October 2007 to provide a structured voice for family mediation in the UK. If you are looking for a mediator then you should ensure that they are recognised by the Family Mediation Council. The ADR Group, College of Mediators, FMA, NFM, Resolution and the Law Society are all members and this ensures that their family mediators work to agreed minimum professional and training standards.
- Family Mediation Database. This is currently accessible through www.familymediationhelpline.co.uk and provides users with the details of the nearest accredited family mediation services.
- Information can also be obtained in local family courts and from the Community Legal Advice Helpline – CLA Direct on 0845 345 4345.

Full contact details of these organisations may be found in the Appendix.

Will the children have to attend mediation sessions?

In all cases where children are involved the mediator should have regard to their needs and interests. The law provides that a mediator should have arrangements designed to ensure that both parents are encouraged to consider 'whether and to what extent each child could be given the opportunity to express his or her wishes in the mediation.'

The mediator should consider whether and when the children may be directly involved in mediation. The mediator should not ordinarily invite children to be directly involved unless specifically trained to do so and is alive to issues such as confidentiality and the dynamics inherent in doing so.

It is extremely important that a mediator who wants to involve children in the mediation process should undertake specific training covering these issues.

Positive benefits of mediation

This is a 'conflict resolution' process, so in other words it is a means by which parties address and agree the issues between them and therefore avoid contested court proceedings. Even if they do not resolve all their issues, the fact that they have attempted to mediate is positive.

Mediation promotes co-operation between the parties, and looks at both their needs in the round rather than from just one side, so compromise is more likely. Furthermore, it creates options other than winning and losing which is generally how parties will perceive their case once the court battle lines are drawn up.

Because each party has a say in the mediated agreement, it tends to include more specific details and actually reflects both their wishes, whereas if the matter proceeds to court there will be an enforced result and sometimes neither party will achieve his/her aims. A mediated agreement may subsequently form the basis of an agreed order to be submitted to the court, that is, a consent order.

However, the subject matter of any negotiations forming part of the mediation process is privileged from disclosure in subsequent court proceedings. During the course of mediation sessions parties may discuss contact arrangements, but ultimately fail to come to an overall agreement and one party may decide to make an application to the court for a contact order. A party would *not* be able, within the context of those proceedings, to refer to what had been discussed at the mediation sessions. This is the same in terms of any other negotiations that take place with a view to settlement, more commonly known as without prejudice negotiations. This is important because if parties were afraid that anything they said could be used against them by the other party, they would never negotiate. Matters discussed in the mediation session are confidential except when a criminal offence is disclosed.

Mediation is thus a way of encouraging the parties to compromise and agree without putting them under pressure. It does not mean though that if parties do not manage to dot all the 'I's and cross all the 'T's at the mediation session that either of them should decide to change completely their position just to be awkward. It is not constructive, although it has been known to happen.

What is a Mediation Assessment Information Meeting (MIAM)?

Since 6 April 2011 parties will be 'expected to explore the scope for resolving their dispute through mediation before embarking on the court process.'[4] This is part of the Pre-Action Protocol. Separating couples need to 'assess' whether mediation would be a better way of resolving their disputes instead of going to court and will need to attend what is known as a Mediation and Information Assessment Meeting (MIAM). This is not a mediation session. It is a fact finding exercise to find out if mediation would be right for them.

It is actually only the party who wishes to apply to the court, the Applicant, who is obliged to attend subject to certain exceptions referred to below. He or she will need to find a family mediator. At the meeting the mediator has to explain what mediation has to offer and explore whether mediation would or would not be suitable. Prior to April 2011 there was no obligation on privately paying separating couples with children to attempt mediation. This was in direct contrast with couples in need of public funding who would be refused legal aid unless they attempted mediation.

The problem with all of this is that there is nothing to stop a party who has no intention of settling from attending a MIAM and, even if they attend mediation, then saying it has failed and proceeding to court anyway. Other parties may simply feel frustrated about the delay before they can actually make the application. There is also the question about funding the MIAM because unless a party is in receipt of public funding they will be expected to pay the costs of it. In any event, an

---

[4] Family Procedure Rules 2010, Practice Direction 3A.

Applicant is not expected to attend a MIAM where any of the following scenarios apply:

- The mediator decides that the case is not suitable for a MIAM.
- Where there has been an allegation of domestic violence between the parties and this has resulted in a police investigation or the issuing of civil proceedings within the last 12 months.
- If the parties are in agreement on the issues then they do not need to mediate.
- If the whereabouts of the other party are unknown to the Applicant.
- If the prospective application relates to family proceedings which are already in existence and ongoing.
- The prospective application is to be made without notice to the other party or it is urgent. An emergency application would be necessary, for example, if any delay by attending a MIAM would cause a risk of significant harm to the child.
- Social services are involved as a result of child protection concerns in respect of any child who would be the subject of the prospective application.
- The Applicant has contacted three mediators within fifteen miles of the Applicant's home and none is able to conduct a MIAM within fifteen days of being contacted in which event the Applicant does not have to attend.

If the Applicant subsequently makes an application to the court then he/she will have to file a completed Family Mediation Information and Assessment Form (Form FM1) confirming attendance at a MIAM or giving the reasons for non-attendance. At the first hearing the court will want to know whether mediation has been considered by the parties and in considering the conduct of the parties the court will take into account any failure to comply with the Pre-Action Protocol and may refer the parties to a meeting with a mediator before the proceedings continue further.[5] The court cannot make the parties mediate.

The Family Justice Review recommended that attendance at a MIAM and a Separated Parents Information Programme (PIP) should be required of anyone wishing to make a court application and that, although it cannot be compulsory for a prospective Respondent to attend a MIAM, he/she should be encouraged so to do.[6] A PIP is a programme specifically designed to improve parents' awareness of the potential impact their dispute is having on their children and to improve their relationship with each other. The idea is that it will enable them to reach an amicable agreement about their children's future care without involvement of the courts. Currently PIPs are only available once the parties have begun the court process.

It may well be that the Respondent will simply decline to take part in a MIAM or any dispute resolution service. The Government has indicated that it intends to make further statutory reform to reinforce the existing Pre-Action Protocol, and ensure that in *every* case evidence of attendance at an initial meeting with a

---

[5]   Practice Direction 3A, Part 4.1.
[6]   Family Justice Review Final Report – November 2011, p.35.

mediator at a MIAM via the completion of a form FM1 by the mediator is required before a case can proceed to court.[7] There would be exceptions, such as for domestic violence for example.

We look at the detailed recommendations for reform below.

The debate on compulsory mediation

There has been considerable debate about whether mediation should be compulsory or not. An argument against making it so is that it is supposed to be a voluntary process and it defeats the purpose of it if couples are required to attend compulsorily. Some believe that the threat of litigation is necessary to bring people to the negotiating table. Mediation is considered unsuitable where there is domestic violence or abuse and/or the imbalance between the parties is such that a mediator cannot hope to rebalance it.

Also it might not be appropriate at a particular stage and if it was compulsory would be likely to fail. That being said it should not be ruled out completely and may be suitable if circumstances change. In a case where the Saudi Arabian father had abducted the five children of the family from London to Riyadh four years earlier, and after the parties finally came to a judicially led mediated settlement, Mr Justice Thorpe in the Court of Appeal stated that there is, 'no case however conflicted which is not potentially open to successful mediation. This demonstrates how vital it is for there to be judicial supervision of the process of mediation.'[8]

Current developments and reform

There is concern that the Government regards Dispute Resolution Services and particularly mediation as the 'all cure' for parties in dispute. While DRS will work in many cases it will not work for everyone. The Government supports the view of the Family Justice Review Panel that, 'All mediation in which disputes about children are being discussed should be child centred – that is the welfare of children should be central to it.'[9] It has announced that the amount of public funding available for mediation will be increased from £15 million to £25 million. The Government proposes to make a number of reforms to the mediation and dispute resolution services[10] available for pre-court proceedings further to the recommendations of the Family Justice Review Panel:[11]

- The Government is looking into setting up an online information hub as well as a helpline offering support to all separating families.
- ADR is to be rebranded as Dispute Resolution Services (as discussed above).
- We have considered the proposed reforms the the Pre-Application Protocal and to MIAMs above.

---

[7] The Government Response to the Family Justice Review – *A system with children and families at its heart* – Ministry of Justice & Department for Education, February 2012, Cm 8273, p.72.
[8] Al Khatib v Masry 2004 EWCA Civ 1353 [2005] 1FLR 381.
[9] Family Justice Review Final Report – November 2011, para. 4.105.
[10] The Government Response to the Family Justice Review – *A system with children and families at its heart* – Ministry of Justice & Department for Education, February 2012, Cm 8273, pp.71-79.
[11] Family Justice Review Final Report – November 2011, pp.150-172.

- The Government recognises that in order to be able to assess and advise on which Dispute Resolution Services are appropriate for the parties, mediators need to be highly skilled, professionally trained and accredited individuals. Their professional judgment is key to weeding out cases unsuitable for mediation which includes cases of domestic violence.
- The exemptions in the Pre-Application Protocol will apply.
- The mediator who carried out the MIAM will need to track progress to make sure that one party is not stringing the matter out prior to any court application being made.
- In terms of finding an accredited mediator, the Government is considering how the Family Mediation Database can be improved and will work with the Family Mediation Council and encourage them to support their members and make their services better known to the public, and to work with both the Family Mediation Council and the Legal Services Commission to ensure that accreditation standards are harmonised and that mediators are able to access Continuing Professional Development. The Government has commissioned an independent review into the Family Mediation Council to consider its effectiveness and what changes might need to be implemented in terms of meeting the demands for the provision of mediation services.
- We considered form FM1 above.
- The Government recognizes the benefit of Parent Information Programmes (PIPs) which help parents focus on the needs of their children and to reach an agreement about arrangements for them. It is exploring how it can promote the take-up of such courses in the initial stages before the parties have become entrenched in their positions and court proceedings have been commenced. Currently PIPs are only available once parties are in the court process.
- Judges shall retain the power to order parents to attend PIPs where the judge deems it appropriate.

Collaborative Law

See Chapter 7.

Family Group Conferences (FGCs)

As the name suggests, FGCs promote the involvement of the extended family in decisions about the future plans concerning child arrangements. Although mainly used for public law local authority care cases, they are useful and used in private law cases where there is an extended family which is very involved with the child.

The Family Rights Group has developed a guide on the use of FGCs in public law proceedings endorsed by CAFCASS and the Family Justice Council.[12]

---

[12] Using Family Group Conferences for children who are or may become subject to public law proceedings (Family Rights Group 2008) available from www.frg.org.uk.

Current developments and reform

The Family Law Review recommended that the benefits of FGCs should be more widely recognised and their uses should be considered before proceedings and that more research is needed on how they can best be used, their benefits and cost. It also recommended that a pilot on the use of formal mediation approaches in public law proceedings should be established.[13]

In its response the Government agreed there would be advantages in researching what features of FGCs offer the greatest benefits[14] and in terms of establishing a pilot on formal mediation approaches in public law, it will identify areas in which formal mediation is currently used and work with the Family Mediation Council, Her Majesty's Courts & Tribunal Service (HMCTS), the Legal Services Commission, Local Authorities in England & Wales, Cafcass, Cafcass Cymru and other organisations with an interest in developing options for undertaking a pilot.[15]

Parenting Plans & Agreements

In 2008 the Department for Children Schools & Families (DCSF) introduced a 48 page document on Parenting Plans, *Putting your child first – A guide for separating parents* which is available from CAFCASS. The emphasis is on putting children's needs first and avoiding them being caught up in conflicts and arguments. Parents are required to think about all aspects of their children's lives and the arrangements they are making for them. There are tips on how best to support children through the transition and beyond, and a lot of 'dos' and 'don'ts' and suggestions on where to go for help and support. It points out that parents should be acting in the children's best interests and remembering that children are entitled to a relationship with both their parents. There is also a checklist of matters that the parents need to address to resolve short term and long term issues remembering that arrangements should be flexible to meet children's changing needs.

Current developments and reform

The Family Justice Review recommended that parents should be encouraged to develop a Parenting Agreement to set out the arrangements for the care of their children post-separation, and the Government and the judiciary should consider how a signed Parenting Agreement could have evidential weight in any subsequent parental dispute.[16] The focus should be on a child's day to day arrangements and care rather than on status in relation to residence or contact; the agreement would set out in advance what the ground rules were for the child's care in certain given

---

[13] Family Justice Review Final Report – November 2011, pp.33, 129 paras. 3.171, 3.176 & 3.177.

[14] The Government Response to the Family Justice Review – *A system with children and families at its heart* – Ministry of Justice & Department for Education, February 2012, Cm 8273, p.58.

[15] Ibid, p.65.

[16] Family Justice Review Final Report – November 2011, pp.34, 135 (para. 4.12) & 144 (paras. 4.49-4.50).

situations so that both parents know the position hopefully reducing the number of potentially disputed issues.[17]

The Government agrees that the use of parenting agreements is beneficial and its intention is that parents will be supported to reach such agreements through Dispute Resolution Services. In terms of a signed Parenting Agreement having evidential weight, the Government will need to determine how the court's procedures and powers would need to change to achieve this.[18]

Avoiding the legal process but using legal advice

Clarification of legal position

If a father is divorcing or separating then it is likely he will be taking legal advice in relation to that as well as financial matters, and this will include maintenance for the children, where they are to live and their schooling. The children are likely to be at the forefront of any dealings with his solicitor.

Using the advice constructively

Ideally the advice given should be used to help resolve the issues with the mother. Focusing on finding solutions which are positive to everybody is the key to resolving issues without conflict. The difference between the parties resolving conflict themselves and an adversarial position is that the former focuses on the need to find a solution and the latter on winning. At least that is how it is perceived. To the extent that they can do that the legal process becomes redundant and costs are reduced. But again, this is an ideal scenario and many parties never reach this stage because either or both of them simply have no intention of meeting the other half way.

We will look at the choice of solicitor in Part II.

---

[17] Ibid, pp.34, 144 para. 4.51.
[18] The Government Response to the Family Justice Review – *A system with children and families at its heart* – Ministry of Justice & Department for Education, February 2012, Cm 8273, p.68.

Chapter 3
What about the children?

Telling the children

When parents separate and the father leaves, a child's world is turned completely upside down. Everything changes and the established pattern of life no longer exists. Children are faced with an abrupt change in their lives, especially so if their father suddenly leaves without warning and they had no idea that there were any problems at home. It affects their sense of security.

When, where and how

Children should be kept informed about what is happening between their parents as, after all, the changes are affecting them too and more than may be apparent. How, when and where they are told about the divorce and what they are told and understand can have a significant effect on their reaction. The way this is done can either reduce or increase their worries and fears.

All of this depends upon a number of factors including their age and understanding. How a child aged three is told that 'daddy has left' will be different from telling a child aged thirteen; all children are different. They will have views, issues and wishes too. The way they convey them will depend upon their age and understanding.

Timing is of the essence. Parents do not want to break the news to the children suddenly but they must not delay for too long either. If the decision to separate is final then parents must make that clear, because otherwise the children may pursue a false hope that their parents will be reunited. Parents should tell their children jointly if that is possible. The children need to be assured at all times that they are loved. They need to be told this on an ongoing basis and shown that they will be loved whatever happens.

The children may worry about any changes. Parents need to be specific and realistic about practical changes in their children's lives. They may be changing home, school, and having to make new friends. If either parent has a new partner then they will have to deal with that new relationship too.

How the children might react

Relevant factors

It is very difficult to be exact about the impact of divorce/separation on a specific child although there has been much research into children's different reactions and there are a number of factors to consider:

- Their age and ability to understand, express and explain what they feel. Children's cognitive development varies.
- Gender. Girls react better than boys do apparently!
- Their nature.
- Their parents' relationship.
- Social background.

General reactions

Children may:

- Feel a terrible loss and miss the daily presence of their father in their life.
- Convince themselves that 'this is not happening' and go into a state of denial.
- Think that if they shut out the problem then it will simply go away.
- Feel very angry and lash out at the father for leaving them, believing that he has betrayed them and has 'broken' up the family.
- Become withdrawn and introverted.
- Believe that they have in some way contributed to the 'break up' and feel it is their fault that their father has left because he no longer loves them as a result of something they have done.

When children realize that the situation is not going to change, despite anything they say or do, they can become very depressed. Parents need to look out for behavioural and emotional changes in their children at this time. Depression is apparently one of the most common psychological/psychiatric disorders and children are not immune, particularly when their parents separate. Feeling sad or depressed is a normal reaction to a tragedy, change or a significant loss.

General symptoms for children of all ages

These symptoms vary from child to child. Some may display many symptoms and others only one or two. Here are examples to look out for, some of which have been provided by former clients. Once again this list is not exhaustive:

- Crying, feeling sad, helpless or hopeless.
- Feeling discouraged or worthless.
- Loss of interest or pleasure in activities they used to enjoy.
- Bad temper, irritability.
- General lethargy, fatigue and loss of energy nearly every day.
- Fearful, tense, anxious, withdrawn.
- A drop in performance at school.
- Disruptive/destructive behaviour.
- Mood swings.
- Imagined illnesses where there is no medical cause.

- Appetite variations.
- Changes in sleeping habits.
- Bedwetting.
- Nightmares.

Reactions at different ages

The symptoms referred to above straddle the age groups and much depends upon the social environment and background from which the children come. If the parents are dysfunctional themselves, then the likelihood is that the children will be too.

If parents separate when children are babies or infants, the children will not remember a time when their father lived with them so they do not suffer the effects of the separation itself. There will not have been a change in their routine or life so far as they are aware. As we have seen when we looked at the father's role, the majority of fathers do not have the general day to day care of babies and very small children/toddlers, so obviously the impact of the separation is not felt by these children in the same way as it is felt by the father. In these situations it is the father's ongoing role that becomes significant and more crucial. We touched on this in Chapter 1 and we look at this in depth in Chapter 4.

Small children between the age of about 5 and 10 are more likely to say they do not feel well or that they do not want to go to school. Their way of expressing they are not happy is by their actions rather than their words. They may become more aggressive and uncooperative or withdraw into themselves. For young children in particular there is a need for consistency in their lives and they are most seriously affected where it is lacking. The loss of daily contact with their father rocks their foundations. It makes them feel insecure. Little children may not fully understand that their parents have stopped loving each other and, even if they do grasp that point, they may think that their parents will stop loving them too. Or, as we saw above, they may think that their father is leaving because he does not love them any more. They may become mistrustful.

Children between the age of 11 and 16 are very aware of discord, situations and atmospheres. They can feel guilty about parental conflict especially if they believe they are the source of the conflict between their parents. Older children may feel deep sadness and loss. Their schoolwork may suffer and behavioural problems are common. As teenagers they may experiment with drugs and/or alcohol and generally go off the rails. Teenagers may have trouble with their own relationships and experience problems with self-esteem that will follow them into their adult life.

How the parents' relationship impacts on the children's reaction

The effects of the relationship breakdown on the children are determined during the relationship and depend on the level of conflict between the parents. After a split, parenting and raising children may be more difficult. If there were conflicts or disagreements over parenting before the split, those problems will usually be worse and not better afterwards. Interestingly enough, the termination of a destructive relationship will probably be beneficial to the children because it removes them from an antagonistic and stressful environment. For these children this will be a welcome release from an adversarial and dysfunctional home life, and better for their psychological well-being.

What a father can do to help

We have looked at ways to resolve issues amicably in Chapter 2 and we will look at the post-separation relationship in Chapter 4. As indicated above, the parents' relationship has a direct bearing upon how they handle and react to the needs of their children. How skilfully parents can handle or mishandle their interactions with each other, and the children, makes a difference. Recognizing that children have a right to expect to continue to have the love and support of, and to enjoy a happy relationship with, both parents is very positive.

Put them first

A father can really help his children by letting them know that, whatever happens, he will always be fully committed to them and will love them, listen to them, and take account of their views. Because children tend to feel insecure at this time it is crucial to keep commitments and promises made to them. If a father cannot do that he must explain to them why not, otherwise they are left feeling that he does not really care even though that is just not the case at all. What an adult may not consider to be a big issue may be a major issue for a child. Children's reactions will be influenced by a father's ability to provide continuing emotional support and this sense of security. The children will fare best knowing that both parents remain involved with them, even though the family no longer lives together.

Be alert to signs of distress

It is necessary to be alert to any signs of distress that they portray and to look out for warning signals. By carefully observing his children, a father will see if they have anxieties and concerns and can give them the attention they need. If there is cause for concern it helps if a father can talk to the mother or at least agree that help from a qualified health professional – generally the GP in the first instance – could be beneficial.

Things a father should *not* do

Most of these points apply to both parents, not just fathers.

- After the parties have separated, and while they sort out all the arrangements, they should try to avoid the children being caught in the crossfire.
- Long legal wrangles or pressure for the children to 'choose sides' can be particularly harmful to them and can add to their distress. Children should not be faced with having to choose which parent is the better parent.
- Do not talk about the children within their earshot.
- Do not argue in front of the children.
- Do not manipulate, pressure or lie in order to make the children take sides.
- Do not use the children as messengers or spies.
- Do not exclude the children's involvement with the other members of the family, for example grandparents.
- Do not withhold information from the other parent.
- Do not speak negatively about the other parent. When children hear negative remarks about one of their parents they internalize it. This holds true for remarks concerning step-parents, grandparents and extended family members and any other significant person in the children's lives.
- This is not a time to use the children as a sounding board or an emotional prop.
- Do not make it difficult for the children to express their feelings. They need to vent them. Do not tell them how they should feel.

The children's wishes

A child's perspective

Children have a different perspective from adults. It should never be assumed that because the children do not talk about their concerns that they do not have any. However, they do like to be consulted and for their views to be heard. What are their views? Have these been taken on board? It is important to listen to what they have to say.

What are the children thinking?

A father needs to take into account what the children really want when making arrangements and talk to them, but remember that children often feel torn as they have divided loyalties and because they do not want to hurt their mother, or for their father to be cross with them, may sit on the fence. The children may have concerns and expectations regarding, for example, a father's new partner. Children may feel resentful of a new partner if they see that partner as the reason why their father moved out. They may think that he loves his new partner more than them.

Needs and requirements in light of age and understanding

It is necessary to look at what the children's needs are and consider what the difficulties are for them. It is very stressful for a child to see one or either or both his/her parents emotionally stressed. Children, even very small ones, are sensitive to atmospheres and pick up on when something is wrong. This in turn impacts on them and they are affected.

Where mature children are involved it is important to listen to their views. Their views may have an important influence on the terms of what is being discussed between the parents and the end result.

In any settlement where there are dependent children, their needs and welfare will need to be reflected in the terms of any agreement and, of course, in contested proceedings the child's welfare is the first consideration of the court and will be treated as paramount.

Stepchildren

The significance for them of the breakdown of the second relationship

In Chapter 1 we looked at how the family unit is changing. In Chapter 4 we look at remarriage and the introduction of a child to a new partner and potential stepparent. But what about the scenario whereby children have already been through the natural parents marriage breakdown, and one or both of the parents remarry and then one or both those second relationships fail? This scenario is, unfortunately, quite common because over half divorced parents marry again and sadly second marriages are more likely to fail than first ones, and therefore there will be many stepchildren affected by these breakdowns.

The breakdown of the first relationship is going to be bad enough for the children, but if there is a second split the children will go through trauma again, especially if they have become attached to the step-parent. In this situation a child's loyalties may have been torn between the natural parents and now they may be torn even further.

All the factors we have looked at above apply here as well.

Recent developments and reform: the child's voice

There has been considerable debate about the 'pros' and 'cons' of children giving evidence and we look at these recent developments and the current situation in detail in Chapter 14. We also consider the circumstances where a child may be made a party to court proceedings, his/her separate representation and the rights of the child generally.

In terms of their involvement in the court process itself, many children complain that when their parents' separate they are given very little information about what is happening, and they are neither told nor really understand what is going on, particularly when proceedings are commenced. Many also feel frustrated that they are not really given the chance to speak about how they feel and say what they want. In short they do not believe they have a voice.

In its Final Report, the Family Justice Review emphasized that children's interests are central to the operation of the family justice system and that decisions should take the wishes of children into account and they should know what is happening and why. The Review made a number of recommendations[19] in relation to children and young people that the Government accepted:[20]

- It is recognized that reform is necessary to reduce the emotional strain on the children and young people at the centre of family disputes.
- In July 2012 the Government established the Family Justice Board (FJB). David Norgrove has been selected to Chair the FJB, following his Chairmanship of the Family Justice Review. Essentially the FJB's role will be to oversee the recommendations made by the Family Justice Review and their detailed implementation.
- A Young People's Board should be set up to support the work of the FJB.
- The new board is expected to find ways to support children and young people quickly and will develop age-appropriate information so children have a clear understanding of what might happen to them and will provide children with a range of ways in which they can make their views known.
- The Government is aware that professionals must have the necessary skills to support children and young people to express their views. Through developing national standards and guidelines, and drawing on the latest research and work of those already contributing in this area, the idea is that professionals will feel more confident in working directly with children and young people and in reflecting those children and young people's views.

---

[19] Family Justice Review Final Report - November 2011, pp.6, 26, 45-49.
[20] The Government Response to the Family Justice Review: *A system with children and families at its heart* – Ministry of Justice & Department for Education, February 2012, Cm 8273, pp.34-36.

Chapter 4
Post-separation fatherhood

The post split father/child relationship

What is going to happen?

What happens to the father/child relationship after the parents' relationship breaks down? How does he maintain a meaningful relationship with his children? We have already talked about the importance of a father and his role. We touched on maintaining that role in Chapter 1. Many fathers say that, post split, their fathering role is never quite the same, but that they do manage to carve out a satisfactory role for themselves. For those who do achieve continuity in the fathering role there are, at the very least, transitional problems and glitches along the way. Very few indeed can achieve a completely smooth transition. Others report that they are unable to maintain a role at all.

Carving out a new role?

In the next chapter we look at how and why the father's relationship with the mother is so important for maintaining quality contact with the children. Sustaining an active and supporting role in the children's lives is weighted against a father if the inter-parental relationship is poor, and this is the case no matter how much a father loves his children and wants to spend time with them. This is seen by a father as the biggest obstacle to contact and has serious implications for his relationship with his children. Fathers often have to jump through hoops in their attempts to fulfill a meaningful role.

Where inter-parental relationships work well, the father/child relationship generally does too. This does not mean that if the parents have problems then the father and his children will too, just that it will be harder for a father to be involved and build the relationship he would like to have with his children. He will have to make a conscious effort to be a part of their lives and for fathers who *do* want to be a regular part of their children's lives it can be very tough.

Fathers feel that after the parties split there is always the danger that their relationship with their children will slide. Sometimes the battle against the mother for contact is too much and fathers give up fighting for it, or put up with severely reduced contact. To an outsider looking in, it may appear that the father has just walked away from his children because he simply does not care about them and wants to shirk his responsibilities. The 'dead beat dads' as the media calls them.

Appearances can, of course, be deceptive. Fathers also state that one cause of major problems is the mother's new partner and the stepfather of their children.

Choices for fathers

Giving up

Into this category fall those fathers who have had to make extreme efforts to maintain contact in a hostile climate. They may have had to deal with severely frustrated contact and/or court proceedings, but have still been unable to obtain any decent level of contact with their children. The emotional, physical and financial costs of continuing to pursue contact have taken their toll and they see their decision to abandon the fight as in the best interests of everyone, particularly their children. They argue that they are not opting out but making a sacrifice. These fathers do not wish for their children to be embroiled in bitter court proceedings and caught in the middle between their parents wrangling over them. Many of these fathers remain bitter and harbour resentment against the mother who they regard as vindictive and manipulative, and disillusioned with a legal system which they believe does not address the problems of being a non-resident parent.

Hanging in there

These fathers may have to face exactly the same problems as in the category above; they cannot communicate with the mother and face the same hostility. They are determined to keep the father/child relationship going by surmounting obstacles made by the mother so as to maintain a degree of contact with their children, if nothing else. They feel deeply unhappy with their situation, the continuing struggle, the enduring bitterness and conflict, and at times feel like giving up too. These fathers continue to maintain a presence, even if only a shadowy one, and take every opportunity to press for more contact if and when the occasion does arise.

Reinventing a role for father

Fathers say that the reality is that, being removed from the children for the bulk of the time, impacts upon their role as fathers. Understandably a 'two-day a fortnight father' feels he is losing out on the day to day routine of the children. Of course, this is a direct consequence of a father leaving the family home – which generally happens even if he did not initiate the separation – and for those fathers who did not want to separate in the first place this may be more of a tragedy. It is very difficult to recreate the same role in an abnormal situation where fathers are, in effect, stepping in and out of the children's lives. This is why children are often spoilt on contact visits, as the father tries to compensate for not being there all the time. Of course, this can backfire because the mother often says that the father disturbs the children's normal routine and equilibrium and therefore objects to contact. So this becomes a Catch 22 situation for the father.

Making the most of contact: pointers for fathers

Faced with the reality of limited contact, compared with the relationship that the father used to be able to enjoy with his children, is it understandable that fathers are tempted to spoil their children when they are with them on their contact visits or holidays.

Make contact as normal as possible

Clearly fathers want to treat their children, but it is when it turns into a competition between mother and father as to whose company the children enjoy most that difficulties arise. A complaint mothers make is that fathers deliberately go out of their way to undermine them. They do this by spoiling the children, and giving them a better time than mothers are able to provide on a day to day basis. This causes resentment, although in the circumstances it is only to be expected that fathers may want to indulge their children when they do see them.

Keeping the children entertained
Fathers sometimes worry about what they should do to entertain the children on contact visits. They worry that the children will be bored. When the parties were together they had a routine and probably the children were happy with that. Fathers might be surprised to find that their children are often just happy spending time with them. The problem stems from the fact that fathers want to make contact special because of the limited time they have to spend with their children.

Disciplining the children
On contact visits, fathers generally tend to be more lenient. Fathers do not want to spend the time with their children disciplining them. One father told me that his little boy was very badly behaved on his Saturday contact visit, but he did not want to discipline him because that would probably have meant ruining the day, and so he let it pass as the time he had with him was very precious.

Avoid making any negative comments about their mother
Children sometimes repeat things that their mother may have said about their father which may not be altogether pleasant. It is better for the father to ignore the comment, or to deal with it casually, rather than to make a big issue out of it or respond with some vicious barb because, whatever she has said, she is still their mother. This works both ways. If a father has negative feelings towards the mother he should avoid directing them toward the children.

Be prepared to give a little

No agreement should ever be so carved in stone that it cannot be varied if necessity dictates. This applies even if there is a court order setting out the arrangements. Unfortunately, many parents rigidly adhere to these agreements, fearful that the slightest element of flexibility will weaken their position. It is a question of being flexible in response to a reasonable request.

Do not pressurize the children

Children need time to adjust to a change in their circumstances, different routines and unfamiliar surroundings. They now have two homes and in the initial stages moving between both parents' homes is emotionally trying. Parents must think about how all this is affecting them. Children need to be surrounded by items with which they are familiar. They are more comfortable and relaxed knowing that they have their own possessions in both homes and that they will be there when they return.

Dealing with problems

Reasons for resisting contact

There are many reasons why children may resist contact. The most common reasons, with which many fathers are already familiar and that they may have to face, are as follows:

- They may not like his new girlfriend or wife or members of her family, particularly if she has children of her own. There may be stepsibling rivalry.
- The children reach an age when they have other commitments. They may want to go out with friends, they may have to study for exams, have extra curricular school activities, and other interests that have become very important to them. Because they cannot spend so much time with their father this does not mean they no longer love him. It does not necessarily mean that they do not want to see him or that their mother is preventing them from seeing him. Fathers have to review contact arrangements and to reconsider their own role as the children grow older.

What to do if the children won't see their father

A father cannot force his children into wanting to spend time with him. This just makes matters worse. For example, if they do not like his new partner or they feel that he walked out on them, then the father has to take a step back and accept the situation. They may lash out at their father because they are hurting and he must not lash back. In time they may be able to rebuild their relationship with him. A father can often re-negotiate the relationship with his child but only when the child is ready. Sometimes he just has to be patient as with time they may accept the changes in his life; as they grow older they will have a better understanding of the situation. However, this is easier said than done.

Fathers feel rejected and insecure when their children do not want to see them.

They think that their children do not love them any more and this hurts. They fear that they are losing their children. It does not help if a mother does not want to encourage the father's relationship. It may give her the excuse she has been looking for to reduce the contact. It is very difficult for a father to know what is best to do. All he can do is to make it clear he loves his children unconditionally and that he is there if they need him.

After this period of time has elapsed are fathers in a better position? Problems may ease in relation to the children once financial matters are resolved in a good many cases, but mothers do hold the trump card. You can tell a father that time will heal and when the children are a little older they can decide with their feet, but you try telling that to a father of a two-year-old child who is totally distraught that he cannot see his child. It might be a solution but it is hardly a satisfactory one.

External influences: dealing with new partners

Adjustments to be made

The break up may have been caused because one party has found a new partner. If not for that reason, they may have found someone since the split. They may decide to live together and subsequently marry. The new partner may have children of his/her own. Whatever the facts, a number of adjustments have to be made for both parents and the children. Sometimes the partner who has been left on their own can be very resentful of the other party's new found relationship and happiness, and problems bubble under the surface which can then manifest themselves in contact problems. The children themselves may have issues.

Introducing the children to a new girlfriend

One of the problems for a father with a new partner is introducing the children to her. When does he do this? What will they think? How will they react? He needs to be aware of his children's feelings. Loving parents will be concerned with any effect on the children. If the parties are arguing over contact and an application to the court has been made, the court will want to know whether the father is offering a stable environment since the court will not want the children exposed to different partners over a short period. Is the relationship stable? A father does not want to introduce his children to his new girlfriend, for them to become attached to her and then for her to suddenly disappear. This breeds insecurity.

Older children may be critical (or even jealous) of their father's new girlfriend. This is another example of where they may think that he does not love them any more, or as much, or be able to spend time with them. These are issues that will have to be dealt with.

Their mother may oppose the father introducing the children to his new girlfriend on the grounds that it is too soon, too disruptive and, even if initial contact takes place, she may firmly object to overnight contact taking place until the children have adjusted. She simply may not like his new partner. We look at reasons for a mother's opposition to contact in Chapter 5. This can cause a problem if prior to the father forming a new relationship he had overnight contact with the children. If the children react well to a new partner it makes it easier. If they do not like her, then there are problems.

The mother's new partner and its relevance to the father/children relationship

There is often resentment on the part of a father when the mother finds a new partner, they start living together and/or she remarries. A father's fear is not just that the new man might supplant him in the children's affections. The resentment often flows from the fact that the stepfather can see his stepchildren anytime he wants but the natural father can see his children only as agreed or by order of the court. That is a dire situation for a father to be in. It is intolerable.

Of course, a father can be deliberately awkward and if he wants to sabotage the mother's new relationship may use the children as pawns and oppose everything the mother wants to do, for example in relation to the children's schooling or medical treatment.

In one particular case the father was a bully and there had been physical violence to the mother during the marriage, which was why she divorced him. They had one child, a little boy. She remarried and had another child and her son developed a very good relationship with his stepfather. The natural father then began a major 'contact campaign'. He said that the mother was denying him contact, and not consulting him on issues relating to his son. The mother had not denied the father contact but the father took issue with the mother over everything relating to their son. She found it difficult to deal with him and if he did not agree with something he would threaten a court application, and then go and make it. This mother lived under the continual threat of the father making an application as soon as a contentious point arose between them. Instead of trying to resolve matters with her amicably, his solution was to make an immediate application to the court. On several occasions the first indication the mother had that there was a problem, was when she was notified of a forthcoming hearing in the post.

And another thing...

When parents remarry the mother/child bonds tend to be strengthened while the father/child ties are strained. Apparently, second wives are less likely to want to raise someone else's children, although there are many cases where both parties have children from previous marriages and it does not pose a problem at all.

Mother moving away

Generally, the further the distance between the children and the father, the harder it is for him to maintain contact with them and less likely that he can visit regularly. That is bad enough. Should a mother want to move to the other side of the world the situation becomes critical. For a father who has a regular pattern of contact with his children and/or has already had to surmount innumerable obstacles to ensure that he has a degree of contact, this is a nightmare scenario. Even where the mother is committed to contact with the father taking place, the reality is that no matter what her best intentions are, if she is on the other side of the world, at best that contact will be severely limited.

The welfare of the child is paramount, so is it in the children's best interest to see their father maybe a couple of times a year? How will the child be able to build a strong relationship with both parents? The move abroad prevents this from happening. Inevitably a father's contact would be severely reduced to holiday contact and he would therefore be denied involvement in the general upbringing of his child. Unless the father happens to be a millionaire, and most are not, he will not be able to afford to visit his children frequently.

If a mother wishes to relocate out of the UK with the children and the father does not agree she must make an application to the Court for leave to remove them. We will look at this in Chapter 17.

Chapter 5
Friend or foe: dealing with your ex

Working together

Acting in the children's best interests...

Parents must try to avoid settling old scores by using their children as pawns. They need to cooperate and support each other for the sake of the children, keep the lines of communication open and put their children first. Even though they no longer live together in the same household, fathers will always be fathers and they and their children need quality and quantity time together. They are ex-husbands and partners but not ex-fathers!

Facilitating contact

A mother needs to facilitate contact and encourage the children's relationships with their father. There will always be exceptions. For example, where a father has abused, neglected or deserted a child, or where there has been domestic violence and the mother opposes contact, what is in the best interests of the child will be something the court will have to decide. We look at a mother's justification for preventing contact further below. How the court deals with these issues is addressed in Part II.

In cases where both parties are genuinely acting in their children's best interests, and the problems in the above paragraph do not apply, they may find some way to sort out the contact arrangements. In previous chapters we have talked about avoiding conflict and agreeing arrangements but we have not looked at the arrangements themselves.

Contact schedules

Parties may work out a contact schedule and agree dates for contact, where that contact will take place, how long the contact visits will be, including collection and return times. They should consider the arrangements for staying contact and holiday contact. Will the children stay overnight? What are the holiday plans? What is feasible? If the children have a routine, that will need to be factored into the arrangements. Do the children have extra-curricular activities? Can contact arrangements be made to fit around them?

Both parties have to expect that very occasionally arrangements need to be altered. Although last minute changes should be avoided, sometimes this cannot be helped due to some unforeseen event. For fathers who travel abroad on business, agreeing a rigid contact schedule in advance can be very difficult because it is not always possible to schedule business arrangements and trips around contact. Sometimes business plans are changed at the last minute too and are not within the father's control. Flexibility is required on the part of both parties if contact arrangements are to work well.

The parental relationship

Although the parties' relationship has come to an end, their parental relationship is ongoing. They need to work on that relationship together as parents for the sake of the children. Conflict between parents makes contact very difficult. Probably the most accurate test as to whether the parties have adjusted after their split is to look at the level of conflict between them. It is not a good sign if parents are constantly at each other's throats and it is certainly not healthy for children to be caught in the crossfire.

The goal of everybody, advisors included, should be to reduce conflict between former partners thereby reducing the negative impact on the children.

Parental Interaction

A father's relationship with the mother is highly significant when it comes to his ongoing relationship with his children. Fathers confirm that the 'type' of relationship they have with the mother has a direct bearing upon the quality of contact they enjoy with their children, and that the majority of disputes arise from ongoing or recurring conflict.

Relationships between former partners fall into a number of categories. They may have a relatively positive relationship and can separate out their issues, enabling each parent to have a quality relationship with the children. They may be amicable or able to tolerate each other for the benefit of the children. In this way the 'emotional' disruption of the break up is reduced. On the other hand, they may have a very negative relationship where conflict has a nasty habit of breaking out at the slightest sign of tension between the parties, and where there is a lack of support, cooperation and trust. This causes 'emotional' stress for everybody involved.

What type of relationship do the parties have?

Friends

Parties may fall into this category because for one reason or another they have decided to separate, but the decision is mutual and often based on the best interests of the children. They may have just drifted apart and although they may not 'love' each other any more, still like and respect one another and recognize that each parent has a valid contribution to make to the children so they work together.

If one party does have any negative feelings towards the other, he/she does not let those feelings interfere with the parental relationship. Because they put the children's welfare above their own they have workable and flexible child arrangements and emotional disruption to the children is minimized. This type of relationship is not very commonplace and more parties fall into the next category.

Formal acquaintances

If parties fall into this category then they will probably be less at ease with each other and child arrangements will therefore be on a more formal footing. There may be conflict between them in relation to their own issues, but they manage it and do not allow this to spill over into their relationship with the children. So, although they will not be friends, they will make compromises for the sake of the children and make agreements in their best interests which still have the necessary flexibility to work well. Both parties will make joint decisions over important matters relating to the children and exercise their parental responsibilities well. This relationship allows the children to maintain a healthy relationship with both parents.

Warring parties

If parties fall into this category then there will be a lot of anger, bitterness and resentment in their own relationship which has not been dealt with which spills over into the parental relationship. They will find it very difficult to separate out and discuss child issues and argue over the smallest points always re-opening old wounds when they try to negotiate.

Their relationship is strained and, even if they can come to some form of agreement regarding the children, there is little flexibility in the arrangements. This means that contact will be difficult and the children will be caught up in the midst of it all and have torn loyalties. Members of each party's respective families may become involved in the squabbles and the children will be affected by the poor relationship.

Sworn enemies

If parties fall into this category their own relationship problems dominate and they cannot communicate on child issues. They see each other as enemies and dwell on all the negative aspects of their relationship and lose focus. There is a great deal of anger for one reason or another and it is not dealt with so matters do not improve. Since the parties cannot agree child arrangements, they invariably resort to court proceedings to battle it out, and this in turn causes more conflict. The contact is constantly frustrated and they enter a vicious circle of conflict.

Everybody is affected and children become pawns. Every opportunity is used to score points against each other. A father in these situations often fights harder for contact in the initial stages, but over a period of time may gradually withdraw to reduce and/or avoid conflict because he cannot continue with a full scale war for various reasons. In such circumstances the father and children both suffer.

Disconnected partnerships

Into this category fall those relationships where, after the parties split, the father moves away completely and all contact is discontinued. The father generally withdraws from his former partner's life.

Parents may start off in one category and move into another. Many couples start off in the warring parties' category and then move into the formal acquaintances' category. This may be due to time healing matters between them or because they have made the conscious effort to improve their relationship for the sake of the children. Open communication between parents is the key. It is important for each parent to continue to communicate with the other no matter how they feel.

Communicate to negotiate

It takes two...

It cannot be emphasized enough that in order to resolve matters both parties need to communicate. Each party will have views and want those views heard, but the way those views are communicated to the other party can make a difference. So how can they communicate constructively and productively?

Communicating effectively

The common ground between the parties should be to find a solution that is in the best interests of their children. If they keep that goal in sight, then they will both attempt to communicate. Neither party can force the other to communicate nor to make an agreement, but for a father there are things he should bear in mind if he plans to try and resolve child issues with the mother. He needs to:

- Be clear about the issues he wants to discuss and think about areas of potential conflict.
- Decide where he is going to meet the mother. Think about a neutral location.
- Start off with issues that are not in dispute.
- Think about the children's wishes. Has he talked to them and asked them what they want?
- Listen to what the mother has to say and explain why he holds a particular view on a certain issue.

- Be prepared that there are things he may need time to consider and not feel that he has to give an immediate response and also be prepared to compromise. Maybe neither party has considered all the options. Give and take is important in these situations.
- Decide what his boundaries are. How far is he prepared to negotiate? What is negotiable and what is not?
- Keep reminding himself that he is communicating to resolve matters amicably in his children's best interests not his.

Maternal gatekeeping

As we have seen, where the parents own relationship is poor then problems with contact are compounded. In such circumstances fathers are faced with a dilemma. They want to see their children but are often thwarted. Fathers mention situations where the mother prevented contact with the children, and the health, safety or wishes of the children had nothing to do with the refusal!

Sabotaging the father/child relationship

When fathers leave the family home and there is conflict, one of their concerns is that they are going to be dependent upon the mother to facilitate contact and to promote the father-child relationship. Fathers refer to mothers actively trying to sabotage their relationship with their children and trying to 'poison' the children against them in order to destroy a previously loving relationship.

In the United States this is known as Parental Alienation Syndrome. This is where mothers attempt to programme the children and use psychological tactics to destroy the relationship, even though outwardly they may appear to support contact. There are a number of factors to consider including the strength of the father/child bond in the first place, the ages of the children, what the children might actually decide they want for themselves and external influences such as the mother's new partner.

What do fathers consider to be sabotage?
Sabotage does not just relate to the contact visits, but the whole father/child relationship. Mothers may try to exclude fathers from issues relating to the children and in effect sideline or in drastic cases oust them from their lives altogether. The following list is not exhaustive but it includes common complaints made by fathers against mothers:

- The mother calls the father at the last minute to change the contact arrangements or to cancel the visit by which time the father is probably on his way.
- The father arrives to pick up his children to be told that they are ill.
- The father arrives to pick up his children and there is nobody at home.
- The father calls to speak to his children and the mother either makes an excuse

for him not to speak to them, says they are out, busy or refuses to allow him to speak to them.
- The children do not receive the cards and presents that the father sends through the post because the mother withholds them.
- The mother does not inform the father about medical, schooling and other important matters and constantly tries to make important decisions about the children without consulting the father. For example, when the father does not attend a parents' evening or school event, about which the mother has failed to inform him, she then tells everyone that he cannot be bothered and is not interested in the children.
- The mother encourages the children to regard her new partner as their father.
- The mother says that the father is irresponsible and that he does not care for the children properly when they are with him.
- The mother blames the father if the children are badly behaved saying that it is his contact visits that disturb them.
- The mother says the father tries to undermine her relationship with the children on their contact visits.

Sabotage by mother or justifiable position?

Although from a father's perspective a mother may appear to be sabotaging contact, this may not be her intention at all. Some mothers may genuinely believe they are acting in the best interests of their children, even if it is an ill-founded belief and without any justification whatsoever. Fathers would argue that many mothers are being deliberately obstructive as a means of exacting revenge on them. Unfortunately, this is true in a number of cases, but there are situations where a mother has real cause for concern; matters are often neither black nor white but a variable shade of grey.

Examples of reasons for maternal sabotage provided by fathers

The following list is not exhaustive:
- The mother regards the father as a bad lot. He is not worthy to be the father of her children. Even though the parental relationship has failed this should not adversely impact on the father's relationship with his children. One father told me that he felt very guilty that he could not make his wife happy and he was totally responsible for the breakup of their marriage, but that she was now trying to punish him by being as awkward as possible when it came to contact.
- The parties may be caught up in an acrimonious financial battle, and a complaint sometimes made by fathers is that some mothers use contact as a tool to engineer a better financial settlement. By the same token, mothers sometimes claim that fathers put financial pressure on them as a means to force them to agree to more generous contact. Power struggles ensue...
- The mother may really hate the father. If he was the one to break up the relationship or walked out on the family she may use the children to exact her revenge on him. Alternatively, she may still want to be with the father and

cannot accept that the relationship is over and uses the children to exert some pressure.

- The mother has found a new life for herself and does not want the father to be part of it. She sees his intervention as bothersome and no longer desires to be in touch with him and wants to cut him off.
- The children may be all the mother has, she has become emotionally dependent on them, and is possessive of their love and jealous of their relationship with the father and fearful that in some way he might take them away from her.
- The mother feels resentful towards the father's 'generosity' to the children on contact visits, feeling she cannot compete.
- The father may have a new female partner; she resents her, neither likes her nor wants her as a rival for the children's affections, so finds reasons why the children cannot have contact with their father.
- The mother may have a new male partner and she wants to establish her new family unit and for the children to think of him as their father.

A mother's justifiable concerns
Some examples:
- When the parties initially separate everybody involved is disrupted, especially the children. There are many adjustments that need to be made. A mother may argue at this time that if the children have weekend staying contact with their father this will cause disruption and that it will take her several days to re-establish their routine therefore overnight contact is out of the question. Fathers complain about this, but the fact is this is often true. The problem for fathers is where this is an ongoing issue, even after a period of time, when both parties have settled into their new routines and homes.
- The father may have remarried or have a new female partner and there are problems over introducing the children to her and when staying contact may be appropriate. There are various factors to consider. The children may react well to the situation or they may not, and do not want to stay overnight anymore. Mothers report children being very distressed and bedwetting. Fathers see this as an excuse for avoiding contact.
- The mother may have genuine concerns about the welfare of the child. She may have reason to believe that the father is not looking after the children properly on contact visits. They may return from contact visits dirty, or with only half the clothes she sent them with, and they may not have been fed properly.
- In a situation where a father has set up home, not with another woman but with another man and the mother is worried about the environment in which the child will be placed.
- Where there has been domestic violence.
- Where there has been abuse/maltreatment or the mother suspects it.
- Where the mother has other reasons to believe that the children are or might be in danger. Examples of this would be where the father was an alcoholic or drug addict or was mentally unstable.

A final word…

Many mothers go to extreme lengths to ensure their children have flourishing relationships with their fathers and try to separate their own relationship from the parental one. These mothers actively support fathers' desires to stay involved with their families. By all accounts contact is an extremely sensitive and emotive issue and striking a balance is very difficult because each parent may have a different agenda and view of what is in the best interests of the children. Each case has its own specific set of circumstances, but one thing is certain: a child has two parents for a reason and should have every opportunity to build a loving relationship with both of them.

Chapter 6
In brief: the law and legal system

The law in outline

The Children Act 1989

This Act is the principal statute dealing with children. The Act was introduced to simplify the law relating to children and to consolidate and unify the court system. When the Act came into force in October 1991 most of the existing children legislation was repealed.

The Act is divided into two parts: the first part relates to private law and the second part to public law. Under the Act private law means the law between individuals, for example parents, and relates to their rights over, responsibilities towards and proceedings in respect of children. Public law means the law relating to the responsibilities and proceedings in respect of children where public bodies are concerned. This covers local authority care cases.

Private law orders
There are five main types of private law order that the court can make under the Children Act and which are of interest to fathers, as follows:

- Parental responsibility order. The Children Act introduced a new concept of parental responsibility.[21] Essentially what parental responsibility means is having the responsibility for taking all the important decisions in a child's life on a day to day basis. Parental responsibility is the most important of the private law orders because everything else flows from it. We look at parental responsibility in detail in Chapter 9.

The four other orders are known collectively as s 8 orders. Essentially these orders govern how parental responsibility is exercised:

- A residence order. If a party has a residence order this means their child will live with them. We consider residence orders in Chapter 17.
- A contact order. If a party has a contact order (usually the father) this requires the person who has residence (usually the mother) to allow the child to visit or stay with the father or for other forms of contact to take place such as telephone calls, letters etc. We look at the different forms of contact in Chapter 18.
- Prohibited steps order. A father would apply for this order to prevent the mother taking a particular step without the prior consent of the court. It is an order for forbidding actions. We consider prohibited steps orders in Chapter 20.

---

[21] Children Act 1989, s 4 (as amended) deals with the acquisition of parental responsibility.

- Specific issue order. A father would apply for this order where he has, or may have, a disagreement about a specific question in connection with any aspect of parental responsibility for his child and he needs the court to direct how it will be resolved. It is an order permitting actions to take place. We consider specific issue orders in Chapter 20.

Public law orders

It is not within the ambit of this book to deal with public law in detail save where local authority proceedings impact upon a father's contact with his child. We will look at this in Chapter 13.

Two further orders of significance to fathers...

These are a:

- Special guardianship order. This is an order where the natural parent retains parental responsibility but the special guardian is given parental responsibility and can make most decisions about the child without consulting anyone else. Rather than make an adoption order which severs ties with natural parents this is a way of retaining links with them and is not nearly so drastic. We consider special guardianship orders in Chapter 21.
- Family assistance order. This is an order made by the court requiring a CAFCASS officer or Local Authority Officer to advise, assist and help with the smooth running of a contact order. We look at this in Chapter 18 under contact and in more detail in Chapter 21.

Recent developments and reform: the child arrangements order

The Family Justice Review recommended that the Government replace residence and contact orders with a new order called a child arrangements order (CAO).[22] It is proposed that this should be the standard post-separation order made whenever a matter relating to a child's upbringing comes to be decided by the court. It would set out the arrangements for the upbringing of the child. The Government has indicated that it will introduce legislation on this at the earliest opportunity.[23] While I am only too aware that the terms residence and contact are seen as having negative connotations and the idea is to make the parties focus on the day to day care of the child, I am not convinced that a CAO will make any significant difference in practise.

There are no plans to remove/replace prohibited steps orders or specific issue orders. The idea is that they should be retained for issues where a CAO is inappropriate.

---

[22] Family Justice Review Final Report – November 2011, pp.22, 34, 149-150.

[23] The Government Response to the Family Justice Review: *A system with children and families at its heart* – Ministry of Justice & Department for Education, February 2012, Cm 8273, p.69.

Underlying principles under the Children Act

When the court makes any order under the Children Act relating to the upbringing of a child it will consider:

- The child's welfare. This shall be the paramount consideration of the court. There are a number of factors the court will review and these are known as the 'welfare checklist'. See below and Chapter 11.
- Whether to make 'no order'. Where the court is considering whether or not to make one or more orders under the Act, it may decide not to make an order or any orders unless it considers that making an order would be better for the child than making no order at all. The Act assumes that parties will endeavour to make their own agreements. In other words, it has to be in the best interests of the child to make an order. This is known as the non-intervention principle.
- There must be 'no delay'. The court will want to deal with matters as quickly as possible. For a child several months is a long time. Delay could be detrimental. This is why the the timing of cases has to be regulated. Delay has been a major criticism of the court system. We look at measures introduced to deal with this in Chapter 11.

How the court decides

The court will have regard to seven factors when considering the welfare of the child:

- The ascertainable wishes and feelings of the child concerned, considered in the light of the child's age and understanding.
- The child's physical, emotional and educational needs.
- The likely effect on the child of any change of circumstances.
- The age, sex, background and any characteristics of the child which the court considers relevant.
- Any harm which the child is suffering or which the child is at risk of suffering.
- How capable each of the parents, and any other person in relation to whom the court considers the question to be relevant, is of meeting the child's needs.
- The range of powers available to the court under this Act in the proceedings in question.

Each of these factors is referred to in detail in Chapter 11.

The courts and court protocol

The courts

Jurisdiction

In private law matters, proceedings can be commenced in any court that has jurisdiction to deal with the case.

The courts have jurisdiction to make s 8 orders in the following situations:
- Where there are continuing matrimonial proceedings between the parents, in other words divorce proceedings or judicial separation proceedings.
- Where there are no matrimonial proceedings – in other words where the parties are unmarried but the child is present in England & Wales, is habitually resident in England & Wales and is not habitually resident in any other part of the UK.[24] There is no exact definition of habitual residence. It is a question of fact to be determined according to the circumstances of the case. A child will normally have one habitual residence and that habitual residence will generally be where the child has lived for a settled period of time. If a child is habitually resident in England and Wales the court's jurisdiction will be retained there even though the child might be temporarily in another country. Similarly, if a child is abducted to another country and the courts of the country fail to order an immediate return of the child under the provisions of the Hague Convention (for which see Chapter 20), jurisdiction will not be lost.

When examining the question of habitual residence, consideration must also be given to 'Brussels II bis'. This is a jurisdictional code and binds all the member states of the EU except Denmark. Essentially it provides a regulatory framework for the recognition and enforcement of judgments and for granting jurisdiction to try disputes about parental responsibility. Parental responsibility includes issues about custody and access in this context, that is residence and contact. Basically the way it works is that jurisdiction should lie in the first place with the Member State of the child's habitual residence, except for certain cases of a change in the child's residence pursuant to an agreement between the holders of parental responsibility.

The courts have jurisdiction to make s 4 orders, that is for parental responsibility, where it can be shown that there is some connection with England and Wales. There does not appear to be any specific requirement.

Which courts deal with children matters?
The courts that deal with children matters in the first instance are the:
- The Family Proceedings Court (FPC) which is part of the Magistrates Court. It is in fact a specially constituted Magistrates Court.
- County Court – at first instance and on appeals from the FPC.
- High Court (Family) Division – for difficult cases and on appeal.

We look at the appeal process in Chapter 23.

Which is the right court for my case?
In 2008 the introduction of the Allocation and Transfer of Proceedings Order (ATPO) changed the way in which cases are allocated between the courts.[25] The

---

[24] Family Law Act 1986, s 2.
[25] SI 2008/2836.

idea was to streamline the system so that cases would be dealt with more quickly and by a judge in the appropriate court with the appropriate level of judicial expertise. Also magistrates' courts were not being properly utilised and the ATPO directs more appropriate cases to the magistrates' courts and ensures that proceedings are only dealt with in the High Court if relevant criteria are met. The ATPO has now been supplemented by Practice Direction 12B of the Family Procedure rules 2010.[26] In relation to private law proceedings under the Children Act 1989 the situation is as follows:

- The Family Proceedings Court (FPC). An application for parental responsibility or an application for contact with a child in care by a parent must be commenced in the FPC **unless** the application for parental responsibility is being made at the same time as a s 8 order in respect of the same child, in which case both applications must be heard in the same court, or there are existing related proceedings such as divorce proceedings for example, in a County Court or a High Court in which case the application should be made to that court. The Family Proceedings Courts do not deal with divorce. The magistrates sit in groups of two or three and the bench should include a man and a woman. Most magistrates are trained volunteers rather than lawyers, although there are increasing numbers of District Judges who now sit in these courts as chairman with one or two lay justices or the District Judge may even sit alone. Lay justices must be a member of the family panel and have been specially appointed to deal with family proceedings.

- The County Court. The judges in the County Court are known as District Judges and hear private law family work. They are experienced in family work and sit alone. County Courts with jurisdiction to hear family proceedings are Divorce County Courts, Family Hearing Centres and Care Centres. The Principal Registry in London is treated as a Divorce County Court, Family Hearing Centre and Care Centre. Applications for leave by a child or applications for enforcement of orders must be brought in the County Court. If there are divorce proceedings these will be filed in a County Court which deals with family cases and an application under the Children Act will be made there within those proceedings.

- The High Court can hear all types of Children Act applications. It will deal with exceptionally complex cases, cases where the outcome of the proceedings is important to the public in general and where there is another substantial reason for the proceedings to be started in the High Court. A substantial reason will only exist where the nature of the proceedings or the issues raised are such that they ought to be heard in the High Court. Some examples of cases which are more likely than not to be heard in the High Court are cases involving removal from the jurisdiction to a non-Hague Convention country, or cases with a complex foreign element or where there are contested issues of domicile. It does not follow

---

[26] This is in addition to the Practice Direction – Allocation and Transfer of Proceedings of 3 November 2008.

that merely because it is a case of intractable contact, or sexual abuse, or a removal to a Hague Convention country, that the case will be dealt with by the High Court.

Tranferring case between courts

The Children Act introduced a unified court system to make transfers between courts easier. Cases may be transferred up as well as down and to a court on the same level. A case may be transferred at any stage of the proceedings. This means that even if a case has already been transferred it may be transferred again if the circumstances dictate. The important thing is that the case is dealt with in the most appropriate court. Essentially the question of transfer must be kept under review at all times and delay will be a determining factor. The fact is that transferring a case will inevitably cause a slight delay because all the paperwork has to be transferred, but the court will make a decision looking at the circumstances of the case and what is in the interests of any child concerned.

Court layout and dress

Family proceedings are more informal than other legal proceedings and generally held in private and not open to members of the public, unlike criminal proceedings. In these circumstances neither the judges nor the advocates wear gowns or wigs. And since 1 October 2008, in the Family Division of the High Court and Court of Appeal, the judges have no longer worn wigs, wing collars and bands when sitting in open court. The layout of the court varies from court to court. Usually the seating arrangements are more relaxed and the court is often a large room with the judge sitting at the head of a table and the parties and their advisors on either side.

The Principal Registry is in High Holborn, London. It deals specifically with family cases. In these courts the District Judge sits on a raised platform, there is a witness box and there are several rows with seating for the parties and their advocates. The Family Division of the High Court is based in London at the High Courts of Justice in the Strand. These courts are similar to the courts at the Principal Registry but much larger and less modern than the former.

There are instances where family proceedings are held in open court, which means the press and members of the public are allowed into court. Of particular relevance to fathers are committal proceedings for contempt of court orders. For example, where a mother refuses to hand over a child for contact and is hostile and repeatedly in breach of court orders, there is provision to apply for her to be committed to prison. This is rare and is explored in more detail in Chapter 18.

We look at the openness of family court proceedings in Chapter 16.

Relevant court personnel

- Counter clerks. These form part of the administrative personnel. They are not legally qualified and therefore do not give legal advice. They have various roles but specifically there are clerks who deal with the issuing of applications, lodging of court forms, payment of court fees and listing of cases.

- Court clerks, Associates and Ushers. When parties and their advisors arrive at court they need to inform court staff that they are present. The court needs to know who is in attendance and the names of the parties and their representatives. In the County Court the clerk will be allocated to a District Judge. Any papers that the Judge needs to review before the hearing must be handed to his clerk. The clerk will be present in court, and generally sits below and just in front or to the side of the District Judge. The clerks have a number of duties: they pass papers to the District Judge when they are handed up from the parties or their advisors, swear parties in if they are to give evidence, liaise with the listing office over hearing dates and draw up court orders made by the District Judge further to the hearing. They are not legally qualified. In the High Court the usher wears a black gown and literally ushers parties in and out of court. The associate's role is essentially the same as the court clerk.

Court address
How should the Judges be addressed?
- Magistrates are referred to as: Your Worship, Sir or Madam.
- Deputy/District Judges as: Sir/Madam.
- County Court Judges as: Your Honour.
- High Court/Court of Appeal Judges as: My Lord (M'Lord), My Lady (M'Lady).
How are solicitors and barristers addressed in court?
- The Judge will refer to them as Mr… or Mrs… or Miss… as appropriate.
- Solicitors refer to fellow solicitors as: My friend, Mr… Mrs… or Miss… as appropriate.
- Barristers tend to refer to each other as: My (learned) friend, Counsel for X.

Recent developments and reform

Establishing a single Family Court for England and Wales
As a result of the recommendations of the Family Justice Review,[27] and to simplify the process, the Government intends to establish a single Family Court for England and Wales, with a single point of entry rather than the current three tiers of court: FPC, County Court or High Court. It is the Government's intention that proceedings in the Family Court should be allocated to the appropriate level of judiciary based on factors such as case type and complexity. The Government accepts the need to preserve the High Court's status in relation to its international work and inherent jurisdiction. The idea is that the creation of a single family court will facilitate wider reforms to enable the more efficient use of court resources, and more effective administration of proceedings.[28]

---

[27] Family Justice Review Final Report – November 2011, pp.72-76 paras. 2.155-2.169.
[28] The Government Response to the Family Justice Review: *A system with children and families at its heart* – Ministry of Justice & Department for Education, February 2012, Cm 8273, p.22 para. 75, 44.

Family Procedure Rules (FPR) 2010

A consultation document *Family Procedure Rules – a new procedural code for family proceedings* was published by Her Majesty's Courts Service (part of the then Department of Constitutional Affairs) in August 2006. The aim was to create one set of court rules for all family proceedings There were four key objectives: modernisation of language, harmonisation with the Civil Procedure Rules, a single unified code of practice and alignment in all levels of court. The Family Procedure Rules (FPR) 2010 came into force on 6 April 2011 and they do indeed provide a single set of rules for all family proceedings. They are supplemented by Practice Directions and forms. They are all important but in terms of private law proceedings under the Children Act, and for the purposes of this book, the particularly relevant Parts are:

- Part 1 – Overriding Objective. The court needs to deal with cases justly having regard to the welfare issues involved.[29] In dealing with a case justly the court, so far as possible, should ensure that the case is dealt with promptly and fairly, in a way which is proportionate to the nature, importance and complexity of the issues, that ensures the parties are on an equal footing, saves costs, and allots the appropriate share of the court's resources to the case taking account of the need to allot resources to other cases. The court must balance all these factors without giving undue weight to any of them. The court has a duty to manage cases and by active case management the court can give effect to the overriding objective. Some examples of active case management are as follows: where the court encourages parties to come to an agreement; identifies what the issues are at an early stage and who should be a party to proceedings; decides which issues need full investigation and the procedure to be followed; gives directions to ensure that the case proceeds as smoothly as possible. The parties are required to help the court to further the overriding objective and this applies to expert witnesses who have an overriding duty to the court. We look at expert witnesses in Chapter 12.
- Part 3 – Alternative Dispute Resolution: The Court's Powers. Practice Direction 3A – Pre-Application Protocol for Mediation Information and Family Mediation Information and Assessment Form FM1. We considered this in Chapter 2.
- Part 4 – General Case Management Powers. The court may take any step or make any order for the purpose of managing the case and furthering the overriding objective.
- Part 5 – Forms and Start of Proceedings. Practice Direction 5A – Forms and Family Procedure Rules 2010 Forms. See below.
- Part 6 – Service.
- Part 12 – Proceedings Relating to Children except Parental Order Proceedings and Proceedings and Proceedings for Applications in Adoption, Placement and Related Proceedings (numerous Practice Directions).

---

[29] FPR 2010 Part 1.1.

- Part 16 – Representation of Children and Reports in Proceedings Involving Children. Practice Direction 16A – Representation of Children. See Chapter 14.
- Part 17 – Statements of Truth.
- Part 21 – Miscellaneous Rules about Disclosure and Inspection of Documents.
- Part 22 – Evidence.
- Part 25 – Experts and Assessors. Practice Direction 25A – Experts and Assessors in Family Proceedings. See Chapter 12.
- Part 27 – Hearings and Directions Appointments.
- Part 28 – Costs. Practice Direction 28A. See Chapter 7.
- Part 30 – Appeals. Practice Direction 30A. See Chapter 23.
- Part 33 – Enforcement. See Chapter 18.

Consequences of failure to comply with FPR 2010

Sometimes a procedural error is made. The court however, can make an order to remedy this and, in any event, the error does not invalidate any step taken in the proceedings unless the court so orders.[30] But if a party fails to comply with a rule or a practice direction or a court order, any sanction for that non-compliance will apply unless the party in default applies for and obtains relief from the sanction;[31] in which event the court will look at the circumstances. Is there a good explanation for the failure? Was it unintentional? Has there been previous non-compliance? Can the hearing date still be met? What effect has the failure had on the parties? These are all scenarios that the court will consider. But if the sanction is the payment of costs then the party in default may only obtain relief by appealing against the order for costs.[32]

Where a rule, practice direction or court order requires a party to do something within a specified time and specifies the consequences of failure to comply, the time for doing the act in question may not be extended by agreement between the parties.[33]

Court forms

Below are listed the main forms to be aware of in private law Children Act proceedings with the forms of particular note highlighted:

- C – Notice of a first appointment.
- **C1** – Application for an order except s 8 orders (for s 8 orders use form C100 unless the proceedings are existing in which case use form C2) and orders related to enforcement of a contact order (for which use form C79). For the record form C1 is not appropriate if applying for a care or supervision order where form C110 would be used.
- **C1A** – Allegations of harm and domestic violence. Supplemental information form.

---

[30] FPR 2010, Rule 4.7.
[31] Ibid, Rule 4.5(1).
[32] Ibid, Rule 4.5(2).
[33] Ibid, Rule 4.5(3).

- **C2** – Application for permission to start proceedings, for an order or directions in existing proceedings, or to be joined as (or cease to be) a party in existing proceedings under the Children Act 1989.
- C3 – Application for an order authorising search for, taking charge and delivery of a child.
- C4 – Application for an order for disclosure of a child's whereabouts.
- C6 – Notice of Proceedings.
- C7 – Acknowledgement of Service.
- C8 – Confidential contact details.
- C9 – Statement of Service.
- 13A – Supplement for an application for a Special Guardianship Order s 14A Children Act 1989.
- C63 – Application for declaration of parentage under s 55A of the Family Law Act 1986.
- C63A – Declaration of parentage under s 55A of the Family Law Act 1986.
- C66 – Application for an order under the inherent jurisdiction of the High Court.
- C78 – Application for attachment of a warning notice to a contact order.
- C79 – Application related to enforcement of a contact order.
- **C100** – Application under the Children Act 1989 for a residence, contact, prohibited steps, specific issue section 8 order or to vary or discharge a section 8 order.
- C(PRA1) – Parental Responsibility Agreement.
- C(PRA2) – Step-parent Parental Responsibility Agreement.

Other forms:
- D8A – Statement of Arrangements for Children form. Applicable to divorcing fathers and fathers dissolving a civil partnership.
- FM1 – Family Mediation Information and Assessment Form.

Forms may be obtained from:
http://hmctsformfinder.justice.gov.uk/HMCTS/FormFinder.do

The role of solicitors and barristers

Both solicitors and barristers may appear in court on behalf of their clients in child cases. Solicitors provide ongoing legal advice to the client and deal with the day to day running, management and preparation of a case. They are responsible for the preparation of court bundles which generally contain the following documents: all the court applications, orders made by the court, statements of the parties, the welfare report, experts' reports and relevant correspondence as applicable to the particular case. They attend court hearings, either presenting the case themselves or attending as instructing solicitor with the barrister they have retained to present the case. The decision by a solicitor to appear at court depends upon the complexity of the case and the issues involved.

Generally, and there always exceptions, solicitors deal with early direction appointments and less contested applications in the court process. They are more inclined to instruct a barrister as the case progresses because the barrister is a specialist advocate. Barristers will be instructed to advise on the issues and briefed to appear on behalf of the client at court and present the case. There are Juniors and Leaders. A party has a Conference with Counsel and a Consultation with Leading Counsel, known as QCs, that is Queen's Counsel.

In children's proceedings an atmosphere of negotiation and cooperation between professionals is encouraged. They are supposed to be non-adversarial. Unfortunately, the very nature of the legal system encourages the opposite.

The court process

The basic procedure in children's cases is the same. The court application and process is addressed in detail in Chapter 12. Here we deal briefly with general procedure at every hearing.

General procedure

The person who makes the application is known as the Applicant and the person against whom the application is made is known as the Respondent. At each hearing the Applicant's advocate introduces the other advocate and the parties to the court. The parties stand while the judge enters the court, nod and remain standing until the judge sits.

The length of the hearing will vary depending upon the issues involved and the stage of the case. The case will be allocated a time in the court list – but sometimes cases overrun and there can be a considerable waiting period, particularly in the High Court.

If a parent has legal representation and does not attend at court it will not prevent the hearing proceeding, unless it is necessary for that particular parent to give evidence or an order has been made for the parent's attendance by the court itself. There are occasions where it is possible to obtain an order without the other party being notified and present at court. These are known as without notice orders and we look at these in Chapters 12 and 20.

The courts are extremely cautious where a party is not represented by a solicitor and fails to attend a hearing. A party representing themselves is known as a litigant in person. We look at litigants in person in detail in Chapter 15. The court will ask the other side to provide documentary evidence that this party has been properly served with the proceedings and is aware of the hearing date. This involves producing a statement of service and/or sworn statement from process servers to prove that the party has been properly notified of the court hearing. If the court feels that there has been proper service of the papers or the Applicant can show that all reasonable steps have been to taken to try and serve the Respondent then an order may be made. Sometimes hearings are adjourned to a later date to allow time for further attempts at service to be made or for any other valid reason such as the non-attendance of a party because of illness. The circumstances of the case and the nature of the hearing will have a direct bearing upon the decision made by the court. We look at this in more detail in Chapter 12.

Unless it is a final hearing, or an interim hearing where the parties are to give evidence and are to be cross-examined (in other words where there are witnesses) it will be a case of the Applicant's advocate opening the case and outlining it to the court. Then the other parties' advocate has the opportunity to make a speech to the court. A judge may ask further questions and there may be some interaction between each party's advocate and the judge to assist the judge in making his/her decision. The judges will then make the order.

At a final hearing the Applicant's advocate opens the case and calls all the witnesses in support of the Applicant's case and questions them on their evidence – that is the witness statements they have filed at court setting out their case and which have been served on the other party. This is known as examination in chief. The Respondent's advocate has the opportunity to cross-examine those witnesses. If the CAFCASS officer who prepared the welfare report is present, he/she may be questioned. Once the Applicant has presented the evidence it is the turn of the Respondent and all of the Respondent's witnesses to give evidence. The Applicant can then cross-examine those witnesses. The Respondent's barrister then makes his/her closing speech followed by the Applicant's barrister. The judge will then give judgment. Sometimes judgment is reserved while the judge considers the issues.

What is CAFCASS?

This is the Children and Family Court Advisory and Support Service. Prior to 1 April 2001 when CAFCASS became operational, the Family Court Welfare Service was responsible for the preparation of the much-dreaded welfare report.

Fathers in particular raised concerns that many Family Court Welfare Officers did not have a social work qualification and that they spent little or insufficient time with a child and his or her family to assess the situation adequately. This was seen as a major failing because the welfare report carries so much weight in Court. CAFCASS is now responsible for the preparation of these reports. Part of CAFCASS's duty is to support children and families to ensure that their voices are heard and to assist the courts to make decisions that are in the best interests of the children affected by family proceedings. Like its predecessor, CAFCASS has been criticised for not delivering these services effectively and for underperforming. CAFCASS has also been criticised for being inadequately funded, having insufficient staff without proper training and no provision for that training.

Many recommendations have been made to make it more effective and plans to overhaul CAFCASS were set out in the CAFCASS 'Every day matters' Consultation paper published at the end of 2005. One of the aims was to reduce delay by assigning a CAFCASS officer to every case referred to it within two days and then assess cases as to their urgency within six weeks so that more problematic cases such as those involving issues of abuse or domestic violence and cases where a parent is intractable about contact would be addressed more quickly – at least that is what was hoped. The idea was to reduce the number of reports made by resolving more cases at an earlier stage thereby freeing up time to deal with the difficult cases. The CAFCASS Safeguarding Framework came into effect in April 2007.

In any event, there were concerns over whether CAFCASS would have sufficient funding and resources to be able to achieve and sustain the proposed improved service to any significant degree. CAFCASS soon ran into difficulties and in May 2008 Ofsted published its first two inspection reports of regional performances and found that there were serious failings and inadequacies. There were problems with meeting targets and although it seems judges remained satisfied with the quality of the reports being produced, with increasing caseloads family court advisers found that they were spreading themselves too thinly, which in itself was putting increasing pressure on the level of service they were able to offer. To help ease this pressure, in 2009 the then President of the Family Division issued temporary guidance on how the service should be used.

However, in July 2010 the Interdisciplinary Alliance for Children (IAC) which is an alliance of legal, medical and child care organisations, sent government ministers with responsibility for justice or child welfare a joint position statement setting out their concerns about the services provided by CAFCASS. In September 2010 the President of the Family Division issued revised guidance to assist CAFCASS in reducing backlogs and unallocated cases. But in November 2010 CAFCASS was declared 'not fit for purpose' by the House of Commons Public Accounts Committee. By 2011 a review concluded that the President's guidance had achieved its temporary aim and the President and the Chief Executive decided that it did not need to be reviewed.

Traditionally CAFCASS has a poor reputation among fathers; they are very mistrustful of the service. Certainly the majority of fathers I have spoken to who have had dealings with CAFCASS have very little to say in favour of it and are particularly concerned about whether CAFCASS officers have either the capability or expertise to assess cases correctly.

CAFCASS is also key in terms of facilitating and monitoring contact and we look at Family Assistance Orders in Chapter 21. There is no question that the service is under pressure which is why the court will consider the issues seriously before being persuaded that a s 7 welfare report is absolutely necessary and that any order requiring one should clearly identify the issues upon which the report is needed.

Current developments and reform

The Government has stated that CAFCASS has reformed many of its working practices to absorb a much higher volume of cases and increased its productivity by 15% since April 2010. The sponsorship of CAFCASS is now to be transferred to the Ministry of Justice from the Department for Education. The intention is to bring CAFCASS's functions closer to the court process, mediation services and to out of court resolution and to give CAFCASS a strong voice within the wider family justice system to champion the voice of children in the courts.[34]

---

[34] The Government Response to the Family Justice Review: *A system with children and families at its heart* – Ministry of Justice & Department for Education, February 2012, Cm 8273, p.27.

Chapter 7
Your solicitor

How do I find a good family solicitor?

As I indicated in the Introduction, I am not suggesting that a father should instruct a solicitor as a matter of course, but if he does decide to instruct one out of necessity or choice, it is essential that the solicitor he instructs is a specialist family practitioner and therefore fully up to speed with family law and recent developments. There are tales of clients who have been given poor legal advice by a solicitor who is not a family law specialist and who have lost out as a result. The choice of solicitor is important because the way a case is conducted can have a major bearing on the outcome. There are many firms that have strong family law departments with specialists who can draw on each other's strengths and have the expertise to deal with all aspects of family law.

Personal recommendation

Most family solicitors obtain new clients through the referral process; either through former clients or business associates such as other solicitors, bankers, accountants and financial advisors. Personal recommendation from friends who have divorced recently or had problems over family issues such as contact is very common. It is worth asking friends which firm of solicitors they instructed and in particular who dealt with their case, why they instructed that firm and the quality of service that was provided. So far as quality of service is concerned, this covers not only the advice given but also how they were treated generally.

Reputation

A father might decide to instruct a firm of solicitors because he has heard they have an excellent reputation for family law or he wishes to instruct a particular solicitor because he has heard about his/her personal reputation. It depends upon the approach he is looking for. A hard-hitting lawyer specializing in family finance may not be suitable for children proceedings. It is all a question of balance. At the end of the day, he needs to have confidence in his solicitor and the solicitor needs to instill confidence into him.

Law Society

The Law Society will be able to assist a father in finding a family specialist in his area. If he wants to find out more information about a solicitor, that is, whether he/she is a Partner and how many years he/she has been qualified, the Law Society will be able to provide this information. The Law Society's Family Law Protocol[35] includes key recommendations as to how solicitors should handle/manage cases. This should be read in conjunction with the Solicitors' Code of Conduct (see below).

The Solicitors Regulation Authority (SRA)

As the name suggests this is the regulatory body for solicitors, a role taken over from the Law Society, and means that the SRA now has responsibility for regulating the profession. Solicitors must abide by the Solicitors' Code of Conduct.[36] Prior to the Code there was simply a Guide to the Professional Conduct of Solicitors and it contained a mixture of obligations and good practice and it was not always clear whether specific principles in the guide amounted to an obligation or were simply an indication of good practice. With the Code this problem has been resolved as it sets out the obligations that are applicable.

The Solicitors' Code of Conduct

All aspects of the solicitor/client relationship are covered by the code. Solicitors are expected to have high standards of integrity and professionalism in both their dealings with society and clients. There are 10 mandatory principles with which it is necessary for anyone providing legal services to comply so as to meet the needs of society and clients:

- To uphold the rule of law and the proper administration of justice. A solicitor has obligations not only to clients but also to the court and to any third party with whom the solicitor has dealings on a client's behalf.
- To act with integrity. A solicitor must have personal and professional integrity. This is central to dealings with a client and also in professional dealings with the court, other lawyers and the public generally.
- Independence. A solicitor must not allow his/her independence to be compromised.
- Best interests of clients. A solicitor must always act in good faith and do his/her best for each of his/her clients. A solicitor must observe a duty of confidentiality to a client, obligations with regard to conflict of interests and the obligation not to use his/her professional position to take unfair advantage of any client.
- Standard of work. A solicitor must provide a proper standard of service to clients. This includes the exercise of competence, skill and diligence.
- Public confidence. A solicitor must instil trust and confidence and behave in a way that maintains that trust.
- There must be compliance with legal and regulatory obligations and any dealings with regulators and ombudsmen must be dealt with in an open, timely and co-operative manner.

---

[35] The Law Society 2010.
[36] The SRA Code of Conduct was first introduced on 1 July 2007 since when it has been amended. The latest SRA Code of Conduct has been in operation since 6 October 2011.

- The solicitor must run his/her business or carry out his/her role effectively and in accordance with proper governance and sound financial and risk management principles.
- The solicitor must run his/her business or carry out his/her role in a way that encourages equality of opportunity and respect for diversity; and
- A solicitor must protect client money and assets.

Resolution (formerly the Solicitors Family Law Association 'SFLA')

Resolution members are solicitors who are all family law specialists. Resolution has a Code of Practice for its members to adhere to which should be read in conjunction with the Law Society's Family Law Protocol. A copy may be obtained by contacting Resolution. Solicitors who are members of Resolution should endeavour to advise, negotiate and deal with issues constructively and quickly with a view to encouraging a settlement and try to avoid conflict. In children's cases the approach is to be conciliatory and the aim is to deal with the issues in a non-confrontational manner. Where children are involved Resolution's code directs family solicitors to see their work as most important and to act accordingly.

Memberships
The Solicitor may be an Accredited Specialist on the Law Society Family Panel or Children Panel or Resolution accredited Family law specialist. A solicitor may also be a lawyer/mediator as we saw in Chapter 2. Additionally he/she may be a collaborative lawyer.

Collaborative lawyers
Collaborative law is a US inspired process. It is based on the principle that parties are much more likely to reach a settlement if both they and their respective lawyers work together and agree from the outset of the case to try and settle the case out of court – with the proviso that if they cannot settle the case and it has to proceed to court, then neither of the lawyers involved in the collaborative process will represent the parties further and the parties will need to instruct new lawyers. The requirement to change lawyers before litigating is a powerful tool to encourage both the clients and their lawyers to remain at the negotiating table.

The parties meet together with their lawyers (who must be specially trained as collaborative lawyers) to discuss financial and children arrangements which means they keep control of the process and play a greater part in the negotiations while being supported by their legal advisors. Generally there will be between 4 and 8 'round table' meetings. Although each party's lawyer is available to give advice during the meetings the emphasis is always on working together to reach a settlement. In order to provide the optimum chance for the parties to settle the case the lawyers can enlist support from other experts including mediators, counsellors, accountants and financial advisers.

The demand for collaborative law is increasing in this country and more lawyers are training to become collaborative lawyers. The Collaborative Family Law Group was established in October 2003 and is affiliated to Resolution. Collaborative lawyers join local practice groups called 'PODs'. Details of these PODs may be found on Resolution's website.

Currently there is no public funding for collaborative law so it is only open to privately paying parties. In any event it might not be effective where one party is unrepresented as there will be an imbalance around the negotiating table. Also it might be used by a party who secretly wants to obstruct reaching an agreement while seeming to support it, and thus causing delay which will only be detrimental. As with any dispute resolution service where urgent action is required it will not be appropriate. And there is the argument that parties who are amenable to it are often the ones who are so reasonable with each other that they have half-settled everything before they even come to the negotiating table. However, bearing in mind the adversarial nature of legal proceedings, collaborative law can only be a positive step forward.

Other considerations which may affect the choice of solicitor

How much they cost

Solicitors charge on an hourly basis, and their hourly rate will depend upon how senior they are and where they are based. It is important to find out how much that hourly rate is before the first meeting. Where funds are limited a party may be entitled to a contribution towards his/her costs. The Legal Services Commission (LSC) replaced the Legal Aid Board in 2000 and will itself be replaced by the Legal Aid Agency on 1 April 2013 to oversee public funding of legal costs. Not all firms undertake LSC funded services so that is something to clarify initially. We look at public funding of legal costs in detail later in this chapter.

Solicitors charge for all time spent on a file. This is called chargeable time. This includes telephone calls made to the solicitor by a client and calls they make to the client or to third parties in relation to the case. All correspondence received and sent out is charged for, including e-mails and faxes. A client will be charged for meetings, perusal of documents, analysis of documents, preparation of documents, conferences with the barrister, attendance at court, travel time to and from court and conferences, and the travel costs.

Case management

If there are a number of solicitors in a firm who specialize in family law it is important to find out if there will be anyone else working on the file and what his/her charge out rate is. It may well be that the Partner instructed may delegate the case to a more junior member of staff, such as an Assistant, to deal with on a day to day basis. The Partner will continue to oversee the file and the Assistant

will keep the Partner informed and refer to the Partner on important matters. From the client's point of view this has two implications:
- There is another point of contact and this is very useful if the Partner is often unavailable, in court, on holiday or ill, and
- This should reduce the costs.

Sometimes clients are not very happy about a more junior member of staff dealing with their case because the whole reason why they may have instructed a firm in the first place is that they want a particular solicitor to act for them. The reality is that Partners with busy practices will have to delegate work to a junior member of staff because they cannot handle all the work themselves and it is not cost effective for them to do so. However, Partners who manage their practices well will not delegate work to a more junior member of staff who is incapable of dealing with it. They will inform the client, and explain why they are delegating the matter and that they will oversee the file. They should also introduce their Assistant to the client at the earliest opportunity. Every practice must have at least one person who is 'qualified to supervise', have made arrangements to ensure the proper supervision and management of the practice as a whole and have a system in place for supervising the work done for clients.

If clients have any concerns about the quality of work or the advice they are receiving they should feel able to raise them. Clients should never feel that they cannot question the progress of their case. The client is paying for the advice received and if there are queries about who is dealing with the work, or any of the work being undertaken, it should be questioned sooner rather than later in order that any problems can be addressed and rectified.

Personal qualities to look out for

Family solicitors have different styles. Feeling confident and comfortable with the solicitor instructed is crucial.

Affability
Obviously the solicitor/client relationship is a professional one, but the very nature of the work makes it much more 'personal' as family clients have to provide solicitors with intimate details of their lives. Therefore it is very important for a family client to be able to relate well to his/her solicitor and to build up a rapport with him/her. A client wants and needs a solicitor who is approachable, not gruff and standoffish. Clients like to feel that they can trust their solicitors implicitly and that they are patient, sympathetic and empathetic but also constructive, objective and polite, but firm when needs be.

Availability
The nature of family work is such that the solicitor will have a very hectic schedule and cannot always be there at the very instant a client calls. He/she may be on the

'phone or in a meeting or at court. If a client leaves repeated messages and calls are not returned then he needs to find out if the messages have been passed on or where his solicitor is and why he has not received a response. A solicitor's secretary can be of invaluable assistance to a client. It is important to build up a good rapport with the secretary because at the very least she will be able take an accurate message in her boss's absence and she may be able to deal with the query. Obviously she cannot give legal advice, but she will be familiar with the file so is a very good point of contact.

Ability

Clients also need someone who is in command of the subject and can advise thoroughly on their case, who has a grasp of all the issues and who can instill confidence and, of course, who acts constructively.

Characteristics to avoid

Arrogance

Solicitors who denigrate other solicitors to boost themselves are unprofessional because they inflame the situation between the parties. In family cases this is particularly detrimental and can do a great deal of damage. Confrontational solicitors will turn the process into a battle because they like to win. The whole case is in danger of turning into a battle of egos between the parties and their solicitors because this unconstructive behaviour promotes conflict.

Aggression

Sometimes family lawyers have to be very tough to fight their client's corner, but a party cannot negotiate if his/her solicitor turns every issue into a battle. Being tactical is a completely different point. Negotiation requires skill and is time consuming but is likely to be far more productive than aggressive correspondence. In fact the Family Law Protocol advises that solicitors should communicate in a non-confrontational manner to preserve dignity and encourage agreements. Resolution have produced a Guide to Good Practice on Correspondence.[37]

Antagonism

A father should watch out for actions backfiring. He has to live with the consequences of any legal action taken long after his solicitor closes the file. If the solicitor makes his job more difficult then he should consider instructing a different solicitor.

---

[37] 2009 www.resolution.org.uk

The solicitor/client relationship

Client Care under the SRA Code 2011

Chapter 1 of the Code deals with client care. The basic aim is to ensure clients are given sufficient information about every aspect of their case and are kept informed. A client must be provided with information at the outset relating to the management and costs of his/her case and the complaints procedure. This information will be set in the letter of engagement and terms of business letter (the costs letter) which we consider below.

Giving and receiving advice

Instructing the solicitor
It is for the client to instruct the solicitor and for the solicitor to advise the client. The client should listen to the advice, but if he is dissatisfied with all or part of it and feels unhappy about pursuing a course of action proposed then he should make his instructions understood and not be forced into taking any action with which he is uncomfortable. If he has doubts about the advice he should take a second opinion.

Seeking clarification
If anything is unclear the solicitor should be asked to explain, otherwise the client may find himself going down a path he never intended. The solicitor will advise on the facts provided by the client, so a client needs to tell the solicitor everything to enable him/her to advise properly. Sometimes a solicitor will only be able to give initial advice, if full details of the case have not been provided.

Help to keep the costs down
In order to keep costs down, the client should try to be as organized as possible and be clear about what he wants to discuss with the solicitor before making the call or attending the meeting. By producing any information/documents requested as quickly as he can and dealing with any queries his solicitor raises promptly, he should be able to cut down his costs.

Terms of business and costs

The terms of business letter
All solicitors are required to inform clients in writing about their terms of business in accordance with the SRA Code. The terms of business letter or letter of engagement should set out details of the solicitors who will be dealing with the case and an explanation of their responsibilities, identify the client's objectives, explain options available to the client, the next steps to be taken and explain the client's responsibilities, that is what is expected of them – this generally includes

responding to the solicitor's enquiries and providing necessary documentation, for example. The terms of business letter will explain how the work is to be managed and expected levels of communication between the solicitor and client.

In relation to costs, a solicitor will need to set out details of the hourly charge out rates for any fee earner who will be working on the case and explain how expenses and disbursements will be incurred and that any bill will be subject to VAT. Details relating to billing arrangements, settlement of payments, money laundering regulations, methods of payment, late payments and disputing a bill should all be included. A solicitor has a duty to keep a client informed as to the level of costs and of any changes in the charge out rates so that the client is fully aware of his costs position at all times. If the matter is likely to proceed to a contested hearing, the solicitor should provide the client with an estimate of costs and include the barrister's costs in that estimate.

The terms of business letter will be provided to the client in duplicate. The client will be required to sign and date one copy and return it to the solicitor together with two forms of identity in respect of the money laundering regulations. When a party instructs a solicitor to act for him it is known as the 'solicitor/client retainer' and when a client returns a signed and dated terms of business letter it acts as confirmation of that retainer and the basis upon which the solicitor is instructed to act. A client can terminate the retainer by giving written instructions to his solicitor at any time and the terms of business letter itself will include details relating to termination of the retainer. The solicitor can terminate the retainer only with good reason and on giving reasonable notice. Until a client's costs are paid the solicitor is entitled to retain the file of papers. This is known as a 'lien' on the file.

Complaints

The terms of business letter should include details of whom to contact in the event of a complaint. One of the main changes implemented by the SRA Code is that the client must be informed in writing of his/her entitlement to complain and that following a complaint, he/she must be told in writing how the complaint will be handled and be given a time scale within which he/she will receive an initial and/or substantive response to the complaint. If the matter is not resolved the client has the right to complain to the Legal Ombudsman[38] and should do so within six months after the firm's final written response to the complaint.

Payment of costs

The client is responsible for payment of his solicitor's bills for the work carried out on his behalf. A bill should include a summary of the work undertaken. It will set out the solicitor's costs and stipulate the period of time these costs cover. The solicitor's costs are profit costs and disbursements. Profit costs mean all the

---

[38] Legal Ombudsman PO Box 6806, Wolverhampton, WV1 9WJ; Tel: 0300 5550333
E-mail: enquiries@legalombudsman.org.uk (www.legalombudsman.org.uk).

chargeable time spent on the file during the period of the invoice and are subject to VAT. Disbursements are the other expenses the solicitor has incurred on the client's behalf. Some disbursements are subject to VAT such as counsel's fees, telephone, postage and copying. Some disbursements do not attract VAT including court fees and oath fees.

Costs queries

Bills are to be paid within 30 days of an invoice otherwise interest becomes payable. A client can request a breakdown of the bill and if he wants to challenge a bill he may do so. The terms of business letter should contain details of what steps to take if the client disputes the amount of the bill. The information may also be printed on the back of the invoice and will explain what to do if he does not accept the bill.

Different considerations apply as to whether the case involved court proceedings or not. If not and the bill has not been paid, a client has one month to ask his solicitor to apply for what is known as a Remuneration Certificate from the Legal Complaints Service.[39]

This is a certificate stating that the sum charged is fair and reasonable or, as the case may be, what other sum would be fair and reasonable. As well as applying within one month of the bill, a client will have to pay half his costs, VAT and all the expenses. In the meantime, while there are outstanding costs, the solicitor will be entitled to charge interest. To avoid paying interest the client can write to his solicitor saying that he will pay the whole bill on condition that the solicitor obtain a Remuneration Certificate and if this is unacceptable the firm will have to return the payment. If there have been court proceedings then he could ask for a detailed assessment of his costs.

Orders for costs

It is not usual for a costs order to be made in children's proceedings even though in family proceedings the court may exercise its discretion and make an order.[40] Consideration of all the factors will generally lead the court to conclude that there should be no order. The following are reasons for not making an order for costs:

- An order for costs will diminish the funds in the family pot.
- If a party has a reasonable case to put forward about what is in a child's best interests he/she should be able to make an application without worrying about the threat of a costs order hanging over him/her if unsuccessful.
- Where the parties are the parents, the courts will be mindful that they will have dealings together in the future over arrangements for the children and making a costs order is likely to inflame the situation which will not be in the best interests of any children involved.

---

[39] Legal Complaints Service, 8 Dormer Place, Leamington Spa, Warwickshire CV32 5AE.
[40] Family Procedure Rules 2010, Rule 28.1.

When would the court exercise its discretion? An order for costs might be made on a fact-finding hearing where there have been serious allegations of misconduct against a party which are then found proven. This might be where there has been domestic violence, for example.

Not following good practice may have cost implications. For example, prior to issuing proceedings, solicitors should notify the intended Respondent of their intention to commence proceedings at least 7 days in advance unless there is good reason not to. The Law Society Protocol comments that it is bad practice for Respondents to then issue proceedings to pre-empt Applicants issuing, unless there is good reason for doing this. If Respondents want to proceed this way their solicitors must warn them of the court's disapproval of such action, the possible costs implications and the impact of such action on the rest of the case.

Costs assessments

If the court makes an order for costs it may either assess the costs summarily, that is there and then, or make an order for a detailed assessment which will take place at a later date. In family proceedings it is better if a summary assessment is made as this avoids delay and expense, but if the issues are very complex this is not always possible.

Where the hearing is one day or less there will generally be a summary assessment at the end of the hearing. If no written statement of costs has been filed (which it should be at least 24 hours before the hearing) the court can still deal with the summary assessment. It could make the assessment in the absence of a statement, adjourn for a short while for one to be prepared, adjourn the summary assessment to a short appointment (which must be before the same judge) or order a detailed assessment.

Costs will be assessed on either the standard or indemnity basis. If costs are assessed on the standard basis the court will allow costs which are proportionate to the matters in hand and will resolve any doubt as to whether costs were reasonably incurred in favour of the paying party. But if costs are assessed on the indemnity basis there is no requirement of proportionality and any doubt as to whether costs were reasonably incurred will be resolved in favour of the receiving party.[41] Indemnity orders are made infrequently in family proceedings.

The costs must be paid within 14 days of the assessment unless the court orders otherwise.

Wasted costs orders

If a legal representative has acted improperly, unreasonably or negligently and thereby caused a party to incur unnecessary costs it might be appropriate for the court to order the legal representatives to compensate the party for all or part of those costs, by making a wasted costs order against the firm.

---

[41] Civil Procedure Rules 1998, Rule 44.4.

Public Funding of legal costs

If a client is funding the case himself, he is a private client, but if a client cannot afford to fund his costs he may be entitled to public funding. Legal Services Commission (LSC) funded services are only provided by solicitors who have a contract with the LSC. For family work the contract must actually cover the specific type of case. The solicitor will complete an application form with a financial assessment form. The client will need to give full details of his finances to his solicitor for him/her to assess his financial eligibility. He has to show that his capital AND income are within the current financial limits and these change on an annual basis. We look at the financial criteria in more detail below. Consideration also has to be given to whether the Applicant will benefit sufficiently from the application to justify the likely costs. In contact cases this means showing that the likely outcome of the case will cause 'a significant improvement in the arrangements for that child or children viewed objectively.'

Any funding certificate may be limited in terms of the work the solicitor can undertake, and the amount of costs that can be incurred. If the client's position is unreasonable or it is deemed that there is no prospect of the application proceeding then LSC may decide to withdraw funding because the case has to be one that has a chance of success. There have been cases where a father's funding certificate has been withdrawn after it was made clear by the CAFCASS officer in the welfare report that his residence application was unmeritorious. In any event once funding has been granted it will be regularly reviewed.

What funding is available in family proceedings?

Family help
This covers assistance in resolving a dispute through negotiation or otherwise, where necessary to obtain disclosure of information from another party, or to obtain a consent order following an agreement of matters that were in dispute. It does not cover representation at a court hearing. It does cover help with mediation. This is limited to giving legal advice and assistance to support family mediation and includes assistance in drawing up an agreement reached with the other party. The financial criteria for family help are as follows:

- If you are in receipt of Benefits such as Income Support, Income-related Employment and Support Allowance and income-based Jobseeker's Allowance you will be eligible and will automatically receive funding for family help. The value of your home and any other assets are not taken into account.
- If you are not in receipt of Benefits then both your income and capital will be taken into account and that of your partner unless your partner happens to be the person you are in dispute with! The amount of your disposable income, that is after payment of tax, national insurance, child support and maintenance has to be below the financial threshold and, even if you satisfy those criteria, if you have disposable capital of more than £8,000 (disposable capital includes

savings, valuable items such as jewellery or cars and assets such as your home) you will not be eligible for funding.
- If you are a parent, expectant parent or person with parental responsibility (see Chapter 9) you do not have to meet these financial criteria to qualify for advice where the local authority is intending to start care or supervision proceedings (see Chapter 13).

If you 'win' your solicitor or advisor will first put any monies received to pay the legal bill and you receive what is left. The deduction is called the Statutory Charge. However, you would not have to pay if this would cause serious financial hardship and payment can be postponed. For example, in a situation where a party has been awarded a property and that is to be his/her home and that of any dependents or the money awarded or retained is to be used to buy a home for the party and/or any dependents.

Legal representation

This level of service is so that a party can be represented in court by a solicitor or barrister if he is taking or defending court proceedings. This is the same level of service previously called Legal Aid. There are two forms available:
- Investigative help. The funding is limited to investigating the strength of a claim. In other words you will only receive it for so long as it takes the solicitor to assess the merits of the case and if the case is strong enough.
- Full representation. The funding is provided to represent a party in legal proceedings.

The financial criteria are the same as for Family Help save that there is a sliding scale for disposable income. A certificate will not be backdated, but in some cases involving children the solicitor can act immediately. If a case is urgent the solicitor may be able to apply for emergency Legal Representation.

With Legal Representation a party may have to pay a contribution depending upon his financial status and this will be calculated for him. Contributions from income are by way of monthly instalments but contributions from capital have to be paid as soon as he accepts the offer of a certificate.

In terms of the costs a party pays, if he wins this depends on whether the other side is ordered to pay his costs and in fact does so. If he loses, then the most he will normally have to pay towards his solicitor and barrister's costs is his contribution under his certificate. The court will not normally order him to pay his opponent's costs but it may do depending upon his conduct and will be dependent upon his own financial position.

The Community Legal Advice Helpline offers free advice on eligibility for public funding. It may be contacted on +44 (0) 845 345 4345. Calls cost 4p per minute from a BT landline. Alternatively send a text with the words 'legal aid' and your name to 80010 and an advisor will return your call.

Legal Aid reform and the implications of the Legal Aid, Sentencing & Punishment of Offenders Act 2012

At the time of publishing the second edition of this handbook in 2007 there were radical proposals afoot to make substantial cuts to legal aid and to reform the legal aid system. Since then there have been more radical proposals for reform and to reduce costs. In December 2008 the Legal Services Commission (LSC) and the Ministry of Justice (MoJ) launched a consultation *Family Legal Aid Funding from 2010* in relation to proposals to reform payments from 2010 for solicitors and barristers carrying out family legal aid work.

The proposals included introducing a fee scheme called the *Private Family Law Representation Scheme* for those solicitors representing clients in private family law cases from the issuing of the proceedings to the end of the final hearing. The scheme would replace hourly rates with standard fees. There was also a proposal to create a simplified single fee scheme called the *Family Advocacy Scheme* to cover payments to both solicitor advocates and barristers for public and private family law cases, the idea being to bring in a single, graduated fee scheme. This would mean paying barristers and solicitors the same fees for the same work.

There were warnings that with fees being squeezed there would be a major exodus out of family law leaving parties unrepresented and vulnerable children more vulnerable. Nonetheless, in 2009 the MoJ introduced new fee structures for family legal aid which did indeed replace hourly rates with fixed fees.

The controversial Legal Aid, Sentencing and Punishment of Offenders Act 2012 makes serious cuts to legal aid including its removal from all private law children cases subject to limited exceptions, for example, where a child is at risk of abuse – which is defined to include physical or mental abuse and includes sexual abuse, violence, neglect, maltreatment and exploitation – funding will be available. Funding for domestic violence will continue but with most private law cases becoming ineligible there is a worry that people might be motivated to make false accusations of domestic violence simply to obtain legal funding. Anyone seeking legal aid to bring a case of domestic violence must claim within a 12 month time limit.

As we saw in Chapter 2 the Government is focusing on funding dispute resolution services such as mediation and on directing parties in private law cases to mediation rather than on funding them to proceed to court. Despite all the funding for mediation there is no guarantee that it will work and then there will be an increase in litigants in person coming before the courts. We consider acting in person in Chapter 15.

Chapter 8
Paternity & Parentage

Paternity

If the paternity of a child is in dispute and a man wishes to establish whether or not he is the biological father of the child there are a number of statutory provisions which may assist him. We look at these in detail below. There are various reasons why he might be anxious to establish paternity. For example, if he wants to make an application under the Children Act for a parental responsibility order or an order for residence or contact and a dispute as to parentage arises, the court will not make any orders under the Children Act until the paternity dispute is settled. Alternatively, he might want to prove that he is not the biological father of the child. For example to avoid a potential claim for financial provision for the child.

Starting point

Presumption of legitimacy
If a man was married to the child's mother when the child was born then there is a presumption that he is the father of the child, and this is so even if by the time the child is born the parties are divorced. This is known as the 'presumption of legitimacy'. The presumption may be rebutted by evidence which shows that it is more probable than not that the child is not the husband's – for example, it is proven by the fact that the pregnancy was rather too long. The best form of evidence will be that derived from bodily samples, which can be DNA tested. We look at DNA testing below.

Where there is no presumption of legitimacy
If a man was not married to the child's mother there is no such presumption. What about registration of the birth? If his name is on the birth certificate that may be evidence of paternity but that does not prevent the mother from subsequently denying his paternity or he himself denying it. This also applies to married men despite the presumption of legitimacy. There might be a scenario where a man believes he is the father of a child who has been registered as another man's child on the birth certificate. For example, the man had been having an affair with the mother around the time she became pregnant. He may decide he wants his name on the birth certificate and needs to know what steps to take to achieve that.

So how does a man establish paternity?

Establishing Paternity

There is no unified statutory procedure for establishing paternity in England & Wales. Which procedure is used will depend upon the circumstances. The standard of proof for establishing paternity is the balance of probability, not proof beyond a reasonable doubt.

A right to establish paternity?
According to the European Convention on Human Rights a man has a right to challenge or prove paternity by taking court proceedings.[42] The court will weigh up the man's right at least to have the opportunity to dispute or prove his paternity.

Application for a declaration of parentage under the Family Law Act 1986
If a declaration of parentage under the Family Law Act 1986[43] is made, the court notifies the Registrar General who has discretion under the Births & Deaths Registration Act 1953 to re-authorise the re-registration of the child's birth. The original birth certificate is annotated to show the birth has been re-registered.

Is it possible for a man in a scenario like the one we looked at above, to make such an application so that the birth certificate will be amended to include details of his paternity?

Under the Family Law Act the child him/herself or one of his/her parents may apply. Anybody else who tries to apply will be prevented from doing so by the court unless the court considers that that person has a 'sufficient personal interest' in the outcome of the application. On this basis the man in our scenario should be able to show to the court that he has a sufficient personal interest in the outcome to be allowed to apply.

Even so, the court may refuse to hear the application if it decides that determining the issue of paternity would not be in the best interests of the child. What about the child's right to know who his/her father is? We look at this further below; but the bottom line is the court will need to strike a balance between the rights of the child, mother and father and in doing so must consider the welfare of the child.

Obtaining a declaration of parentage under the Child Support Act s 27
A declaration of paternity can be made under this Act but is only effective for Child Support purposes. In England & Wales if the man who is alleged to be the parent of the child in question denies paternity a maintenance assessment cannot be made until the issue of paternity has been resolved. The effect of the declaration of paternity is that the 'father' is liable to pay maintenance even if he continues to dispute his paternity. The maintenance is back-dated to the date the mother made her application.

We look at proposed reforms to Child Support in Chapter 24.

---

[42] ECHR Arts 6 (1), 8 and 14 and see Chapter 25.
[43] Family Law Act 1986, s 55A.

Proving Paternity by scientific means

Blood samples and DNA Testing

By far the best way to establish paternity is by means of DNA testing. There have been two important changes to the law which have made it easier to obtain bodily samples for testing and therefore proof of paternity. These are the:

- Blood Tests (Evidence of Paternity) Amendment Regulations 2001

  Under the Family Law Reform Act 1969 it was only possible for the court to direct the use of blood tests in order to resolve a dispute about paternity. Thanks to the Blood Tests (Evidence of Paternity) Amendment Regulations 2001, bodily samples other than blood may now be taken. Refusal to take a blood test for religious reasons is no longer a stumbling block now that these Regulations are in place.

- Child Support, Pensions & Social Security Act 2000

  The Family Law Reform Act 1969 did not give the court express power to direct the taking of a sample from a child for the purpose of establishing paternity unless the person with care and control of the child, which in the bulk of cases is the mother, consented. This caused enormous difficulties. The Family Law Reform Act was amended by the Child Support, Pensions & Social Security Act 2000 to enable the courts to authorize the taking of a sample from the child even when the mother refuses consent, provided the court considers that it is in the best interests of the child concerned.

The correct procedure must be followed when instructions are to be given to a testing company. Only companies which are accredited by the Ministry of Justice (MoJ) may be instructed; it must be made clear in the court order for DNA testing that the testing is made pursuant to the Family Law Act 1969; samples should not be taken from children without the express order of the court; all requests for DNA testing should be by letter of instruction (unless the issue is confined to paternity testing where the testing company may have its own standardised form) which should emphasise to the company that their DNA experts' overridding duty is to the court; clear and informative instructions should be given about the 'familial' relationships to be analysed and the DNA experts should set out the results of the tests which should be explained in clear language.

Can I just apply for the court to order a DNA test?

It is not possible to make a freestanding application for a DNA test – in other words the court will only make a direction for the use of blood tests or bodily samples in the context of existing proceedings, such as, for example, under the Children Act. It follows on from this that the best option for a man who has good grounds to believe he is the father of a particular child, and where the mother refuses to acknowledge his paternity, is to make an application under the Children Act. It is not unknown for a mother to react to the 'father's' application for parental responsibility (or contact, or residence) by denying that he is the father of her child. Since the issue of paternity will have to be determined before the application under the Children Act can proceed, at least the matter will be before the court.

How will the court approach the case?

The court has a discretion to refuse direct testing and even to hear the issue of paternity at all. However, where paternity is a major factor in the case the court is unlikely to refuse to hear the application. The court could refuse to direct a test if it is not in the child's interests. That being said, it is almost always in the interests of justice to establish the truth and for the child to know the true identity of his/her father. DNA testing is the most reliable means possible of proving that. Bear in mind however, that the welfare test (see Chapters 6 and 11) does not apply as this is a procedural matter and not one which concerns the upbringing of the child.

My ex won't give a sample for DNA testing. What can the court do?

In civil proceedings the courts cannot compel any adult to provide a sample. So an adult male whom the mother alleges is the father of her child may refuse to provide one. The Child Support, Pensions & Social Security Act 2000 makes it clear that samples may not be taken from anyone other than the child except with his or her consent. Consent is required from an adult before DNA testing may be undertaken.

Nevertheless, if the court has made a direction for tests and an adult party refuses to provide a sample so that a test may be carried out, the court can draw inferences as to why the test was refused. For example, if a mother alleges that a man is the natural father of her child and he denies it, but then chooses to exercise his right not to consent to being tested, then the court may well draw the conclusion that he is the father of the child. Drawing adverse inferences is not ideal but it does sometimes have the effect of encouraging a party to take a test.

The child's right to know who the biological father is

Most courts have taken the view that it is generally in the best interests of a child to know who his/her biological father is. The Adoption & Children Act 2002[44] gives an adult who has been adopted some right of access to his original birth certificate, and in a case before it the European Court of Human Rights has recognised that everyone should be able to establish details of their identity.[45] Where children are born as a result of assisted reproduction (see under Parentage below) familial relationships become very complicated in terms of biological parentage and legal parentage. The general consensus seems to be that it is important for a child to know about his origins. We look at the whole issue of Human Rights in Chapter 25.

---

[44] The Adoption and Children Act 2002, ss 60 and 74.
[45] Mikulic v Croatia [2002] 1 FCR 720.

Does a man have a right to know he's the biological father?

Not according to a case decided by the Court of Appeal in 2007, where the Court ruled in favour of a mother who wanted the father never to know he had a daughter conceived as a result of a one-night-stand. The Court ruled that he had no right to know he was a father because, as a "one-night-stander", he did not fall within the definition of family life required by Article 8 of the European Convention on Human Rights. This meant that he had no rights under that Act and as a result was denied both the option and opportunity to play any part in his child's life.[46] The fact is that when considering a case such as this the court will need to consider all the competing rights: in other words, the rights of the child and the mother as well as those of the father; then it must carry out a balancing exercise, and of course, always has to consider the welfare of the child.

It should be noted though that, had the mother in this case decided to keep the child, rather than put her up for adoption, and then pursue the father for a claim for financial provision under the Children Act, the fact that the child was a product of a one-night-stand would be no bar to the mother proceeding with a claim against him and an order being made for him to provide for the child!

Can a paternity case be re-opened now that DNA is available?

A case before the European Court of Human Rights concerned a married father who had disputed the child's paternity since the child's birth but to whom DNA tests were unavailable at that time. A blood test was directed but the result was not conclusive and he was unable to disprove his paternity and rebut the presumption of legitimacy. Later when DNA testing became available he was able to establish conclusively that he was not the father, but the court would not reopen the proceedings on the basis that scientific progress could not be used as a ground for so doing. The European Court of Human Rights said this was not the right approach because a balance had to be struck between protecting the legal certainty of relationships and the husband's right to have the legal presumption of legitimacy reviewed in light of the DNA evidence. The domestic court should interpret existing legislation in light of scientific advances.

---

[46] Celia Conrad, 'Right to know – A recent court decision is another nail in the coffin of fathers' rights', Letter to the Editor, in *The Times* November 27, 2007

Parentage

Who's the father now? Altering the legal status

There are certain circumstances where the status of fatherhood will be transferred from someone who is the biological father to someone who is not the biological father by statute.

The Human Fertilisation & Embryology Act (HFEA) 2008

Advances in medical science and in the field of assisted reproduction have meant that more and more parties can now become 'parents'. The law has been revised to take account of these scientific advances and is now set out in HFEA 2008 which lays down the criteria for parentage. Essentially HFEA enables someone who has no biological connection with a child to be the mother, father or parent provided they meet these criteria.[47]

HFEA sets out provisions for when those who have children through assisted reproduction will be treated as the mother, father or parent. These provisions apply where the child has been born as a result of treatment provided in the UK under licence, for example through a licensed fertility clinic. It follows that they do not apply where the parties have made their own informal arrangements – in such cases the sperm donor will remain the legal father as well as being the biological one. By virtue of being recognised under HFEA as the child's parent, a party has the right to register the child's birth and state that he/she is indeed the child's parent.

Fathers and HFEA 2008

HFEA states explicitly that a child may have only one father.[48] Under HFEA:

- When a man consents to his sperm being donated for the purpose of licensed fertility treatment, he will not be treated as the father of the child.[49]
- If a married woman has IVF treatment and the sperm which is used to fertilize her eggs is not her husband's, he will still be treated as the father of her child unless it is shown that he did not consent to the treatment.[50] It should be noted that HFEA actually provides that a husband will also be presumed to be the legal parent (as will a civil partner) when donor insemination takes place in a non-licensed setting so long as the insemination is 'artificial' rather than through sexual intercourse. This is in direct contrast to two people who are not married or in a civil partnership where the only way they can fall within the provisions of HFEA is to receive treatment services in a licensed clinic.

---

[47] The various categories of parent and the criteria necessary are set out in HFEA 2008 ss 33 to 53.
[48] HFEA 2008, s 38.
[49] Ibid, s 41.
[50] Ibid, s 35.

- If an unmarried woman and man receive licensed fertility treatment and the sperm which is used to fertilize her eggs is not his, for him to be classified as the father of her child 'agreed fatherhood conditions must be met' which essentially means that he must consent to the treatment, be alive at the time of the treatment, and his consent must not be withdrawn prior to treatment. In practice this means that if the parties separate before the eggs are implanted into the mother and the man withdraws his consent to the treatment, then his original consent to treatment is no longer valid.[51]
- Where the sperm donor dies:
  (i) before the creation of the embryo, or
  (ii) after the creation of the embryo, but before it is implanted
  and he consented to the use of his sperm and the treatment in the event of his death (such consent to be in writing and not withdrawn before his death), and to be named as the father on the birth certificate and nobody else is to be treated as the father of the child or as a parent of the child, then he will be treated as the father of the child which will have been borne by the woman as a result of her being implanted with the fertilized eggs using his sperm.[52]
- Where the parties are married and the husband dies:
  (i) after the embryo was created
  (ii) and the embryo was not created using his sperm
  and he consented to the placing of the embryo in his wife after his death (such consent to be in writing and not withdrawn before his death), and to be named as the father on the birth certificate and nobody else is to be treated as the father of the child or as a parent of the child, then he will be treated as the father of the child borne to his wife as a result of her being implanted with the embryo.[53]
- Where the parties are not married or in a civil partnership but an embryo has been created through licensed fertility treatment and the man dies:
  (i) before the embryo is implanted
  (ii) and the embryo was not created using his sperm
  provided immediately before his death 'agreed fatherhood conditions' were met (see above) and nobody else is be treated as the father of the child or as a parent of the child then he may be named on the birth certificate as the father of the child borne to the woman as a result of being implanted with the embryo created in the licensed fertility treatment.[54]

---

[51] Ibid, s 36.
[52] Ibid, s 39.
[53] Ibid, s 40.
[54] Ibid.

Surrogacy

HFEA also sets out the criteria for who is to be categorized as a parent where a child has been conceived as a result of a surrogacy arrangement – which is an arrangement whereby a woman agrees with a couple (heterosexual or homosexual) that she will conceive using the sperm of the male or one of the males (as applicable) and will hand over the child at birth to the couple with the intention that they will become the child's parents. There is provision under the act for a parental order[55] to be granted in specified circumstances which means that the parties who commission the surrogacy will be the child's parents. Special circumstances include the treatment being licensed, the application for a parental order being made within 6 months of the birth of the child, the Applicants being UK domiciled, over the age of 18 and the surrogate mother of the child agreeing unconditionally to the making of the order. The court must be satisfied that no money has been paid except for expenses reasonably incurred.

Mothers, female parents and HFEA 2008

A woman who gives birth to a child, irrespective of whether she is the genetic mother, will be the legal mother unless the child is subsequently adopted. Changes implemented by HFEA have had an impact on fatherhood because a woman's civil partner will now be the presumed 'female parent' of any child born to her partner unless there is evidence to prove she did not consent to the procedure.[56] Where a child has a female parent under HFEA no man is to be treated as the father of the child[57] which means fathers are taken out of the equation.

The Adoption & Children Act 2002

Adoption also has the effect of transferring the status of fatherhood from the biological father to the adoptive one. A couple in a civil partnership or living as partners in an enduring family relationship may adopt under the Adoption & Children Act 2002.[58]

Does biological parentage matter?

HFEA 2008 again…

The 1990 Human Fertilization & Embryology Act stated that before offering anyone treatment a fertility clinic was obliged to take account of the needs of the child to have a father. The importance of a father was made clear. This requirement was removed by the 2008 Human Fertilization & Embryology Act and fertility

---

[55] Ibid, s 54.
[56] Ibid, s 42 and see also ss 43-44 which state that where no second parent is established under s 42, a female partner can also achieve legal parenthood when the 'agreed female parenthood conditions are met.'
[57] Ibid, s 45.
[58] Adoption & Children Act 2002, ss 50 & 144(4).

clinics no longer have to consider a baby's need for a father when single women and lesbian couples seek IVF treatment. So does biology matter?

Biological and psychological parents

In the case of Re G[59] the children were born by anonymous sperm donation to a lesbian couple. They split and the High Court made a shared residence order to enable the non-biological mother achieve parental responsibility and an order prohibiting the biological mother from moving any significant distance away. She flouted the order and the Court of Appeal then awarded residence to the non-biological mother and stated that the biological parent cannot take precedence over the other parent, and that children's views as to whom their psychological parents were should be taken into account. According to the Court of Appeal, when deciding such disputes 'blood ties' were no longer deemed an advantage when both parents had cared for the children. This was a rather worrying decision for a natural father.

The case was appealed to the House of Lords which said that the unusual facts had distracted the lower courts from the principles of universal application. While not raising a presumption in her favour, the fact of biological parentage was an important and significant factor in determining what would be best for the children, and a child should not be removed from the primary care of his/her biological parents without compelling reason. So, according to this judgment, biology does still matter. In Re G Lord Nicholls said that in reaching its decision 'the court should always have in mind that *in the ordinary way* the rearing of a child by his or her biological parent *can be expected* to be in the child's best interests, both in the short term and also, and importantly in the longer term.' (The italics are mine!) The decision in this case was very important as it highlighted the debate about the legal status of various categories of 'parent' such as the psychological parent, the non-biological lesbian parent as in this case, parties who use a surrogate mother to have a child, and sperm donors.

When the sperm donor is known to the parties

We considered the situation under the HFEA 2008 where the sperm is donated by a stranger for the purpose of licensed fertility treatment, but what about the legal status of the sperm donor where he is known to the parties? This is important because as a result of a change in the law enabling an adult child to contact the Human Fertilisation & Embryology Authority to discover the identity of his/her father[60] fewer men have been donating their sperm to sperm banks and there are now more cases where lesbian couples ask someone they know to donate sperm to enable them to have a child.

---

[59] Re G (Children 2006 UKHL 43).
[60] HFEA 2008, s 24 made changes to the Register of Information held by the Human Fertilisation & Embryology Authority. One of the changes was that it reduced the age at which a donor-conceived individual can seek information about their donor from 18 to 16 although identifying information will not be provided until they are 18 (s 31ZA).

The case of Andy Bathie[61] who donated his sperm to a lesbian couple and was then pursued for maintenance by the Child Support Agency highlighted an anomaly in the law and a dilemma for informal sperm donors. There is something radically wrong with a system where it was clearly the intention of the parties that the biological father would not have any legal rights in relation to the child conceived with his sperm and yet be obliged to pay child maintenance. What made this case all the more significant was that the previous week the Court of Appeal had denied a biological father the right even to know about the existence of his daughter because she was the product of a "one-night-stand" – but he too could have been made to pay maintenance for her had the mother kept the child and chosen to pursue him for it, and yet in that case blood ties were deemed unimportant.

There are of course cases where it is the intention of the parties that the male donor will play some role in the child's life. There might be the scenario where the male donor has a same-sex partner and the agreement to donate the sperm only comes about because the male donor and his same-sex partner want to have a 'child' and to play some role in the child's life. And then there are the cases where either heterosexual couples or same-sex partners wish to have a child through a surrogate. A situation could arise where a child is born to a third party, as a result of impregnation by the intended male parent or his donated sperm, and is then placed in the care of the intended parents by way of surrogacy in which case a parental order could be made under HFEA 2008[62] to confer parenthood (as we have seen above).

Legal implications
Whatever the scenario, all parties should consider the legal implications of sperm donation. Once the child is born the known donor could apply for parental responsibility – which we look at in the next chapter – or even contact. The parties need to bear that in mind. In view of the House of Lords' decision in Re G the court is likely to support the right of the father to be involved with the child born to the lesbian couple if he were so minded to make an application to it for parental responsibility.

What is clear though is that biological parentage does not guarantee success. As Lord Kerr pointed out in the case of Re B (A Child)[63] it is only 'as a contributor to the child's welfare that parenthood assumes any significance.' Which means that if the child's welfare is better served by living with say the psychological parent then that would be the order the court would make.

---

[61] Celia Conrad, 'Fathers and biology – The situation of Andy Bathie, who donated his sperm to a lesbian couple and is now being pursued for maintenance, highlights yet another anomaly in the law', Letter to the Editor, in *The Times* December 5, 2007.

[62] HFEA 2008, s 4

[63] Re B (A Child) [2009] UKSC 5 [2012] 1 FLR 551.

Chapter 9
Parental responsibility

What is parental responsibility?

The Children Act defines this as all the rights, duties, powers, responsibilities and authority which by law a parent of a child has in relation to the child and his property.[64] It means having the responsibility for taking all the important decisions in the children's lives relating to their day to day care, religion, education, and medical care. The emphasis is on 'responsibilities' towards the children and not rights over them. Parental responsibility is to be exercised for the benefit of the child not the parent. The duties involved in parental responsibility will change from time to time depending upon the age and maturity of the child. A mother will have parental responsibility automatically on the birth of the child[65] but for a father whether he has parental responsibility or not will depend on his own particular circumstances.

Married fathers and parental responsibility

If the father was married to the child's mother at the time of the birth then he will have parental responsibility automatically. This will include the married father under the HFEA 2008 which we considered under parentage above.[66] Married parents both have 'joint' parental responsibility. There has to be a legal marriage and not just a religious one for the married father to have parental responsibility.

Unmarried fathers and parental responsibility

Registering the child's birth
So far as the unmarried father is concerned he will not have automatic parental responsibility, but since December 2003, as a result of an amendment to the Children Act by the Adoption & Children Act 2002, provided he registers his children's birth jointly with the mother he will obtain it. An unmarried father will also include a man who is treated as the father under the HFEA 2008.[67] Therefore there is the facility for both the biological father and the father whose status has been conferred by statute to be named as the father on the birth certificate. As the law currently stands an unmarried father does not have the right to register the birth on his own and a mother is not obliged to include his details on the register.

---

[64] Children Act 1989, s 3.
[65] Ibid, s 2(1).
[66] HFEA 2008, s 35.
[67] Ibid, s 36.

The father has to attend with the mother at the Register Office at the time of registration for his details to be included on the birth certificate and so that they can both sign the birth register.

At the same time, if he is not present a mother cannot include his details unless she has obtained a statutory declaration acknowledging that he is the father and wishes to be included on the register. A statutory declaration is a signed statement where the party affirms or swears an oath before a solicitor or any other person who is able to witness an oath. A statutory declaration form can be obtained from the local Register Office. Even if the father does not attend with the mother, and no statutory declaration has been made at the time of registration, the register may be amended at a later date and the father's details included. Also, if the father refuses to attend or to make a statutory declaration that he is the father, the mother can make an application to court for a declaration of parentage (see under Paternity above) which means that his name will be recorded on the register without his agreement.

Reform of the birth registration process
In 2008 the then Government issued a White Paper, *Joint Birth Registration: Recording Responsibility*.[68] The plan was to change the law to make it a requirement for fathers to be named on the birth certificate. These changes were incorporated into the Welfare Reform Act 2009, Schedule 6, with the effect of amending the Births and Deaths Registration Act 1953 by introducing s 2A which relates to information concerning the birth of a child whose parents are not married. The only problem is this amendment is **not** yet in force, but when it does come into force there will be three key changes to the law:

- The requirement for both parents to joint register the birth of their child. If either parent wants to register solely then the registrar will have to explain to that parent that it has to be a joint registration unless impracticable, impossible or unreasonable to do so – for example, if the mother has reason to fear for her safety or that of her child if the father is contacted in relation to the registration. If there is no good reason for her not to be able to provide details of the father then the registrar will request she returns with information about him in order to continue with the registration.
- Where the mother wants joint registration but the father does not, the mother will be able to provide information that allows the registrar to contact the father who will be obliged to take a paternity test. If he is proven to be the father then the child's birth will be registered jointly.
- Where the mother does not acknowledge that a man is the father he will have the right to ask to take a paternity test. If he can prove his paternity then he will be able to have his name recorded on the birth certificate.

---

[68] Cmd 7293.

Other ways to acquire parental responsibility

The amendments to the Children Act by the Adoption & Children Act have enabled more unmarried fathers to acquire parental responsibility; but not all unmarried fathers will be covered by these provisions and therefore it is necessary to consider the other ways to acquire it, which are as follows:

- By entering into a parental responsibility agreement with the mother.[69] This must be on a prescribed court form which will be form C(PRA1). An unmarried man treated as a father under the HFEA[70] will also be able to acquire parental responsibility this way. An agreement may be terminated by order of the court either on an application of a person with parental responsibility, or with leave of the court, on an application by a child with sufficient understanding.
- By applying to the court for a parental responsibility order. This includes an unmarried man treated as the father under the HFEA.[71] We saw in Chapter 6 that this is the most important of the five main private law orders made under the Children Act. The court will look at the degree of commitment which he has shown towards his child; the degree of attachment which he has shown and which exists between him and his child; and his reasons for applying for the order. If he satisfies the test, the presumption is that a parental responsibility order should be made. Where a father has shown himself willing and anxious to pick up the responsibility of fatherhood, then the law should give him parental responsibility. At all times the welfare of the child must be the court's paramount consideration.
- By being appointed a guardian either by the mother or the court. Note, however, that he will assume parental responsibility only in the event of the mother's death. We consider the whole issue of guardianship and special guardianship in Chapter 21.
- By obtaining a residence order from the court. This automatically gives him parental responsibility. We will look at residence applications later.
- By marrying the mother. Once again this includes an unmarried man treated as the father under the HFEA.[72]

The married stepfather and parental responsibility

There may be a situation where the mother has children from a previous relationship and remarries. Her new husband treats the children as his. They are children of the family. However, marrying the mother does not automatically give a stepfather parental responsibility, unlike the natural father.

---

[69] Children Act 1989, s 4(1)(b).
[70] HFEA 2008, s 36.
[71] Ibid.
[72] Ibid.

What are the ways a stepfather can acquire parental responsibility?

The Adoption & Children Act 2002 amended the Children Act to insert a new section in respect of the acquisition of parental responsibility by step-parents.[73] This provides that a stepfather will be able to acquire parental responsibility as follows:

- If he is married to the mother, and she agrees to him having parental responsibility, provided the natural father also agrees (where he has parental responsibility), he can then enter into a parental responsibility agreement. This must be on a prescribed court form which will be C(PRA2).
- He can make an application to the court himself as a step-parent for a parental responsibility order.

Limitations

Parental responsibility does not give a stepfather the right to consent – or refuse to consent – to the making of adoption orders in respect of the child, or the right to remove the child from the jurisdiction. In all other respects he will have the same parental responsibility for the child as the natural father. Once he obtains parental responsibility he will be able to apply for any s 8 order and will not need the leave of the court.

The unmarried stepfather and parental responsibility

There may be a situation where the mother has children from a previous relationship and cohabits with another man who treats her children as his. The mother's unmarried partner cannot acquire parental responsibility in the same way as the married stepfather. However, there are other options. He could apply for a residence order which would give him parental responsibility. The court will have to be convinced that the circumstances warrant it. It is also possible to apply under the Children and Adoption Act 2002 for an adoption order[74] which can be granted to a couple who are not necessarily married but in an 'enduring relationship.' Also, if he has lived with the child for a period of at least three years, he could apply for a residence or contact order even without parental responsibility.

Civil Partners and parental responsibility

There is also a scenario where one of the partners in a same-sex relationship already has children and the other partner plays a significant role in those children's upbringing. The Civil Partnership Act 2004 came into force on 5 December 2005. The Act enables two same-sex individuals who are not close relatives to obtain legal recognition of their relationship by registering a civil partnership provided each is over 18 and neither is married nor in an existing civil

---

[73] Children Act 1989, s 4A.
[74] Adoption and Children Act 2002, ss 49(1) and 144(4).

partnership. The formation of a civil partnership creates rights and responsibilities. A registered partner can now acquire parental responsibility of his/her civil partner's child in the same way as a step-parent by:

- Agreement between the parent (and any other parent who also has parental responsibility) and the civil partner in which case the civil partner can enter into a parental responsibility agreement.
- Making an application to the court himself for a parental responsibility order.

Same-sex male cohabitees and parental responsibility

There may be a situation where the natural father has children from a previous relationship and cohabits with another man who treats the natural father's children as his. The father's partner cannot acquire parental responsibility in the same way as a civil partner stepfather. He would be in the same situation as the unmarried stepfather (see above).

Sperm donors and parental responsibility

As we have seen, when a man donates sperm through a licensed fertility clinic in accordance with the provisions of the HFEA 2008 he will not be treated as the father of the child. The issue of parental responsibility arises in those cases where an informal agreement has been reached between the parties and, for example, a male friend donates his sperm to a couple of female lesbian friends who wish to have a child. In law the donor father will be the child's father and therefore able to apply for parental responsibility.

In considering the case law on this issue, it would seem that if the court decides that granting parental responsibility is likely to threaten the stability of the child and the child's immediate family and be an unwelcome interference into it, then it will not be granted. Also, although s 2 A of the Births and Deaths Registration Act 1953 is not yet in force, as we have noted, it makes it a requirement for the unmarried father to register. Therefore, once it does come into force, in a case such as this, the father would have the option of requesting a paternity test and of his name being entered on the birth certificate giving him parental responsibility.

If the male donor is in a civil partnership, and because the donor in an informal arrangement is in law the child's father, the civil partner may apply for parental responsibility. Where the male partners cohabit without being in a civil partnership the non-donor father could apply for leave to make an application for a shared residence order.

Current developments and reform in relation to fathers acquiring parental responsibility

In Chapter 6 we looked at proposals to replace residence and contact orders with a child arrangements order (CAO). The Family Justice Review recommended that the new CAO should be available not only to those fathers who already hold parental responsibility but to those without it.[75] The Government is in agreement with this. The 'category' of father is not specified but obviously includes an unmarried father who has not managed to acquire parental responsibility. The Family Justice Review also recommended that where a father needs parental responsibility to fulfill the requirement of care set out in the order the court will need to make a parental responsibility order.[76] Having said that, and as we have seen above, in the majority of cases a father will acquire parental responsibility anyway. What the Government has stated is that unmarried fathers who acquire parental responsibility this way should not have their parental responsibility limited to the duration of the order.[77]

Is parental responsibility really necessary?

For a father, parental responsibility enables him to be involved in the day to day decision making relating to his children, so for a father who does not acquire it automatically, and who wants to be involved, this is a big issue. For example, without it he may have difficulty obtaining information about his children from their school or doctor. For an unmarried father, who lived with the mother and was involved in the day to day care and decision making relating to their child, it can be a rude awakening to find that without parental responsibility he is not in a position to question the upbringing of his child. There are situations where parental responsibility is absolutely necessary for an unmarried father:

- In the case of adoption; without parental responsibility his consent will not be required.
- If there is a residence order in force and the mother wants to change the child's surname she does not need his consent if he does not have parental responsibility.
- In the case of abduction; there have been difficulties where unmarried fathers without parental responsibility have applied for a child to be returned under the Hague Convention as it is not clear whether there has been a breach of a 'right of custody' within the meaning of the Convention. Parental responsibility is considered sufficient to establish a right of custody.

Exercising parental responsibility

Common sense dictates that where both parents have parental responsibility they should consult with each other and not take important steps unilaterally. In practical terms, when the parents live apart it is the parent with whom the child

---

[75] Family Justice Review Final Report November 2011, pp.22, 34, 150.
[76] Ibid.
[77] The Government Response to the Family Justice Review: *A system with children and families at its heart* – Ministry of Justice & Department for Education, February 2012, Cm 8273, p.70.

lives who normally carries the responsibility for day to day decisions.

As explained in the previous section, in some situations the consent of more than one person with parental responsibility will be required. For example, all persons with parental responsibility are required to give consent to an adoption order being granted, even if that consent is given individually. Additionally, where one parent with parental responsibility is considering making an important decision which will have life-changing consequences for any child concerned, the other parent with parental responsibility should be consulted. Parents acting in their children's best interests will consult and make joint decisions. Unfortunately, when it comes to major issues such as name changes, relocation, medical treatment, religion and education where the parents cannot find an amicable solution the court will have to decide the issue for them. We consider the use of specific issue orders and prohibited steps orders in detail in Chapter 20 and the court's approach to major issues such as name changes and relocation in Chapter 17. The bottom line is that the court must make an order (these are not instances where making 'no-order' is an option) and, in making that order the deciding factor for the court will be that the welfare of the child is the paramount consideration.

In some circumstances it might be necessary to make the child a ward of court. This means that no major decision relating to the child's welfare may be made without the consent of the High Court.

Can a father apply for a parental responsibility order where his child was not born in the UK and does not reside here?

Irrespective of whether the child is resident here or was not born in the UK, it is possible to obtain a parental responsibility order.

Can a father lose parental responsibility?

He will not lose it due to someone else obtaining it. This is because, as indicated above, more than one person is allowed to have parental responsibility. In fact, there is no limit to the number of people who may have parental responsibility at any one time. But he can lose parental responsibility in the following circumstances:

- The natural father will lose it on death or if his child is adopted. Adoption automatically extinguishes parental responsibility.
- An unmarried father who obtained a parental responsibility order could lose it if the court makes an order ending it. For example, if he inflicted serious injury on his child. It could also be revoked on the successful application of another person who has parental responsibilty or, with leave, on an application by the child himself. These conditions also apply to a stepfather who has obtained a parental responsibility order.
- If an unmarried stepfather or same-sex partner acquired parental responsibility

by being granted a residence order he will lose it automatically when the residence order terminates.

What happens if the father entrusts his children to the care of someone else?

It is not possible to transfer or surrender parental responsibility, but the father can delegate responsibility for a child on a temporary basis. For example, this could be to a school for a school trip or to a nanny or child minder. Temporary carers do not acquire parental responsibility, but may do what is reasonable while the child is in their care for the purpose of safeguarding or promoting the child's welfare. This includes a stepfather who does not have parental responsibility. For example, this could cover emergency medical treatment.

When does parental responsibility come to an end?

Parental responsibility will come to an end as regards any issue in relation to a child's upbringing as soon as the child itself is mature enough to make a decision about that issue. A balance needs to be struck between parental responsibility on the one hand and the wishes of a mature child (having listened to that child's views) on the other.

In terms of children being able to take responsibility for their own actions, it depends what it is they want to do and their age and understanding and therefore this will vary from child to child. The law prescribes certain ages where it deems that the child will have reached a certain level of maturity to do certain things. For example, at the age of 16 a child could:

- Leave school. If a child attains the age of 16 years during the period from 1 September to 31 January, the child may leave school at the end of the spring term following his sixteenth birthday. In any other case the child may leave school on the Friday before the last Monday in May.
- Marry or enter into a civil partnership with parental consent or a guardian's consent or that of the court.
- Endorse his/her consent on a deed poll to evidence a change of name.
- Consent to sexual intercourse.
- Consent to surgical, medical or dental treatment.
- Ride a motor bike.

At the age of 18 children reach the 'age of majority' and are fully-fledged adults and in the eyes of the law capable of making their own decisions – unless they are mentally handicapped and incapable of making their own decisions, in which case different considerations will apply.

Further developments and reform

In its Final Report, the Family Justice Review stated that parental responsibility was poorly understood by separating parents and that the Government should find a way of providing information to the parties so that they would have a clear understanding of what it is. What was significant in their findings was that some parties thought that the balance of parental responsibility shifts when the parties separate with one party assuming full responsibility for their child.[78] The Government in its response indicated that it will 'consider how best to raise awareness of parental responsibility and to support parents in focusing on their child's needs, both in terms of timing and channels of communications.'[79]

As we have seen above, parental responsibility is the most important aspect of the parent/child relationship because whether a party has parental responsibility or not will determine the whole nature of that relationship and orders which may be made under the Children Act. It therefore follows why the Family Justice Review, when making its recommendations for reform in respect of parental responsibility, has inevitably covered points in relation to shared residence, parenting agreements, residence and contact orders, grandparents, prohibited steps orders and specific issues orders, removal from the jurisdiction and name changes within the context of parental responsibility. For ease of reference however, I have dealt with each of these subject areas separately, and the recommendations in relation to them, in the relevant Chapter on that subject area in this book where we consider each of these points specifically.

---

[78] Family Justice Review Final Report - November 2011, pp.20-21 paras. 106, 108, 111.

[79] The Government Response to the Family Justice Review – *A system with children and families at its heart* – Ministry of Justice & Department for Education, February 2012, Cm 8273, Making parental responsibility work, p.65.

Chapter 10
Formalizing arrangements

Child arrangements for divorcing fathers

The court will not allow the divorce to proceed unless it is satisfied that adequate arrangements have been made for any 'relevant' children. The court will need to be satisfied as to the following:
- Where they are to live.
- With whom they are to live.
- What contact the other parent will have with them.
- Who will be looking after them on a day to day basis.
- What their health is like. If they need special arrangements because they are disabled, the court will want to know that these arrangements have been made.
- What their schooling arrangements are.
- Their maintenance.

It should be borne in mind that exact details may not be known at this time. For example, the home may have to be sold.

What is meant by the term 'relevant children'?

The court will be concerned with any child who was born to the parties, or who has been treated as a child of the family, who is:
- Under 16, or
- Between 16 and 18 and still at college or at school full-time or who are training for a trade, profession or vocation.

These are 'relevant children'. This includes adopted children and stepchildren but does not include foster children.

How does the Court know if the arrangements proposed are adequate?

When parties divorce, the party petitioning for a divorce, that is the Petitioner, will have to file at court the Divorce Petition together with form D8A known as a 'Statement of arrangements for children form'. In this form the Petitioner will set out the proposed arrangements for the children on divorce dealing with all the points upon which the court needs to be satisfied. The proposals will generally be that the children continue to live with the mother but have 'contact' with the father. The judge considers the arrangements for the children at the same time that he considers what is known as directions for trial, that is, at the same time he considers the divorce papers. If he approves the proposed arrangements a notice of satisfaction confirming this will be sent out to the parties.

How will the father find out what arrangements are being proposed?

If the wife is the Petitioner she will lodge her statement of arrangements for children form at court with her petition for divorce. She may agree the content of the form with the father before it is lodged, in which event an agreed form is lodged. A father will worry about committing himself to agreeing to the mother's proposals that he have 'contact', particularly where it is unclear what the exact contact arrangements are and what her definition of contact will be.

If an agreed form is not lodged, her statement of arrangements form will be served on the father with her divorce petition. He will receive what is known as an acknowledgment of service form with the petition. On that form there is a section asking whether he agrees with the Petitioner's proposed arrangements for the children and if he does not whether he is prepared to see a mediator. If he does not agree he can file his own statement of arrangements form.

Agreeing the arrangements does not preclude a father from making an application to the court for an order reviewing those arrangements at a later date. For example, if subsequently problems develop or there is a change in circumstances making the current arrangements unworkable. The court will decide a particular issue at any given time. In other words, the statement of arrangements form is *not* a binding document.

If the father is the Petitioner this process will be the other way round.

If the judge does not approve the arrangements what will he do?

He may decide any of the following:
- He needs further information about the arrangements being proposed. For example, it may not be clear from the form who is looking after the children while the mother is at work.
- There should be an appointment for both parents to see him in Chambers. He may wish to clarify several points with them.
- A CAFCASS officer should prepare a report about the children. He/she will meet with both parents to talk about the proposals and talk to the children too. The report with the Reporter's recommendations will be sent to the court.
- The arrangements proposed should be in the form of a court order because this would be better for the children. An application for an order would then have to be made, but the court will only make an order if it would be better for the children than making no order at all.

Child arrangements for unmarried fathers

Their position is completely different. When unmarried parties split there are no formal requirements for the children and no statement of arrangements for children form is submitted to the court. The court is not involved and will not be unless an application is made to it to rule on the arrangements.

Child arrangements for married stepfathers

If there are relevant children, that is who have been treated as children of the family, then the court will be required to consider the arrangements for them in the same was as for the divorcing father.

Child arrangements for unmarried stepfathers

This will be the same as for unmarried fathers above.

Child arrangements for Civil Partners

In any proceedings to dissolve a Civil Partnership where relevant children are involved, the court is required to consider the arrangements for them. In the same way as on divorce the court may direct that dissolution may not be made final until it is satisfied that adequate arrangements have been made for the children.

Child arrangements for same-sex male cohabitees

This will be the same as for unmarried fathers above.

Current developments and reform

In September 2012 The Department for Education prepared draft legislation to remove the requirement for the court to consider arrangements for the children in any proceedings for divorce (and also judicial separation and nullity), or dissolution of a civil partnership where there are 'children of the family.' Any differences between the parties as to the future arrangements for the children will be dealt with by way of a free-standing application under the Children Act 1989 in the same way as the current arrangements in existence for unmarried/cohabiting parties.

Deciding whether to make an application to the court

Considering the options

Having tried everything he can to reach an amicable arrangement with his estranged spouse or partner, a father has several options:

- Cave in and accept what he is being offered. In Part I we have looked at the reasons why fathers sometimes do this.
- Continue trying to come to an agreement with the mother without issuing court proceedings. As we saw in Chapter 2, he might try and enlist the support of third parties to help him. Many fathers state that this is only a short-term option. This is because mothers frequently move boundaries and promise to sort out the arrangements, thereby stringing matters out. The issues are not resolved between the parties because, so far as the father is concerned, the mother has no interest in resolving them. The parties may not even be communicating so there is no possibility of mediating and even if they are and they do, if they still cannot resolve the issues between them then the likelihood is that a court application will be made.
- Set out his requests formally, through a solicitor, and still try to reach an amicable agreement. By this stage fathers are generally resigned to having to issue proceedings. Unfortunately, the very fact that a father might instruct a solicitor to write a letter setting out his concerns and setting out his requests for contact is often enough to put the mother's back up and to inflame the situation. The father is in fact placed in an extremely difficult position; whatever he does he is caught.
- Issue court proceedings. An agreement can still be reached, but most fathers who find themselves in this position state that, as soon as they issue proceedings, mothers refuse to discuss matters as they feel the application is a personal attack upon them. All cases vary, however, and sometimes one party making an application may make the other party sit up and think about the implications of what they are doing and this gives them the impetus to resolve matters. Invariably matters proceed at least several stages before the matter is compromised anyway.

What are the objectives?

What does a father want to achieve and what are his long-term goals? If he is looking for flexibility, a court order will provide him with a rigid timetable to comply with, and any deviations from it may mean further applications to the court. If a mother is presented with a court timetable she may not be willing to consider any changes, telling the father that this is as a result of the court application that he made and he must accept it.

But if contact with his children is being severely limited then he may feel he has nothing to lose by making an application. Here a rigid timetable may be better because at least it would provide him with some contact. The most common question that fathers ask is, 'What is reasonable contact?' What can they expect from the court? We will look at this in Chapter 18.

Furthermore, any decision imposed by the court upon the father is going to be made by a judge who will adjudicate on the evidence put before him/her and how well the case is presented. How a father stands up to giving evidence will impact upon the outcome of the case. A criticism against judges – justified or not – is that they are biased against fathers and detached from reality. One father told me that he was advised not to proceed to court when it was discovered who the judge would be, on the basis that this judge was, as his barrister informed him, anti men and bad-tempered as a result of suffering from arthritis. The whole point is that any control a father has over the decision-making process, in relation to probably one of the biggest decisions to affect his life, is passed to someone who does not know him or his children at all and only has a snapshot of his life. This is the reality no matter how much deliberation and consideration a judge may make over a decision and no matter how experienced that judge is. This is a hard call for fathers when they are relying upon the legal system to assist them.

An awkward case would be where the father has a degree of contact, or may even enjoy regular contact with his children, but seeks more and/or from time to time the mother goes into maternal gatekeeping mode. He may have reached an agreement with her but she chips away at it so that contact visits/times are topped and tailed or chopped about. He may find that she stops communicating with him over a number of the issues affecting the children and 'forgets' to give him information she would normally share with him. For example, she might decide to go away and leave the children with the nanny or the au pair and fail to inform him. In fact, any ongoing change in attitude should be looked at carefully because it can be the prelude to bigger problems.

Fathers complain that mothers do not fully appreciate the meaning of joint parental responsibility and resent the fact that a non-resident father with parental responsibility will want to exercise that parental responsibility in relation to the children too. One father complained to me that his former wife held the view that, so far as she was concerned, since she had given birth to their daughter, she alone had parental responsibility. She refused to acknowledge that he did too and failed to consult him about important decisions relating to their daughter's welfare. As we saw in Chapter 9 the Government has indicated that it will consider how best to raise awareness of parental responsibility. This is all positive but the problem is that in some cases it is not so much a case of a parent failing to understand what parental responsibility means, but a case of knowing perfectly well what it means and being deliberately awkward nonetheless.

Before resorting to legal proceedings a father should find out about the legal process, the extent to which the legal process can help him achieve his goals but also its severe limitations. Many fathers who have been through the process and expended thousands of pounds, often exhausting their assets in the process, have little to show for it. They do not regard the process as 'father friendly' and see the courts as biased against them.

In my view, which I expressed to the Constitutional Affairs Committee in January 2005, it is not so much a gender issue but a parent issue. It is a balance between the 'resident parent' and the 'non-resident parent' irrespective of gender. This is because the non-resident parent, who in the majority of cases is the father, is on the back-foot when it comes to contact applications. The burden of proof is on that non-resident parent to show why contact should be ordered and that is very hard.

The Constitutional Affairs Committee disagreed and concluded that the courts are not consciously biased towards fathers generally or non-resident parents. They felt that delay in the court process exacerbated problems and that if cases could not be settled then the courts should take responsibility for case management and keeping delays to a minimum. Essentially this was the view of the Family Justice Review, and the Government has indicated that making it clearer that there is no in-built legal bias towards either the father or the mother is what is necessary. In Chapter 6 we looked at a child arrangements order, which will replace a residence and contact order and thus remove the term non-resident parent, but it remains to be seen whether this reform will make a difference in reality.

The fact is for fathers, the very idea of having to make an application to the court to see their own children, and for a stranger to decide how often they can see them, is the most desperate scenario for them. Worst of all they feel totally helpless because, unable to reach an agreement with the mother, they have no choice but to apply to the court.

Chapter 11
Key principles under the Children Act 1989

What factors will the court consider if an application for a s 8 order is made?

In Chapter 6 we briefly considered the welfare principle, the no-order principle and the no-delay principle:

The welfare principle

When a court determines any question with respect to the:
- Upbringing of the child or
- Administration of the child's property or the application of any income arising from it, the child's welfare shall be the court's paramount consideration.[80]

As we have seen this means the welfare test does not apply where the court is considering a procedural issue and the matter does not involve questions about the child's upbringing. It therefore follows that the welfare test would not apply where the court is considering an application for leave to apply for a s 8 order[81] but it will apply in relation to the substantive s 8 order application itself as that will involve questions about the child's upbringing. Similarly, it would not apply where the court is considering an application for someone to be joined as a party to the proceedings or for the ordering of a blood test as these are again procedural. However, in all cases the welfare of the child will still be one of the factors the court will take into account in reaching its decision.

How many legal presumptions are there under the Children Act 1989?
Currently there is only one presumption and that is that the welfare of the child is the paramount consideration. There has been considerable debate as to whether there should be a presumption of shared parenting post-separation/divorce and whether the Children Act should be amended to include legislation to give effect to it. The Government plans to introduce a presumption that a child's welfare is furthered by the involvement of both parents where that is safe and in the child's best interests. We consider the hotly debated, and somewhat emotive, subject of shared parenting in detail in Chapter 17 and Part III.

---

[80] Children Act 1989, s 1(1).
[81] See Chapter 12.

The difference between a legal presumption and judicial guidance

In the case of Payne v Payne[82] which is a case about relocation, and which we consider in Chapter 17, the Court of Appeal gave considered guidance on the circumstances when a resident parent's application to relocate would be allowed and set out a series of factors which should be taken into account. The question to be asked is what weight should be attached to them? The bottom line, which was confirmed by the Court of Appeal in a later case,[83] is that the guidance in Payne is invaluable because it helps to promote consistency in the decision-making process; but at the end of the day it is just that, and the only legal principle enunciated in the case is that the welfare of the child is paramount.

However, although guidance from the Court of Appeal does not have statutory force, it does carry weight and is invaluable for judges in the lower courts when making their decisions, who will follow that guidance.

The welfare factors

Before the Children Act came into force the only guidance on how to apply this principle was to be found in the case law. Now the court has a list of seven factors to which it refers when it is applying the welfare principle in contested s 8 proceedings.[84] The aim of the checklist is to provide a consistent approach for the courts, the parties and advisors with which to work.

None of these factors is given any priority and the court is left to assess the relative importance of each factor in the circumstances of every case. If a father is applying for a residence order, he needs to show that the children are better off living with him: he will have to consider their physical needs, daily care and routine and see if what he can provide is better for his child, bearing in mind the court does not equate welfare with material wealth or the fact that one parent can offer more. Welfare covers physical, psychological, emotional and moral needs. It is very broad. Where the court is considering the welfare of siblings in the same proceedings, it must apply the welfare test separately to each of them.

The checklist is not exhaustive and the court can also take any other relevant factors into account:

- **The ascertainable wishes and feelings of the child concerned (considered in the light of the child's age and understanding).**

We have already referred to the welfare report and this is *one* of the ways in which the child's wishes and feelings can be made known to the court. The CAFCASS report should consider the child's wishes, as well as the maturity of the child, and the extent to which the parents may have exerted influence over the child in forming any views. A court is not obliged to follow the suggestions made in the report. We look at situations where a child might be made a party to the

---

[82] Payne v Payne [2001] EWCA Civ 166 [2001] 1FLR 1052.
[83] MK v CK [2011] EWCA Civ 793.
[84] Children Act 1989, s 1(3).

proceedings, his/her separate representation, situations where he/she may give his/her own instructions in detail and the approach taken by judges in terms of interviewing children in private in Chapter 14. Although the wishes and feelings of a child are very relevant, at the end of the day this is only one of the factors to be taken into account and does not determine the issue to be decided.

Another issue to consider, involving a child's welfare, is the extent to which a child can consent to, or refuse, medical treatment. If a child is sufficiently mature he can consent to treatment and only the court can override his consent.

- **The child's physical, emotional and educational needs.**

Physical needs will include a child's accommodation and general day to day needs such as food, hygiene, warmth, care, safety, health and medical needs. In terms of education parents are under a duty of care to ensure that their children receive a full-time education suitable for their age, ability and aptitude and also that any educational needs that they have are met. Parents must meet their children's emotional needs which includes providing love and security, play and language, praise and recognition and giving them responsibility – this is met by allowing the children to grow in confidence and helping them gain personal independence to make them fully rounded individuals.

The court will look at how close the child is to brothers and sisters and others with whom he/she may lose touch if a particular order is made. The court considers circumstances very carefully before splitting brothers and sisters. It would be unusual to separate siblings close in age but, where there is a large age gap, it has happened particularly where the children are already living with a different parent. The court will consider the child's immediate needs and long-term needs and sometimes these will not be the same.

- **The likely effect on the child of any change in circumstances.**

If the current arrangements for a child are working satisfactorily, the court will be unlikely to change them. This attitude is often referred to as maintaining the status quo and means the person with whom the child is living, generally the mother, is at a considerable advantage. This is one of the major problems for fathers to overcome because it is very difficult to shift the court from this starting point. Continuity of care is considered as the most important part of a child's sense of security, and disruption of a child's routine is to be avoided if at all possible. The court will look at all changes in the child's circumstances and the possible effect of any change on a child should not be underestimated. For example, if another adult is going to be introduced into the child's life because one parent is to remarry or cohabit with someone new, or the child is going to have to move to a new home or school.

Fathers also worry because they know that in most cases the longer the status quo is maintained the harder it is to change it and if there are delays they will be more prejudiced. The philosophy behind the Children Act is that any delay is likely to prejudice the child and therefore a timetable is imposed. Ironically, once proceedings have started this may help, but fathers complain that very often the reason why they issued proceedings was because the mother dragged her feet in sorting out the contact and continually moved the boundary lines.

- **The child's age, sex, background and any characteristics of the child which the court considers relevant.**

There is no presumption of law that a child of any age should be with one parent or the other but courts invariably order that very young babies live with their mothers. A teenager can generally cope with living with either parent. As seen above age also has a decisive influence on the importance a court will attach to a child's wishes. If children are from a multi-racial background, then the court will need to look at this background and how they have been brought up and what influence both parents' culture has had on the children to date. The same applies where the parents come from a different religious background.

- **Any harm that the child has suffered or was at risk of suffering.**

This will cover any past or future harm to the child. Harm is a very broad term and means any ill-treatment of the child or impairment of the child's health or development.[85] Ill-treatment will cover any physical injury such as sexual abuse and psychological injury. Health means physical or mental health, including harm a child has suffered or is at risk of suffering as a result of seeing or hearing the ill-treatment of another person. Development means physical, intellectual, emotional, social or behavioural development. When the court considers this factor, it has to compare the child's health or development in question with what could reasonably be expected of a similar child. The court also has to be satisfied on the evidence that there is a real possibility of harm in the future which is not always easy to establish.

The court also considers the harm caused to a child by not seeing both parents. Contact is the right of the child, *not* of the parent. The child has a right to know his other parent. This is something mothers find very hard to deal with in these circumstances.

- **How capable each of the child's parents and any other person in relation to whom the court considers the question relevant is of meeting the child's needs.**

This factor involves the court looking at the parents or other proposed carers to assess their ability to care for the child. They must be able to provide basic care and meet the child's day to day needs, keep them safe, give them emotional warmth, stimulation (which includes encouragement, cognitative stimulation and social opportunities), show them guidance, teach them boundaries, give them skills and provide stability.

---

[85] Children Act 1989, s 105(1) & 31(9) & (10) inserted by Adoption & Children Act 2002, s 120. See also under Domestic Violence, Chapter 19.

The parent's conduct will be relevant to the extent that it may affect their suitability as a parent. If a father has a criminal record that will be a factor the court will consider.

In disputes between natural parents and another, for example a grandparent, the courts tend to presume that unless there is positive evidence to the contrary it is in the children's best interests to live with their natural parents. We looked at the question of rearing by the psychological parent as opposed to the biological parent in Chapter 8.

Whether a parent works will influence the care of the child. The parent's lifestyle and sexual orientation may be relevant. A parent who suffers from mental or physical illness, which could mean sudden or long-term stays in hospital, might also be less suitable as a full-time carer.

If a parent is proposing to share care with someone else, that person's capabilities will also be considered. This means that new partners or spouses, relatives and friends may be relevant as well as nannies and child minders.

- **The range of powers available to the court under this act and proceedings in question.**

This factor encourages the court to think laterally and to consider every option open to it including that of making no order at all. The court has the power to make any order in favour of any person irrespective of who has applied. For example, in the course of a residence application the court may decide it is better for the child to live with a grandparent even though the grandparent may not have been a party to the application. In s 8 proceedings it could also make a family assistance order so as to provide help to the family from CAFCASS or a local authority. We look at the use of family assistance orders in Chapters 18 and 21.

The no-order principle

As we have seen, the court will not make an order unless it considers that doing so would be better for the child than making no order at all.[86] The reasoning behind this is one of non-intervention and the belief that, in the main, parents know what is right for their children and will act in their best interests.

Where an order would definitely be made

Where there is a real danger that one parent may abduct the child, it would be an advantage to have in operation the restrictions on removal from the UK contained in a residence order. Another example would be where one party makes an application and the other party makes a cross application. In this instance the court has to make an order to decide the matter.

---

[86] Children Act 1989, s 1(5).

Avoidance of delay

The court must have regard to the general principle that any delay in determining the question is likely to prejudice the welfare of the child.[87] To a child one year is a long time. A child's sense of time is very different from that of an adult. Delay causes uncertainty for all the parties concerned and can be very detrimental to the relationship between the children and the parent who is not living with them, particularly if the other parent exploits that delay and causes problems over contact. The court is required to draw up a timetable and give directions to enable it to deal with the matter without delay. In fact the Family Procedure Rules 2010 make it clear that cases need to be 'dealt with expeditiously and fairly by active case management.' Also, the court must have regard to Article 6 of the European Convention on Human Rights, which requires that proceedings should be determined within a reasonable time.

Sometimes delay is not a bad thing. For example, if a judge delays making a final decision because he or she is awaiting the result of an expert's assessment, or a s 7 welfare report which will clearly further a child's interest, then that delay will be acceptable. A court might adjourn the proceedings to see how contact arrangements are working and then will be in a better position to make a final order which will be workable for all the parties concerned and therefore less likely to flounder a few months later.

---

[87] Children Act 1989, s 1(2).

Chapter 12
Preparing your case for court

Automatic right to make an application or not?

Those with an automatic right to apply for any s 8 order

We looked at the five main private law orders that are of particular interest to fathers in Chapter 6 and dealt specifically with parental responsibility in Chapter 9. As for residence, contact, prohibited steps or specific issue orders:

- A parent has an automatic right to apply for any of these s 8 orders, so this includes the natural father, married or not. The unmarried father is entitled whether or not he has parental responsibility. This does not include former parents who have had their child adopted. This is because parental responsibility is extinguished at the time of adoption and the child will be treated as the legitimate child of his adopted parent or parents.[88] The birth parents will not be treated as parents and will need the leave of the court, that is the permission of the court, to apply for any s 8 order (see below).
- A guardian has an automatic right to apply for any s 8 order.
- Those who have acquired parental responsibility by virtue of a marriage or civil partnership to the parent who already has parental responsibility and have the consent of anyone else with parental responsibility (usually the other biological parent) or by order of the court are entitled. This will cover step-parents.
- Any person in whose favour a residence order is in force with respect to the child.
- If the application is for a variation or discharge of an order, any person who was the Applicant for that order or, in the case of a contact order, is named in that order.

Those with an automatic right to apply for a residence or contact order

The following persons have an automatic right to apply for a residence or contact order, but if they want to apply for a prohibited steps or a specific issue order, then they need the leave of the court to make the application:

- A stepfather or stepmother who has treated the child as a child of the family.
- A civil partner who has treated the child as a child of the family.
- Any person with whom the child has lived for at least three years out of the last five years.
- Any person who has obtained the consent of all those people whose legal position would be affected, that is, anyone with parental responsibility or anyone with a residence order, or the local authority if the child is in care.

---

[88] Adoption & Children Act 2002, s 67(1), (2).

The following persons have an automatic right to apply for a residence order:

- A local authority foster parent may apply for residence (not contact) if the child has lived with him/her for a period of at least one year immediately preceding the application.
- A relative may apply for a residence order if the child has lived with him/her for a period of at least one year immediately preceding the application.

Those who need leave of the court to apply for a s 8 order

All other people not within the above require leave to apply for any order. As indicated above, the natural parent of an adopted child would require leave. A child who wants to make his/her own application also falls within this category. In such a situation the court will only grant leave if it is satisfied that the child has sufficient understanding to make the proposed application. We look at applications made by children and their separate representation in Chapter 14. Grandparents and members of the extended family generally fall within this category and we consider them in Chapter 22. Also where a Special Guardianship Order (SGO) is in force no one may apply for a residence order without the leave of the court.[89]

Applying for leave to make a s 8 application

The Procedure to be followed is set out in the Family Procedure Rules 2010. The application for leave should be made on form C2, setting out the reasons for the application. The draft application should be filed at court with it. For example, a grandparent might make an application for leave to apply for a residence order. His/her draft application for that residence order will be filed at court at the same time.

The court may either grant the application for leave on reviewing the papers or fix a date for a hearing, in which case it will give directions about who needs to be notified.

When the court is considering granting leave it weighs up a number of factors including the likelihood of the application succeeding, but the welfare checklist (which we looked at briefly in Chapter 6 and examined in detail in Chapter 11) will not apply and the child's welfare is not the paramount consideration. It will have regard to:

- The nature of the proposed application. For example, if the order is for contact, whether it is for direct contact or indirect contact.
- What connection the Applicant has with the child. Biological connections do not guarantee that leave will be given. The court will look at the psychological relationship between Applicant and child. Grandparents generally fall into both categories.
- Whether there is a risk that the proposed application might disrupt the child's life to such a degree that the child will suffer harm. For example, to his/her

---

[89] Children Act 1989, s 10(7A).

health or development. If the child is in care then disruption will be a key factor.[90]

- If the child is in the care of the local authority, the local authority should have plans in place to safeguard and promote the child's welfare, so the court will consider what plans it has for the child and the wishes and feelings of the child's parents. In one case where the local authority planned to put the child forward for adoption, an aunt was refused leave to apply for residence and/or contact as the mother opposed anyone within her family having contact with the child.[91]

Commencing proceedings

Making an application

In practice, if a father has a solicitor acting for him, he/she will deal with the completion of all the necessary forms and send them to him for his approval. For a father acting in person, it is important he knows the procedure particularly as he will almost certainly have to deal with the mother's legal representatives.

Completing the application form

We looked at court forms in Chapter 6. If the father makes the application he is known as the Applicant and the other parties as Respondents. If a father is applying for one of the s 8 orders – and there are no existing Children Act proceedings – then the correct form to use is form C100. If there are existing Children Act proceedings then the correct form to use is the shorter form C2. A father would use form C1 if he is applying for a parental responsibility order, as would a stepfather. The application form will ask for details about the child or children in respect of whom he wants to apply for an order, his details, the other parties' details and brief details of the order for which he is applying. He must name as a Respondent every person whom he believes to have parental responsibility. The mother will be a Respondent. If an order has already been made within existing proceedings, he must also name as a Respondent anyone who was a party in those proceedings. The Applicant does not need to disclose his/her address on the form if he/she does not want the other party to know her whereabouts or that of any child, but the details must still be disclosed to the court and this must be done on form C8 which should be returned to the court with the application.

What is Form C1A?

Form C100 requires the Applicant to tick a Yes or No box about whether he/she

---

[90] Children Act 1989, s 10(9).
[91] G v Kirklees Metropolitan Borough Council [1993] 1 FLR 805.

believes that the children named in the application 'have experienced or are at risk of experiencing harm from any form of domestic abuse, violence, child abduction, child abuse, drugs, alcohol or substance abuse or safety or welfare concerns by any person who has had contact with, the child?' If the Applicant ticks the Yes box on form C100 then the Applicant needs to complete the supplemental form C1A and set out full details of the incidents. Within the form there is a Response to Allegations of Harm section which the Respondent needs to complete and return with the Acknowledgement of Service form C7 (see below).

The wording of form C1 is slightly different, but that is because it is an older form. It requires the Applicant to tick a Yes or No box about whether he/she believes that the children named in the application 'have suffered or are at risk of suffering any harm from any form of domestic abuse, violence within the household, child abduction, other conduct or behaviour by any person who is or has been involved in caring for the child(ren) or lives with, or has contact with, the child(ren)?' If the Applicant ticks the Yes box then the Applicant needs to complete the supplemental form C1A and set out full details of the incidents.

There was a good deal of concern that the introduction of this question would pave the way to false allegations being made against fathers as a means of blocking a contact application before it has even started. The then Government indicated that the form would deter spurious allegations being made because of the degree to which they have to be described on form C1A, while at the same time protecting those at risk – the purpose of these forms is to alert CAFCASS to the possibility of safety issues, to undertake any preliminary 'paper' assessment of risk, and advise the court accordingly. We look at the court's approach below.

Parenting Plans

We considered Parenting Plans in Chapter 2 when we looked at Dispute Resolution Services and the document on Parenting Plans, *Putting your child first – A guide for separating parents.* Its purpose is to provide parents with information as to what sort of arrangements would be considered acceptable, but also to help them become aware of difficult issues concerning their children that might arise and to work out how to tackle them. *Putting your child first* emphasises the benefit of children having a relationship with both parents.

When completing Form C100 the Applicant will need to confirm if he/she has received a copy of this document, has attended a Mediation Information Assessment Meeting (MIAM) as suggested in the Pre-Action Protocol, and/or attached form FM1. If the Applicant did not use Mediation or attend a MIAM he/she needs to explain why. We looked at MIAMs and form FM1 in Chapter 2. We also consider form FM1 below.

When completing form C1 similar considerations will apply.

Form FM1

As we saw in Chapter 2, parties are expected to explore the scope for resolving disputes through mediation before commencing court proceedings.[92] When the Applicant makes an application he/she must also file a form FM1 stating whether he/she has attended mediation or has not attended. It may be that the case is unsuitable for a MIAM or mediation and in Chapter 2 we considered all the scenarios where attendance is deemed unsuitable. If a party does not fit within any of those categories then he/she will need to explain what the reason is for non-attendance.

Issuing & serving the application

The original court form is submitted to the court together with sufficient copies for service on every Respondent and CAFCASS and the court fee if appropriate.[93] When the proceedings have been issued the court will fix a date for a hearing. This is known as the First Hearing Dispute Resolution Appointment (FHDRA), see below. Unless it is an urgent case the FHDRA should be listed to take place within 4 weeks of the application and not later than 6 weeks from the date of the application.[94] Copies of the application must be served on all Respondents at least 14 days before the hearing (unless the court abridges this time), together with form C1A if applicable, a notice of proceedings form C6 giving the date of the hearing, a blank form C1A and a blank acknowledgment of service form C7. The court will send the application form and notice of hearing directly to CAFCASS and a copy of forms C1A and C7 to CAFCASS on the day of receipt.

It is the duty of CAFCASS to identify any safety issues, that is possible risks of harm to any child in the proceedings, before the FHDRA takes place. CAFCASS will carry out 'safeguarding' enquiries including checks of local authorities and police, and a telephone risk identification interview with each of the parties; if risks of harm are identified CAFCASS may invite the parties to meet separately with the CAFCASS officer; CAFCASS will record and outline any safety issues for the court and at least three days before the FHDRA the CAFCASS officer will report the outcome of the risk identification work to the court.[95] A CAFCASS officer will not initiate contact with a child prior to the FHDRA.

Where a Respondent has a solicitor representing him/her the best way for the Applicant to serve the papers is by sending them first class post to the solicitor's office or delivering them. Where the Respondent does not have a solicitor representing him/her the Applicant might serve the papers by giving them to the Respondent personally or by sending them by first class post to the Respondent's

---

[92] FPR 2010, PD 3A.

[93] There is a leaflet EX160A Court fees: Do I have to pay them? There is also a leaflet EX50 Civil & Family Court Fees (High Court and County Court) which may be obtained from any court office or www.justice.gov.uk.

[94] Practical arrangements before the FHDRA are governed by para 3 of Practice Direction 12B – The Revised Private Law Programme (see below).

[95] Ibid, para. 3.9.

address. The Applicant could always use a process server to deliver the papers. This is more costly but the advantage is that the process server can prepare a sworn statement to confirm that the Respondent was personally served with the papers. If there are potential problems with service this might be a good idea, because the Applicant must file a statement of service form C9 at court setting out how service was effected, that is, when and how. The court will have given the Applicant form C9 when the application was issued. This is because, if the other side fails to come to court, it is necessary to prove to the court that the other party has been given notice of the proceedings and the opportunity to present his/her case to the court and has not been prejudiced in any way.

As well as serving any Respondents, the Applicant needs to be aware that there are sometimes other persons to whom notice must be given so they can decide if they want to be 'joined as a party', that is made a party to the proceedings. We look at applications to be joined as a party later in this chapter. Unlike Respondents they only need to be served with a copy of the notice of the proceedings. They are:

- Any person with whom the child is living at the time of the application.
- Any person with whom the child has lived for three years or more prior to the application being made.
- Any person named in a court order or a party to existing proceedings concerning the child.
- If the child is being looked after by social services, but not subject to a care order, the local authority looking after the child.

The Respondent must complete the Acknowledgment form within 14 days of service, file it at court and serve a copy on the Applicant.

Tell me about the proceedings

In 2004 the then President of the Family Division, Dame Elizabeth Butler-Sloss, produced her *Private Law Programme for Children* addressing, among other things, the delay it was taking for private cases to be listed and dealt with in the courts. This was followed by the Revised Private Law Programme in 2010 and now Practice Direction 12B.[96] Essentially the Programme retains the essential features of the FHDRA – the preliminary hearing where the parties may be helped to reach agreement and to identify the issues between them – but revisions have been made to account for recent developments in private law family matters including concerns over domestic violence and abuse, drug and alcohol misuse and mental illness.

It is now accepted that all court orders, even those made by consent, must be scrutinised to ensure they are safe and take account of risk factors. Additionally, there is a duty on CAFCASS to carry out risk assessments where a CAFCASS officer suspects that a child is at risk of harm. In fact, if CAFCASS is given any cause to suspect that a child is at risk it must make a risk assessment.[97] It is also

---

[96] This Practice Direction supplements FPR Part 12.
[97] Children Act 1989, s 16A.

recognised that it is important to involve children where appropriate in the decision-making process.

In Chapter 6 we considered the principle of the overriding objective[98] which the court must apply in every case to enable it to deal with that case justly. Accordingly, the court will give effect to the overriding objective when applying the Programme and when exercising its case management powers.[99]

What is the purpose of the First Hearing Dispute Resolution Appointment 'FHDRA'

Apart from safety checks and enquiries carried out by CAFCASS before the first hearing which are required for that hearing, and which we looked at above, any consideration and/or discussion of the issues will not take place until the FHDRA itself. This is to ensure that the parties are on an equal footing and can hear what is said to and by each other.[100] At the FHDRA the court will consider in particular:

- Conciliation and dispute resolution – whether and to what extent the parties can resolve safely some or all of the issues with the assistance of the CAFCASS officer and any available mediator.
- Safeguarding – this relates to any risk identification carried out by CAFCASS followed by active case management including risk assessment, and compliance with the 14 January 2009 Practice Direction 'Residence and Contact Orders: Domestic Violence and Harm.' We consider domestic violence specifically in Chapter 19.
- Consent orders – there needs to be judicial scrutiny to ensure any order made is appropriate for the parties.
- The avoidance of delay through the early identification of issues and case management – the court must decide what disclosure it requires and whether it needs witness statements, expert evidence, a s 7 or s 37 report (see below). The court must also consider timetabling and whether the proceedings are to be transferred to the FPC.
- Judicial consideration must be given to the way of involving a child in the proceedings.
- Judicial continuity.

The approach of the court at the First Hearing Dispute Resolution Appointment 'FHDRA'

Conciliation and dispute resolution
The parties and CAFCASS officer must attend the FHDRA and a mediator may attend where available.[101] At the FHDRA the court, in collaboration with the

---

[98] FPR 2010, Part 1.
[99] PD 12B, para. 2.2.
[100] Ibid.
[101] Ibid, para. 4.1.

CAFCASS officer and with the assistance of any mediator present, will seek to assist the parties in conciliation and in resolution of all or any of the issues between them.[102] The Practice Direction does not set out exactly how conciliation should be used but it does state that where practicable the CAFCASS officer should speak to each party separately at court and before the hearing and that the procedure to be followed will be determined by local arrangements.

It is important to note that the hearing is not privileged, in other words the judge presiding over it and the CAFCASS officer can have further involvement in the case. Previously an order could not be made unless the parties were in agreement, but now the judge may make an order even where the parties do not entirely agree, for example, about interim contact. However, despite Practice Direction 12B indicating that the involvement of the child is a matter to be considered at the FHDRA it would seem that the practice of children aged 9 and above attending at court for the FHDRA, to speak to a CAFCASS officer, and which has been the position since 2004, remains unaltered.

Outstanding issues between the parties will be identified and the CAFCASS officer will advise the court of any recommended means of resolving such issues and directions will be given for the future resolution of such issues – what other options are there to resolve the matter? Is the case suitable for further intervention by CAFCASS, mediation by an external provider, collaborative law or use of a parenting plan?[103] It is important to bear in mind that at all times the decisions of the court and the work of the CAFCASS officer will take account of any risk or safeguarding issues that have been identified.[104]

Safeguarding
As we saw above, the CAFCASS officer has to report the outcome of any risk identification work to the court. At the FHDRA the court will inform the parties of any screening report or other information which has been provided by CAFCASS, unless it considers that to do so would create a risk of harm to a party or the child. The court will need to consider whether a risk assessment is required and, if so, when. It will also need to consider if a fact finding hearing is necessary[105] – that is a hearing to assess whether there is any factual evidence to substantiate the allegations being made.

What is important is that any findings are made as quickly as possible to avoid delay and to keep the case progressing, and, moreover, if the allegations are found not to be genuine removing the possibility of the errant parent using them as a means to frustrate contact. Having said that, even if the allegations are found proved there is no presumption against contact although there are likely to be conditions attached to any contact order made. It cannot be emphasized enough the importance of the court getting it right and there needs to be a balance between

---

[102] Ibid, para. 4.4.
[103] Ibid, para. 5.2
[104] Ibid, para. 4.4
[105] Ibid, para. 5.1

speed and thorough investigation of the allegations for the sake of everyone concerned.

Consent orders

Parties often feel under pressure to come to an agreement and to settle the case, and the problem is that if there are still outstanding issues the likelihood is that the agreement will break down, which is not going to be in anybody's interests. The current position is that the court will not make any order without scrutinising the agreement made by the parties. This will be the case whether the agreement is reached at any hearing or submitted in writing.

If safeguarding checks or risk assessment work remains outstanding then the making of the final order will be deferred for such work to be completed and the court will adjourn the case for no longer than 28 days to a fixed date. CAFCASS will need to provide written notification of the work in accordance with the timetable specified by the court. If at that point the information is available the court may be able to make the order at the adjourned hearing in the agreed terms without the attendance of the parties. But if satisfactory information is still unavailable no order will be made and the case will be adjourned again with an opportunity for the parties to make further representations.[106]

Identification of issues and case management

Effective case management involves early identification of issues and reviewing those issues on an ongoing basis. The court needs to identify issues at the earliest stage, assess which issues are agreed and decide which issues need to be fully investigated and heard and those which do not, and the order in which those issues are to be resolved.

If the matter is pending are there any interim orders which the court can usefully make until a final decision is made such as, for example, indirect, supported or supervised contact? What directions does the court need to make to ensure the application is ready for a final hearing? This includes statements and reports. The court may direct that there be a timetable setting out the dates by which certain things need to be done and to which all parties must adhere. The courts are conscious of delay being avoided in children's cases. Delay has been one of the major criticisms of the court system. We have already touched on the no-delay principle in Chapter 6. The court should also consider the need for judicial continuity especially if there has been or is to be a fact-finding hearing or a contested interim hearing.

It may well be that straightforward proceedings started in a county court for a s 8 order may be transferred to an FPC.

---

[106] Ibid, para. 5.3.

Welfare reports

Before a report is ordered the court should consider alternative ways of working with the parties. S 7 of The Children Act deals with welfare reports. A report is not ordered in every case, but only where the court feels it needs one to assist it to make its decision and, if it is ordered, it must be directed towards and limited to welfare issues or other specific considerations identified by the court. In fact, the court should state in the order the specific factual and other issues that are to be addressed in a focused report.[107]

The provision of a welfare report is helpful and sometimes essential but a lack of resources and the resultant delay caused by the preparation of the report means the court must balance the need for the report against the effect which the delay may have on the parties and, in particular, any child involved.

It will be prepared either by the Children & Family Reporter (CFR) employed by CAFCASS or by the Social Services Department of the Local Authority. Most reports are prepared by CFRs. Social Services are usually only involved where the children who are the subject of the application are already known to them – where the child has been the subject of a child protection investigation, for example.

CAFCASS's *Safeguarding Framework*[108] states that there should be a priority allocation system for private law work following the first hearing. The local service manager's role is to keep all cases under regular review whether or not they have been allocated to a duty worker. In terms of priority for allocation, cases should be assessed in terms of high risk, medium risk or low risk. Where the issues in the case are unclear, and it is difficult to make an assessment of the level of risk and the priority to be given to it, then the court should be asked for some guidance.

In order to be able to prepare a report CAFCASS will be sent a copy of the order requesting the report and any relevant court documents, as the CFR will need to see the court file before interviewing both parents and the children. The CFR will want to see how both parents interact with the children and therefore to observe each parent alone with the children in a home environment. CFRs might also interview schoolteachers, the family doctor or grandparents, if their views are relevant. The report will then be prepared and generally this includes conclusions and recommendations about which order would be appropriate for the court to make.

The report carries a lot of weight with the court. For the most part these statements are very conservative in their approach and there has been a lot of criticism that they are heavily weighted in favour of mothers. Many fathers complain that they do not have the opportunity to challenge the report at court. If they want the CFR to attend to give evidence and for cross-examination they have to ask the court to make an order for the CFR's attendance. An order for a CFR to attend will not be made as a matter of course and only if absolutely necessary.

---

[107] PD 12B, para. 5.4.
[108] Working Together Update (2010).

S 37 reports

A s 37 report is not to be confused with a s 7 welfare report. The court has to decide if there is a need for an investigation under s 37.[109] If the court believes that a child is suffering significant harm in the resident parent's care and that an assessment of the kind needed could only take place if the child were not in his/her own home, it may be appropriate for a care or supervision order to be made in respect of that child. The court has the power to make a direction for the local authority to carry out a s 37 investigation into that child's circumstances. The order must contain the date by which the report must be filed. This must be 8 weeks unless the court directs otherwise. The date for the next hearing must be fixed. A copy of the order requesting the report and any relevant documents need to be sent to the Legal Advisor to the Director of the Local Authority's Children's Services.[110] The local authority will provide a report even if it does not decide to apply to take the child into care. The question is what would the court consider to be significant harm in this context?

In an extreme case, for example, where not only has the resident parent been implacable to contact but has also made allegations of abuse which have subsequently been found to have no foundation, and it is believed that the children are being manipulated emotionally because of the resident parent's false and distorted beliefs about the other parent, the court might order a s 37 investigation. Involving the local authority and asking them to assess whether it is appropriate to take the children into care even temporarily is an extremely drastic measure but it might be justified in such a situation.

A s 7 report should not be ordered if a s 37 report is ordered.

Expert evidence

Expert evidence is an area where the courts have sought to control the way in which the evidence is obtained, and over the years there has been considerable guidance in respect of expert witnesses in family proceedings. The instruction of expert witnesses is now governed by Part 25 of the Family Procedure Rules (FPR) 2010 and supplemented by Practice Direction 25A.[111]

Essentially, it makes it clear that the court needs information early on to decide whether expert evidence or assistance is necessary; the court and the parties need to narrow the issues in the case and work towards an agreement where possible; they must be able to obtain an expert opinion on an issue which is not within the skill and experience of the court; early identification of the issues that require an expert's answer is to be encouraged, as must full and frank disclosure of information between the parties, court and any expert instructed.

---

[109] Ibid, para. 5.4 (b).
[110] Ibid, para. 5.4 (c).
[111] It supersedes the Guidance given by the President of the Family Division on 1 April 2008 following the publication on 15 February 2008 of the Practice Direction Experts in Family Proceedings Relating to Children.

To protect children from unnecessary and repeated medical or psychiatric assessments, expert reports are only allowed if the court gives permission. It would seem that no party may instruct an expert for any purpose relating to proceedings without the court's permission[112] although it is permissible to communicate information to an expert to find out whether that expert might be able to assist if instructed.[113] The court will not automatically grant permission for an expert to be instructed and the request will normally be made at the FHDRA. The court welfare report is generally the preferred step to take, but if there is a particularly difficult medical problem with the child, that will have to be addressed by way of the appropriate expert report. For example, where there have been allegations of sexual abuse both a paediatrician's expert opinion and a child psychiatrist's expert opinion might be sought. The expert evidence must be restricted to what is reasonably required to resolve the proceedings.[114] This means that the expert's evidence must be:

- Relevant to the issue the court needs to decide.
- A necessary or desirable means of enabling the judge to make a decision.
- Worth it. That is, the delay to the case and the expense of calling the expert must be outweighed by the value to the child of that evidence being available to the court.

In order to decide whether a particular expert should be instructed, the court will require full information about the expert's relevant expertise, his/her details, availability, fees and whether, for example, the evidence on a particular issue can be obtained by both parties instructing a single joint expert. If so, the court can make a direction for the evidence on that issue to be given by a single joint expert.[115] If there is disagreement as to which expert should be instructed then the court needs to address the problem and where possible resolve it.

Where the court makes a direction for a single joint expert to be instructed, there has to be a jointly agreed letter of instruction unless the court directs otherwise but, if the parties cannot agree on the instructions then upon written request by either party and, provided the other party is copied in on that correspondence, the matter can be determined by the court. There is also the option for both parties to provide separate instructions to the single joint expert as long as each party copies the other party in on the correspondence.

The court may give directions as to the prospective expert's fees and expenses which is why this information should be readily available when asking the court for permission to instruct an expert. In any event, the parties will be jointly and severally liable for the payment of the expert's fees and expenses unless the court directs otherwise.[116] The court should stipulate which documents are to be

---

[112] FPR 2010, Rule 12.74
[113] Ibid, Rule 12.75
[114] Ibid, Rule 25.1.
[115] Ibid, Rule 25.7.
[116] Ibid, Rule 25.8(4) – (6).

disclosed to the expert. The court order dealing with the instruction of the expert, and which should be sent to the expert with his letter of instruction, should set out:

- Which party has responsibility for drafting the letter of instruction and forwarding the relevant documentation to the expert. The letter of instruction has to be filed and served within 5 working days of the hearing.[117]
- The issues the court has identified and the questions upon which the expert's opinion is needed. If the expert has permission to interview a child then the order should specify it.
- The timetable for preparing, filing and serving the report.
- Details of when the report is to be disclosed to the parties and to any other expert where applicable.
- If there is more than one expert then it will be necessary to organise an experts' discussion to see which points they agree on and, in particular, which points they disagree on. Details need to be provided in relation to the preparation for and conduct of that meeting.
- Following on from that experts' discussion there should be statement of agreement and disagreement from them.
- The expert reports need to be available to the court in electronic form as soon as possible.
- Arrangements need to be made for the expert to attend at any hearing. It is incumbent upon the instructing party to ensure that if the expert is to give oral evidence, he/she is kept up to date with relevant developments in the case and sees any new but relevant material that comes to light. A solicitor who fails to comply with this duty would be liable to a wasted costs order.

The expert's duty is to the court, not to the party instructing him/her nor to the person by whom his/her fees are paid. The duty is to assist the court on matters within that expert's expertise.[118] This means that he/she can only provide an opinion on questions that are actually within his/her expertise, skill and experience and if that is the case should make it clear as soon as possible that there are questions which he/she cannot answer and state whether in his/her opinion another expert should be brought in to answer them. The expert must be impartial and provide an opinion that is independent of the party or parties instructing him/her and act according to the best practice of his/her profession. Ultimately the expert must assist the court in accordance with the overriding objective which we looked at in Chapter 6.

In Children Act proceedings the expert's report must be shown to all the parties, the court and any other expert even if it is unfavourable to the party who instructed the expert. The report cannot be disregarded just because that party does not accept what the expert says. But if the single joint expert's report has

---

[117] Practice Direction 28A.
[118] Practice Direction 25A, para 5.7.

serious consequences for one of the parties if the court were to accept that joint expert's findings then, according to the Court of Appeal, he/she should be permitted to instruct his/her own expert.[119] There has been much concern over 'expert' opinions due to the misdiagnosis of child abuse as, for example, in the cases of Angela Cannings, Sally Clark and Trupti Patel. The fact that it was sufficient for one expert to claim on the balance of probabilities that the parent was guilty did little to encourage confidence in the legal system.

It is possible to put written questions to an expert within 10 days of receipt of the report but only to clarify it and any questions must be sent to any other parties at the same time. Any answer will be treated as part of the report. When it comes to the hearing it may well be that, where there are two experts, as a result of an experts' discussion, the issues between them may be limited and a statement of disagreements and agreements (which we considered above) may be drawn up. If the expert's report is uncontentious and consequently the expert is not required to give oral evidence, he/she must be notified. Medical experts should not be required to give oral evidence unless their attendance is absolutely necessary.

A court relies on an expert to provide it with independent assistance in relation to matters within his/her expertise by way of an objective, unbiased opinion. The court will be bound by an expert's evidence if it is on a matter solely within the expert's expertise and the judge accepts the evidence is reliable. The court is not bound to follow the recommendations of the expert if it regards the evidence as merely persuasive and not uncontrovertable. The court only needs to take it into account and if the judge does not follow it, set out express reasons for not doing so in his/her judgment. It is therefore a balancing exercise for the court.

If there is more than one expert in the case and their evidence is conflicted, the court is entitled to prefer the opinion of one expert over another provided the court gives a proper explanation for that decision. With medical evidence cases the starting point for the court will be to consider what is the generally accepted medical opinion and the reasoning behind that opinion and then, if that opinion is challenged by new medical research, the court will have to factor in that evidence when weighing up all the evidence before making its final decision.

Previously experts were given immunity from being sued in respect of the evidence they give in court. After a case in the Supreme Court in 2011 expert witnesses no longer have immunity.[120] Following on from this, and in the same way as solicitors, expert witnesses may be ordered to pay costs wasted by reason of their improper, unreasonable or negligent act or omission. An expert is not immune from disciplinary proceedings by his/her professional body. This was confirmed by the Court of Appeal in the GMC case against Sir Roy Meadows in 2006. In fact, both the court or aggrieved parties may report experts to their professional bodies on the grounds of unprofessional misconduct.

---

[119] Daniels v Walker [2000] 1 WLR 1382.
[120] Jones v Kaney [2011] UKSC 13, [2011] 2 FLR 312.

Witness statements

No party may file a witness statement unless the court makes a direction permitting them to do so. Essentially the court controls the evidence by giving directions as to the issues on which it requires evidence; the nature of the evidence which it requires to decide those issues; and the way in which the evidence is placed before the court.[121] The statement is merely the written form of the oral evidence upon which a party intends to rely at court, and upon which the court makes its decision, and therefore it must be accurate. The court may give directions as to the order in which witness statements are to be served on other parties and whether or not the witness statements are to be filed.[122] Parties generally prefer for witness statements to be exchanged at the same time rather than one following on from the other. This avoids tit-for-tat allegations. Whatever the order made by the court, the court will control the time when this evidence is submitted. Every statement must be signed and dated by the person making it and contain a declaration that he/she believes that the facts stated in it are true.

Disclosure

Orders for disclosure of documents are governed by the FPR 2010.[123] In children's proceedings if an order is made for disclosure it will be very specific – for example, documents relating to a parent's medical records to see if they are physically or mentally capable of looking after a child – the court will need to be satisfied that making the order for disclosure is really necessary. Is the documentation relevant to an issue in the case? Where the documents are personal records the court must perform a balancing exercise between the respective parties' Human Rights. After all where someone's personal records are being sought their Article 8 rights to respect for a private life will be relevant. But what about the situation where the court needs a document which is in the possession or control of somebody who is not a party to the proceedings? The court has several options:

- Make an order under FPR Rule 21.2. The court can make an order requesting the named person to provide the documents or it can make a more formal order specifying the documents or classes of documents a person must disclose; require him/her to specify any document(s) which are no longer in his/her control or which he/she claims a right or duty to withhold – for example, in the public interest; or require him/her to explain what has happened to any documents no longer in his/her control and specify the time and place for disclosure and inspection. The court cannot make an order compelling anyone to produce a document which he/she could not be compelled to produce at the final hearing.
- Witness summons. Make an order for the person in possession of the named documents to attend any hearing and produce them.

---

[121] FPR 2010, Rule 22.1(2).
[122] Ibid, Rule 22.5(2).
[123] FPR 2010, Part 21 and PD 21A.

- Direct a party to obtain and disclose documents. It may be that a person does not have a copy of the document in his/her possession but is able to obtain it by requesting a copy from somebody else. In this instance the court is able to make an order directing the party to take such steps are are necessary to do just that.
- What about obtaining disclosure from the Police? Police information is confidential and will not be disclosed unless there are important considerations of public interest to depart from the general rule of confidentiality. The protection of children is one of the areas where exceptions may be made. There is a strict protocol which must be followed and which deals with requests for disclosure of information held by the police.[124]

What about limiting disclosure of evidence, statements and reports? All parties to the case are entitled to see all statements which are also seen by the court and the CFR, but in very limited cases the court can order that some documents should not be seen by some or all of the parties. This would only be ordered if the disclosure of the documents would be damaging for the child. We look at the whole issue of confidentiality and disclosure of court documents in Chapter 16.

Wishes and feelings of the child
We looked at this in Chapter 3 and look at this again in Chapter 14 when we consider children giving evidence and meeting the judge. Practice Direction 12B states that the wishes and feelings of the child is one of the matters to be considered at the FHDRA. The court will need to consider:
- Whether the child is aware of the proceedings and how the wishes and feelings of that child are to be ascertained, if at all.
- How is the child to be involved in the proceedings, if at all, and whether at or after the FHDRA.
- Whether the child is to be joined as a party to the application. If so, then the court must consider all the appropriate steps.
- Who will inform the child of the outcome of the case where appropriate?[125]

The order
The order shall set out in particular:
- The issues about which the parties are agreed.
- The issues that remain to be resolved.
- The steps that are planned to resolve the issues.
- Any interim arrangements pending resolution, including arrangements for the involvement of children.
- The timetable for such steps and, where this involves further hearings, the date of such hearings – unless the case is resolved, at the end of every court hearing,

---

[124] ACPO Police/Family Disclosure Protocol: Disclosure of Information in Family Proceedings (2004).
[125] PD 12B, para. 5.5.

a date must be fixed for the next one whether that be for the purpose of giving further directions or any other reason.[126]

- A statement as to any facts relating to risk or safety; in so far as they are resolved the result will be stated and, in so far as not resolved, the steps to be taken to resolve them will be stated.
- If the case is to be transferred to the FPC then this is to be stated with the date and purpose of the next hearing.
- If the case is not to be transferred to the FPC then this is to be stated with the reason for the decision.
- Whether in the event of an order, by consent or otherwise, or pending such an order, the parties are to be assisted by participation in mediation, Parenting Information Programmes (PIPs), or by other types of parenting intervention, and to detail any contact activity directions or conditions imposed by the court.[127]

Further hearings and hearing dates

If the matter is not resolved at the FHDRA further directions hearings may be necessary. Unless otherwise directed a party shall attend any directions appointments.[128] To ensure judicial continuity and continuous case management the judge may reserve the case to himself. This is meritorious, but the downside is that sometimes the listing of the case will be delayed because the judge is not available. For example, if at the FHDRA the District Judge has directed that a finding of fact hearing is necessary to determine allegations of domestic violence, both that hearing and the final hearing must take place before the same judge. The court will also consider what directions should be given for the attendance of witnesses and the CFR at the final hearing.

At any hearing the court may confirm a date for the final hearing or the week within which the final hearing is to begin; set a timetable for the final hearing (unless one has already been fixed or the court considers it inappropriate); or set a date for the final hearing or a period within which the final hearing of the application is to take place.

Although a party should attend any directions appointment, proceedings or any part of them can take place in the absence of any party, including a party who is a child, if the court considers it in the interests of the parties. If the Applicant appears but the Respondent does not, the court may proceed with the hearing or appointment provided the court is satisfied the Respondent received reasonable notice of the date of the hearing, or the circumstances justify proceeding with the hearing even in the absence of the Respondent.[129] If the Applicant does not appear but the Respondent does, the court may refuse the application or if it feels it has

---

[126] FPR 2010, Rule 12.13(1).
[127] PD 12B, para. 6.1.
[128] FPR 2010, Rules 27.3 and 12.14(2).
[129] Ibid, Rule 27.4(2) and (3).

sufficient evidence may proceed in the absence of the Applicant.[130] If neither the Applicant nor the Respondent appears the court may refuse the application.[131]

What about the situation where a party fails to attend a hearing and the court makes an order against him/her? He/she may apply to have the order set aside but the court will only grant the application if the party acted promptly after finding out that an order had been made against him/her; had a valid reason for non-attendance and has a reasonable prospect of success at the hearing.[132]

Court bundles

It is the duty of the Applicant to prepare and file at court an agreed and paginated bundle of documents two days prior to any hearing which is not listed for one hour or less or any urgent applications. Chronologies, indexes, position statements of both parties, including a summary of the order or directions sought by each party at the hearing, must be filed one day before the hearing. This is in accordance with a detailed Practice Direction about bundles which came into force on 2 October 2006 and now absorbed by the FPR 2010.[133] So far as litigants in person are concerned special considerations apply. Where the Applicant is a litigant in person and the Respondent is represented by solicitors, the responsibility for preparing the bundle will be with the Respondent's solicitors. The bundle which must contain all relevant documents in chronological order, paginated, indexed and divided into separate sections should be provided to all the other parties not less than four days before the hearing. A failure to comply with any part of the Practice Direction may result in the judge removing the case from the list, or putting it further back in the list and even a wasted costs order against the lawyers responsible.

Time estimates

A time estimate must be prepared in every case, agreed between the parties where possible, and placed in the front of the bundle. It should be prepared on the basis that before giving oral evidence any witnesses will have already read any relevant documentation and it must specify the various time estimates which are:

- Reading time for the judge pre-hearing.
- Time needed for hearing all the evidence and submissions.
- Time required for the judge to prepare and deliver judgment.

If any time estimates change the court must be notified.

The final hearing

The final hearing will be scheduled to take place after any welfare report and any other evidence such as an expert's report and witness statements have been filed.

---

[130] Ibid, Rule 27.4(4).
[131] Ibid, Rule 27.4(5).
[132] Ibid, Rule 27.5.
[133] Practice Direction 27A: Family Proceedings Court Bundles, President's Direction, 27 July 2006 [2006] 2 FLR 199.

This is why it is important that evidence is filed on time and why the court sets a timetable for it to be done in the first place. The court has wide discretion and how it conducts the case will depend upon the issues and the evidence. Do the circumstances warrant there being a full hearing? Is it in the best interests of the child? Does the court have enough evidence to make a decision? Will that evidence affect the outcome of the case? How likely is it that the evidence that comes to light as a result of cross-examination of witnesses will affect the outcome? What are the prospects of success of the application if it proceeds to a full trial?

We looked at the procedure at the final hearing in Chapter 6. We consider publicity and media access in Chapter 16.

Judgment

This must be delivered as soon as possible after the hearing. There is no statutory requirement for all judgments to be recorded in writing although FPCs are required to give written reasons. Any findings of fact made by the court and the reasons for the decision will be kept on the court file. If judgment is reserved the general rule is that judges are required to deliver judgment not later than one month after the hearing. Sometimes the judge will send the parties a draft judgment before it is handed down. Judgments do not take effect until formally handed down and parties may not reveal the content of draft judgments, including the decision reached, to anyone until then. The judgment or order takes effect from the date it is given or made or such later date as the court may decide. A copy of the order must be served on each party and on any person with whom the child is living. We look at the whole issue of whether judgments should be given in public and publication of judgments in Chapter 16.

Post-judgment

There are various issues that may still need to be determined. For example, is permission sought to appeal the judgment? And what about the child who has been the subject of the proceedings? Who is going to explain the judge's decision to him/her? If the child had separate representation and was appointed a guardian that task will probably go to the guardian. If not it might go to the CAFCASS officer who provided a s 7 report. And should the judge write to the child? This will depend upon the age of the child and whether he/she has met the judge.

How long will the order last for?

A s 8 order will cease to have effect when the child reaches 16, but the court does have power – in exceptional circumstances – to make or extend an order beyond a child's 16th Birthday. It also may be varied or discharged by way of an application. In any event, it will cease when the child reaches 18. If a residence or contact order is made in favour of a parent these orders will automatically end if the child's parents live together for a continuous period of more than 6 months.

Other procedural concerns...

Applying to be joined as a party

The application must be made in Form C2. The same applies if a person wishes to cease to be a party. The court may grant the application for a person to cease to be a party without a hearing. If not, and a hearing date is fixed, all the parties must be given notice. Alternatively, the parties will be required to give written representations by a certain date after which the court may consider the request without the need for a hearing.

The court will consider the implications of joining a party. Will it prolong the court case? What about costs? How should the court approach joining members of the extended family? When deciding whether someone should be joined as a party the welfare test does not apply because this is a procedural matter. A person who has parental responsibility will be joined as a party on request because any person with parental responsibility should be a Respondent anyway. Interestingly enough though, a father who does not have parental responsibility is not required to be a Respondent, but if the father then applied to be joined as a party it is likely he would be successful in his application, provided it is made quickly and does not result in any hearing being postponed, in which case his application might be refused.

It may be that the person seeking permission to be joined as a party wishes to apply for a s 8 order. The court will consider the same factors as when a person is applying for leave which we looked at earlier in this chapter. On the other hand a person might want to be joined as a party without wishing to apply for a s 8 order. The court will not grant the request unless it decides that this person has a separate point of view which needs to be put forward. If the court is in any doubt about that or decides that really that person's role is as more of a support to another party then it will be more appropriate for that person to give evidence rather than be joined in the proceedings.

We look at joining children as parties in Chapter 14.

What does it mean to make an application without notice?

This means to make an application without notice to the other party. For example, it would be used in the case of an emergency where it is anticipated that the other parent intends to abduct the children as that parent has not returned them from a contact visit, or there is an urgent medical problem which needs to be addressed. We look at emergency applications in Chapter 20.

An application for a s 8 order without notice is governed by the Family Procedure Rules (FPR) Rule 12.16. The general procedure is that if such an application is made in the High Court or the County Court, the full application should be filed either at the same time or, if it is made by telephone, on the next business day. In the magistrate's court an application can be made without notice with the permission of the court. The application needs to be filed at the time it is made or as the court directs. Service of the order is the same for all courts. The without notice order must be served on the Respondent as soon as possible and the application itself within 48 hours after the making of the order.

The courts do not usually like to make residence/contact orders without hearing from the other party first. If notice can be given, even if it is informal notice by telephone, that is preferable to no notice at all. The court will be cautious because it is obviously only hearing the Applicant's version of events, so the Applicant must give as much relevant information to the court as possible to assist it in making its decision. If the court has been misinformed it is the duty of the Applicant to bring this to the attention of the court, as well as if there is a change in circumstances which would influence the court's decision whether or not to grant the application. The Applicant should file a sworn statement in support of the application at the time of the hearing or failing that undertake to file it as soon as possible. Even so the court might refuse to make an order without notice and direct that the application is made on notice.

If the court does make an order without notice, the order should set out details of the evidence upon which the court has based its decision and state that the Respondent may apply to vary or discharge the order on notice. In any event, an order made without notice will be of limited duration and for a matter of days. If the Respondent does wish to challenge the order then the application should be made on notice!

Controlling further applications being made

The court has the power to make an order that no further applications may be made by a party without obtaining the permission of the court first.[134] For example, where there is a history of a party making unreasonable applications the court might use this power – the party against whom the order is to be made should have the chance to put his/her case why the order should not be made and needs to persuade the judge that he has an arguable case with some chance of success. If the case is meritorious than this should not be too much of an obstacle. But if it is unmeritorious then the other parties and particularly any children involved will have been spared and protected from unnecessary involvement in the proposed proceedings and all that entails. The Applicant's right to a fair trial under Article 6 of the European Convention on Human Rights is not breached because in practice the making of such an order does not prevent that party making further applications, it just means subsequent applications will be monitored by the court. Guidance as to how the court should approach the matter has been set out by the Court of Appeal.[135] In summary these are:

---

[134] Children Act 1989, s 91(14).
[135] Re P (Section 91(14) Guidelines) (Residence and Religious Heritage) [1999] 2 FLR 573.

- When weighing up any decision to control a further application being made the court must have regard to the fact that the welfare of the child is the paramount consideration.
- The court's power to control applications is discretionary and when exercising its discretion the court must take all the relevant circumstances into account. For example, if the welfare of the child dictates that such an order should be made.
- In deciding whether to impose a restriction the court has to consider a party's right to bring proceedings in relation to matters affecting his/her child. See the Human Rights implications above.
- The court should only exercise its power sparingly and with caution – these orders will only be made in exceptional circumstances and more often than not as a last resort.
- The court has the power to decide what type of applications are to be controlled and for how long. It would be exceptional for a court to make an order restricting applications indefinitely. As indicated above, the whole point is that the court can monitor applications and this acts as a safeguard.

Withdrawing the application

Once an application relating to the welfare or upbringing of a child has been issued it may only be withdrawn with the permission of the court and the court may refuse permission if there are still outstanding issues to be resolved, such as, for example, alleged domestic violence. In any event, it will be necessary to make a formal request to the court for the matter to be withdrawn. This may either be made in writing setting out the reasons for the request or can be made orally if the parties are present in court. If written reasons are given and the other interested parties have had the opportunity to make written representations about the request then it will not be necessary to have a hearing.[136]

Recent developments and reform of the court process

Safeguarding checks and a track system

The Family Justice Review recommended that safeguarding checks are completed at the point of entry into the court system and that a track system should be established according to the complexity of the case.[137] The idea is that if parties fail to reach an agreement and an application is made to the court it will either be allocated to a simple track system or a complex track system. The simple track would be used for cases where there are no allegations of domestic violence or abuse and findings of fact are not necessary and presumably where no welfare report or expert evidence is required.

---

xx FPR 2010, Rule 29.4.
xx Family Justice Review Final Report – November 2011, pp.35-36, 163-5 paras. 4.116-4.131.

We already have safeguarding through CAFCASS and CAFCASS Cymru but the Government agrees that this is essential at the point of entry into the court system and, so far as cases settled out of court are concerned, it is equally important to identify safeguarding issues. In terms of a simple track system the FHDRA does currently act as a filter, narrowing the issues and making decisions as to how the case is to be progressed, but we have no formal track system in which to allocate these cases following the FHDRA. The Government has indicated that further work will be necessary to develop and implement a track system and consideration will be given as to how this will work with proposals to improve judicial continuity and avoid unncessary delay.[138]

What about the FHDRA and judicial continuity at further hearings?
The Family Justice Review recommended that the FHDRA should be retained but, where further court involvement is required after this, the judge should allocate the case to either the simple or complex track according to the complexity of the case; and that the judge allocated to hear the case after an FHDRA must remain the judge for that case.[139] In its response the Government stressed that it did not envisage any change to the focus of the Private Law Programme where the court is actively involved in helping parties to explore ways of resolving their disputes at the FHDRA. In terms of progressing cases through a track system following the FHDRA, and as indicated above, the Government will have to work with the judiciary to consider how such a system would work.

In terms of judicial continuity, the Government accepts this recommendation in principle and believes this is the key to ensuring effective management of cases, as the judge dealing with the matter will be familiar with the facts of the case. But the Government has stressed that allocation of cases to individual judges is a judicial matter with the need to take account of local circumstances and to avoid unnecessary delay. The Government has indicated that it will work with the Judicial Office and HMCTS to further promote the existing guidance on achieving continuity in family courts.[140]

---

[138] The Government's Response to the Family Justice Review: *A system with children and families at its heart* – Ministry of Justice & Department for Education, February 2012, Cm 8273, p.77.
[139] Family Justice Review Final Report – November 2011, pp.36, 163-4 paras. 4.117-4.121.
[140] The Government's Response to the Family Justice Review: *A system with children and families at its heart* – Ministry of Justice & Department for Education, February 2012, Cm 8273, p.78.

Chapter 13
Public law

Implications for fathers with children taken into care

Public law is a vast area and relates to the involvement of the local authority and care proceedings. Where there has been violence or abuse Social Services may need to intervene to protect a child 'at risk'. They have to apply for a court order to do this and to show that the child is likely to suffer 'significant harm' because of the level of care provided at home or because the child is beyond your control. Social Services might apply for any of the following orders:

- **Care Order**
This is an order to take your child into care.

- **Emergency Protection Order**
They need this if they feel the child is in danger and want take the children from your care immediately. They have to go back to court for a care order.

- **Supervision Orders**
If Social Services have a supervision order it means you will be supervised when you care for your children.

It is not within the scope of this book to deal with public law procedure in any great detail but it is important to consider these public law orders because a father needs to be aware of local authority powers and the effect of a public law order upon his contact with a child of his in care.

Removing a child from its parent

Lord Justice Munby, President of the Family Division as of 11 January 2013, set out the criteria in a care proceedings case several years ago when he was a High Court Judge.[141] He made it clear that a local authority cannot simply take a child into care and, where the parent(s) do not agree, must have first obtained an order from a family court authorizing removal of the child from his/her parent(s). The local authority would have to obtain an emergency protection order (see above), an interim care order or, in an exceptional case, a wardship order.

A police officer, on the other hand, has the power to remove a child without obtaining a court order first, but only if the police officer has reasonable cause to believe that the child would be likely to suffer significant harm. Neither local

---

[141] Care Proceedings: R (G) v Nottingham City Council [2008] EWHC (Admin).

authorities nor social workers possess that power.

However, like anyone else, a social worker or nurse would be entitled to intervene if that intervention was necessary to protect a baby from immediate violence at the hands of a parent. Furthermore, a hospital might be able to rely upon the Children Act[142] under which a person with care of the child, but without parental responsibility, could take action necessary to safeguard or promote the child's welfare, to justify action taken in relation to a child in its care, but only if there was a medical justification for such intervention. Otherwise, local authorities, hospitals and medical staff have no power to remove a child from parents unless they had first obtained a court order authorising the removal.

The local authority has taken the child into care but the father wants contact. Is he entitled?

Contact with the family is in the best interests of a child in care unless proved otherwise. Contact with children in care is subject to the control of the court. When children are in care they are referred to as being 'looked after' by the local authority.[143]

When a care order is made in relation to children, those children should maintain contact with their parents if at all possible. A child in care is afforded reasonable contact with parents, guardians, or anyone with a residence order in force immediately before the care order was made.

If contact is not forthcoming, a father could make an application for contact. The application would be made under s 34 of the Children Act as it governs public proceedings and not s 8. However, an application can only be made once in every six months, unless the leave of the court is obtained. But if a father is using the application in effect as a means by which he can obtain the return of the child it is unlikely to succeed, especially if the matter has already been fully dealt with by the court.

Although the local authority has a duty to promote contact between the parents and any other person having parental responsibility, it does not have to do so if this is not reasonably practicable or in line with what is in the best interests of the child. The court has to weigh up the pros and cons as to whether continued contact is in the child's best interests. Where a child is in care and an application for contact is made, the court carries out a balancing exercise and weighs up all the factors.

It has been said that contact must not be allowed to destabilize or endanger or frustrate the arrangements planned for the child. The court can require the local authority to justify long-term plans if those plans exclude contact with a parent! The local authority or the child can apply to the court for an order that a 'named' person should have such contact with the child as the court considers appropriate. This includes power to authorize the authority to refuse contact to a named party.

---

[142] Children Act 1989, s 3(5).
[143] Children Act 1989, s 22(1).

In exercising its discretion to determine issues related to future contact, the court should have regard to the child's welfare as paramount and to the long-term plans of the authority for the child's future. At the end of the day contact should continue, but it is evident that so far as children in care are concerned there are a number of hurdles to overcome.

The Public law Protocol and Public Law Outlines

In November 2003 the *Public Law Protocol* came into force for all applications issued by local authorities for care and supervision orders. It stipulated that the maximum length a case should take was forty weeks and only where there were 'exceptional or unforseen' circumstances should a case take longer than that. It also stipulated that there should be judicial continuity, active case management by the court, consistency in terms of standardisation of the steps to be taken during the process and regular case management conferences.

Unfortunately, it soon became clear that these goals were not being achieved with delay being a major problem in particular. On 1 April 2008 the *Public Law Outline 2008* was introduced with the aim of reducing unnecessary delay by setting an appropriate timetable for cases, focused around the needs of the individual child and the promotion of better case management with earlier identification of the key issues in the case. But a review a year after it had been in operation found that there was no consistency in compliance with its requirements by local authorities, and that there was just too much paperwork which needed streamlining. It was replaced by the *Revised Public Law Outline 2010* which came onto operation 1 April 2010.

The Munro Review

In May 2011 Professor Eileen Munro from the London School of Economics published her report reviewing child protection and social work in England. The report states that local authorities should have more freedom to design their own child protection services and that a 'one-size-fits-all' approach to child protection is preventing them from focusing on the needs of the child.

The Family Justice Review 2011 and Government reform

Delay, case management, timetabling & expert reports
The Review set out detailed recommendations for reform. It highlighted the ongoing problem of delay in child care proceedings and it was emphasised that there should be robust judicial case management, more consistency, and legislation to provide a power to set a time limit on care proceedings of six months, which the Government has accepted. In terms of commissioning expert reports, regard must be given to the impact of delay on the welfare of any child. It is agreed that 'there needs to be increased effectiveness in progression of cases through the court

system.'[144] Since 2 April 2012 HMCTS has been piloting a new case management system in the family courts that will track every public law case and give the legal profession ongoing information – updated for every hearing – about the ages of the child or children they are dealing with; the length of time a case has been running; the number of hearings which there have been; any adjournments of hearings; and applications for experts. The national pilot is to run for the whole of the financial year 2012/13. By having a record of data the family courts will be able to understand where public law cases are allocated and what is the consequence, in terms of delay, of the case management decisions that are made. The aim is for the judiciary to complete each case within 26 weeks unless it is not in the interests of the child concerned. The new system will allow the HMCTS to determine where and why this deadline is not being met and what can be changed to improve efficiencies.

The role of the court and the local authority
The Family Justice Review also recommended that courts 'should refocus on the core issues of whether the child is to live with parents, other family or friends, or be removed to the care of the local authority.'[145] The Government agreed that 'it is important that courts continue to consider core elements of children's care plans before making care orders', but it indicated that since care plans often change over time in response to children's changing needs 'it makes sense for the detail to be left to the local authority which has the ongoing responsibility for the plan.' The Government intends to introduce legislation to make the distinction between the role of the courts and local authorities in children's care plans clear. In terms of alternatives to children being taken into care there is already the facility to make what is known as a special guardianship order. This order was introduced by the Adoption & Children Act 2002. If a special guardianship order is made the natural parents retain parental responsibility but it is curtailed so that the special guardian is able to exercise parental responsibility to the exclusion of everyone else. The benefit of the order is that, unlike adoption, ties with the natural family are not severed. We consider the whole issue of guardianship and special guardianship orders in Chapter 21.

Alternatives to court
We looked at dispute resolution services in Chapter 2 and the use of Family Group Conferences and mediation. The Government is considering options for undertaking a pilot on the use of formal mediation approaches in public law proceedings.

---

[144] The Government's Response to the Family Justice Review: *A system with children and families at its heart* – Ministry of Justice & Department for Education, February 2012, Cm 8273, Case Management pp54-57.
[145] Family Justice Review Final Report – November 2011, Public law – The role of the court pp.30, 94-101.

Rights of Children in care

A Government Green Paper, Care Matters: *Transforming the lives of children and young people in care*, was published by the Department for Education and Skills (DfES) on 9 October 2006. Under the proposals children in care would have the right to choose when they leave care once they reach 16, and measures would be introduced to stop them being repeatedly moved between foster homes; ensure they are placed in the best schools; and provide financial security as they enter adulthood. The White Paper, *Care Matters: Time for Change* was published on 22 June 2007 and gave children the right to stay in care up to the age of 18, or even to remain with foster carers up to the age of 21. It was also stated that they would have the support of a personal advisor up to the age of 25. The point is that children should not be forced out of care before they are ready.

Chapter 14
Special consideration for the children

Children and s 8 proceedings

In Chapter 11 we looked at the list of welfare factors the court considers when an application is made to it for a s 8 order, one of which is the wishes and feelings of the child. In the majority of cases, a child's wishes and feelings will be communicated to the court via the CAFCASS welfare report, but in certain cases it may be in the best interests of a child to be joined as a party to the proceedings and to be separately represented. There is also the issue of whether, and in what circumstances, children should be called as witnesses and required to give evidence, and whether judges should interview children.

A right to be heard

Article 12 of the United Nations Convention on the Rights of the Child 1989 states that where a child is capable of forming his or her own views it is the child's right to express his or her views freely on 'all matters affecting the child' and to have those views given due weight. The weight to be given to those views will depend upon the age and maturity of the child in question; and the child should have the opportunity of being 'heard' either 'directly or through a representative or appropriate body, in a manner consistent with procedural rules of national law.'

In considering Article 12 in relation to the separate representation of children in private law proceedings under the Children Act 1989, the Court of Appeal has held that the provisions of the Act are framed widely enough to comply with Article 12 as well as with Article 8 of the European Convention on Human Rights which relates to a right to family life and a child's right to participate in any decision-making processes that will fundamentally affect that child's family life.[146]

Although rights under the Convention are not directly enforceable in the UK Courts, they can be persuasive when the court is considering how to exercise its discretion and decide when children should be made parties to private law Children Act cases. Certainly, their existence has made courts revisit their approach when exercising that discretion.

The children's ascertainable wishes and feelings

The bottom line is that bearing in mind extremely important decisions are being made about the children's welfare and future, where reasonably possible and taking

---

[146] Mabon v Mabon 2005 EWCA Civ 634.

account of their age and understanding, they ought to have a say in the matter. But what is the best way to communicate a child's wishes and feelings? In Chapter 3 we looked at proposed reform in this area and ways to make the child's voice heard. It is important for children not just for their views to be heard but for them to be listened to, and what is clear is that children want to be informed and given accurate information about issues which have a direct bearing upon their lives. There does seem to be a growing understanding of the importance of listening to children. Children often have very definite views and they might be quite different from those of the parent who is looking after them.

The Revised Private Law Programme 2010[147] states that at the First Hearing Dispute Resolution Appointment (FHDRA) the court must consider:

- Whether the child is aware of the proceedings and how the wishes and feelings of the child are to be ascertained, if at all.
- How the child is to be involved in the proceedings, if at all, and whether at or after the FHDRA.
- If consideration is given to joining the child as a party to the application, the current guidance from the President of the Family Division, and who will inform the child of the outcome of the case where appropriate.

While it is recognised that a child's input is valuable, in family proceedings the court will be concerned with the implications and effect on the child of any decision to join him/her as a party or permit him/her to give evidence and to be cross-examined. For example, if the child is an Applicant in the proceedings then he/she will have access to the court file. There might be documents such as medical reports or assessments which might be distressing for the child. This is why, in the majority of cases, there is a tendency to lean towards ascertaining a child's wishes and feelings through the welfare report.

Basically there are five scenarios:

- The child's view is never aired before the court because the parents come to an agreement at an early stage.
- The case proceeds to court, but no welfare report is ordered and the court relies on the parents' assessments of what is in the best interests of their child.
- A welfare report is ordered and the wishes and feelings of the child are communicated to the court through that report.
- The facts of the case dictate that the child be joined as a party to the proceedings and be separately represented.
- The child is old enough and mature enough to bring a case him/herself.

Whatever the scenario, ascertaining the child's wishes and feelings is only part of the equation. The court will have to decide what weight to give to those wishes and feelings and always be mindful that this is only one of the welfare factors that the court takes into consideration. Ultimately the decision taken must be in the child's best interests.

---

[147] Practice Direction 12B – The Revised Private Law Programme para. 5.5.

The child witness

In January 2012 detailed *Guidelines in relation to children giving evidence* in family proceedings were issued by the Family Justice Council Working Party on Children Giving Evidence and chaired by the Rt. Hon. Lord Justice Thorpe, a Court of Appeal Judge. Following a leading case[148] where the Supreme Court held that there was no longer a presumption or starting point against children giving evidence in family proceedings, it was decided that guidance needed to be given in respect of the matters which should be taken into account in such situations. The issue of whether a child ought to be further questioned or give evidence in family proceedings should be addressed at the earliest opportunity. The Guidelines state that the court has an overriding duty to ensure that the child gives the best possible evidence so that the court may make an informed decision.

Competency of the child to give evidence

When deliberating as to whether a child should give evidence, the court will need to assess whether that particular child is competent to give evidence.[149] The child will be competent if he/she understands the nature of an oath or, in the opinion of the court, understands that it is his/her duty to speak the truth and has sufficient understanding to justify his/her evidence being heard. If the child is deemed competent the court must still consider whether it is appropriate for that child to give evidence. The court has to strike a fine balance between the demands of justice and the welfare of the child. The welfare of the child in this instance will be a relevant consideration but not the paramount consideration. Nevertheless, the court must weigh up both the advantages and disadvantages of calling that child as a witness and whether the need to determine the truth is enough to warrant any potential harm giving evidence might do to the child. The court will also consider the question of delay and whether it is merited.

Benefit v Burden

What are the benefits of the child giving evidence? It may be that the court really needs to hear from the child to make a proper assessment in the case, or that the evidence the court already has is insufficient or inconclusive. The child may be very articulate and able to express his/her opinion clearly. There is of course the danger that if some considerable time has passed since the events about which the child is being questioned, that the child's recollection of those events may be hazy and infact unreliable. If there is a recording of events nearer that time (generally from what is called an 'Achieving Best Evidence' interview) that might be an alternative for the court. And what about a written statement from the child? In the majority of cases courts will not allow them. There is always the concern that a child will have been coached by a parent or some other party to write the

---

[148] Re W [2010] UKSC 12.
[149] Children Act 1989, s 96(1).

statement; and this also applies where the child may have written a letter because it may have been dictated by the resident parent. The Law Society's Family Law Protocol[150] states that solicitors should advise clients that it will not assist them to produce statements written by their children.

What are the burdens on the child of giving evidence? For any adult standing in a witness box and being cross-examined is an ordeal, so for a child the burden will be enormous and therefore the impact on children of giving evidence cannot be underestimated. Much will depend on the child him or herself, particularly the child's age and level of maturity and how the child feels about giving evidence. A reluctant child will not make a good witness. It is important the child has a good support network. It may be that the child has a guardian if he/she has been joined as a party (see below) and the views of that guardian or anyone who has parental responsibility for the child will be taken into account.

Supporting and protecting children giving evidence

If the decision has been made for the child to give evidence then the court will wish to ensure the child is shielded so far as is reasonably possible and is supported. Witness supporters are people who are there to provide emotional support and information. They will have received the appropriate training for the role. They are neutral and not involved in the case in any way. They will, for example, help familiarize a child with the court and procedures, support the child through the court proceedings – which means they will accompany the child on any pre-trial visit to court – or be there in the room if the child is giving evidence by video link. The NSPCC and Barnardos have people who are experienced child witness supporters.

The court will have to consider how the child's evidence is going to be given. The courts are used to children giving evidence in criminal proceedings and the 'special' measures implemented in the criminal courts may also be utilized in the family courts. These include:

- Having a screen so the child is hidden from view in court.[151]
- The child giving evidence by live video link.[152] This could be in the court building or somewhere else.
- Instead of the child being asked questions directly by the barristers the questions could be put to the child through an intermediary.[153] An intermediary is literally that – someone who communicates the questions asked, communicates the answers given and explains the questions or answers where necessary, so that the witness understands what is being asked and the advocate is clear on what the response is. The intermediary will be registered with the Ministry of Justice (MoJ).

---

[150] Family Law Protocol 3rd Edition, The Law Society 2010, para. 5.9.12.
[151] Youth Justice & Criminal Evidence Act 1999, s 23.
[152] Ibid, s 24.
[153] Ibid, s 29.

- Using visual communication aids like sign or symbol boards.[154]
- Deciding about media access. It is likely that the court will exclude the press. We look at media access to the court in detail in Chapter 16.

Cross-examining a child is not an easy task for an advocate and is very much an ordeal for a child and all sorts of problems arise. The child might have difficulty understanding the questions. They might be too complicated. This is why the presence of an intermediary explaining the questions is invaluable. The barrister needs to ask focused questions commensurate with a child's verbal and intellectual development otherwise the questions will simply go over the child's head.

Attending Court
The child may not be a witness but may wish to attend court if it is an important court hearing about the child's future. Certainly, where proceedings are held in public a child has as much right to attend court as anybody else subject to the court's power of exclusion! In private proceedings the courts have a practical approach and it will depend upon the circumstances of the case, the nature of the proceedings, the matters to be discussed, the evidence to be given and the particular child.

Meeting the Judge

A judge has a discretion to see a child in private, but for the most part this discretion is not exercised and judges have preferred to rely on other means, particularly the welfare report, to ascertain a child's wishes and feelings. Many judges do not feel comfortable about interviewing children, feeling they lack the expertise and training and having to make an assessment in one short meeting. Then there is the important point that anything the child tells the judge will not be confidential and he will be required to report back anything material which was said to the parties. There has been considerable debate about whether a judge should meet the child or not.

In April 2010 the Family Justice Council issued *Guidelines for Judges Meeting Children* in family proceedings.[155] These Guidelines were approved by the President of the Family Division. The purpose of any meeting is to enable the child to gain some understanding of what is going on and to be reassured that the judge has understood him/her. The Guidelines are not binding on judges, but they are persuasive. They are as follows:

- The judge is entitled to expect the lawyer for the child and/or the CAFCASS officer to advise whether the child wishes to meet the judge and, if so, to explain from the child's perspective, the purpose of the meeting; to advise whether it accords with the welfare interests of the child for such a meeting to take place; and to identify the purpose of the proposed meeting as perceived by the child's professional representatives.

---

[154] Ibid, s 30.
[155] [2010] 2 FLR 1872.

- The other parties shall be entitled to make representations as to any proposed meeting with the judge before the judge decides whether or not it shall take place.
- In deciding whether or not a meeting shall take place and, if so, in what circumstances, the child's chronological age is relevant but not determinative. Some children of 7 or even younger have a clear understanding of their circumstances and very clear views which they may wish to express.
- If the child wishes to meet the judge but the judge decides that a meeting would be inappropriate, the judge should consider providing a brief explanation in writing for the child.
- If a judge decides to meet a child, it is a matter for the discretion of the judge, having considered representations from the parties. He/she will need to decide the purpose and proposed content of the meeting; at what stage in the proceedings (or after they have concluded to explain his/her decision) the meeting should take place; where the meeting will take place; who will bring the child to the meeting; who will prepare the child for the meeting (generally the CAFCASS officer); who else will attend the meeting (although the judge should see the child alone); who will take the notes of the meeting; how those notes will be approved by the judge and how they will be communicated to the other parties.
- If the meeting takes place during the proceedings, the judge should explain at an early stage that a judge cannot hold secrets and what is said by the child will, other than in exceptional circumstances, be communicated to his/her parents and the other parties. The Guidelines do not specify what those exceptional circumstances are. The judge should also explain that decisions in the case are the responsibility of the judge who will have to weigh a number of factors and that the outcome is *never* the responsibility of the child. The judge should discuss with the child how his or her decisions will be communicated to the child, and the parties or their representatives shall have the opportunity to respond to the content of the meeting, whether by way of oral evidence or written submissions.

Joining the child as a party

In 2004 the President of the Family Division issued a Practice Direction offering guidance on when a child might be joined as a party, indicating that such an order should only be made in a minority of cases involving issues of significant difficulty and that other alternatives – such as asking CAFCASS to carry out further assessments or obtaining expert evidence – should be considered first. This Practice Direction has now been replaced by Practice Direction 16A Part 4. The terms are actually identical.

In all cases, when a CAFCASS officer is preparing a welfare report, he/she is under an express duty to consider whether it is in the best interests of the child to be joined as a party and, if so, should notify the court and give reasons why he/she believes joining the child as a party is necessary.[156] In making its order the court will consider the risk of delay. A decision about joining a child as a party should be made as soon as possible. Here are some examples of situations which **might** justify such an order:

- Where the dispute over residence or contact is intractable.
- Where there is implacable hostility to contact on the part of the resident parent which is unfounded.
- Where the child is suffering harm because of either the intractable residence/contact dispute or the resident parent's unfounded hostility to contact taking place.
- Where the child's views or interests cannot be met effectively through the CAFCASS report. For example there might be complex or medical health issues involved or allegations of abuse or domestic violence which cannot be resolved through the CAFCASS officer's intervention.
- Where the child is an older child who is objecting to a course of action.
- Where the child has a certain viewpoint and interests which are inconsistent with or incapable of being represented by any of the adult parties.

Guardians and Next Friends

When a child, who is the subject of family proceedings, is joined as a party to the proceedings, unless the court is satisfied that the child is able, having regard to his/her understanding, to give instructions him/herself in relation to the proceedings that child will need to be represented. The child will be represented by an adult who acts as his/her guardian. In the case of a child who is not subject to the proceedings but needs to be joined as a Respondent, that child will be represented by a next friend. An example of a party who would require a next friend would be a parent under 18 and is the parent of a child who is the subject of the proceedings. It follows that in the majority of cases it will be a guardian who is appointed. Either way it is the guardian/next friend who will instruct a solicitor to act for the child.

The child as a party with a guardian or next friend

A CAFCASS officer will usually be appointed by the court as the child's guardian and in fact Practice Direction 16A states that where a child is to be made a party consideration should first be given to appointing CAFCASS. It is important to check that CAFCASS have an officer who can take on the role and all that it entails. The CAFCASS Practice Note of 2006 makes it clear that if, for whatever reason, a CAFCASS officer cannot be appointed, then some other person or the Official Solicitor may be appointed instead. But the court will only appoint someone to act as a guardian if the court is satisfied that he/she will act competently and has no interests which will conflict with the interests of the child.

---

[156] Practice Direction 16 A, para. 11.3.

If CAFCASS is able to assist, the court makes an order simply stating that CAFCASS has been appointed[157] and CAFCASS will then allocate an officer to the case. The CAFCASS officer will speak to the child and find out what he/she wants and work in conjunction with the solicitor he/she appoints. Sometimes CAFCASS appoints someone from CAFCASS legal in which case it is unnecessary to instruct a solicitor. If CAFCASS is unable to appoint someone without delay, the court may appoint an officer from the National Youth Advocacy Service (NYAS). This is a 'not for profit' children's charity and one of the things it offers is advocacy services to children. A Protocol has been agreed between CAFCASS and NYAS about when NYAS will accept an appointment as a guardian. Generally NYAS will step in where CAFCASS cannot provide a guardian or there are problems between CAFCASS and the family and the court deems it best for a guardian to be provided by NYAS.

The guardian/next friend is the person who reads the court papers, goes to court hearings, prepares statements on behalf of the child and gives oral evidence. It is his/her task to decide on the child's behalf what is in the child's best interests as well as informing the court about the child's wishes. Any solicitor the guardian appoints must represent the child according to the guardian's instructions, unless the child is able to give his/her own instructions – see below.

The child as a party without a guardian/next friend
A child will need the permission of the court if he/she wants to apply for a s 8 order him/herself and this will be given only if the court is satisfied that the child has sufficient understanding to make the application. The application will be for leave to apply. We considered applications for leave in Chapter 12.

The procedure is set out in the Family Procedure Rules (FPR) 2010.[158] Essentially, the child does not need a guardian/next friend if the solicitor acting for him/her considers the child is able, having regard to his/her understanding, to give instructions in relation to the proceedings and the judge accepts the solicitor's recommendations. If subsequently the solicitor forms the view that the child is no longer able to give instructions then he/she must inform the court immediately for the court to consider the appointment of a guardian/next friend. The court itself may revoke any permission it gave for the child to act without a guardian/next friend if it considers the child does not have sufficient understanding to continue. The test is the child's understanding and not his/her age.

The Court of Appeal has recognised that in the case of articulate teenagers the courts must accept that their right to freedom of expression and participation in proceedings outweighs the paternalistic view that the child should be represented by a guardian whose role is to advocate that child's welfare.[159] This ties in with Article 12 of the United Nations Convention on the Rights of the Child 1989

---

[157] Part 16.4 Family Procedure Rules 2010 (formerly Rules 9.5 of the Family Proceedings Ruless 1991).
[158] FPR 2010, Rule 16.6.
[159] Mabon v Mabon [2005] EWCA Civ 634 [2005] 2 FLR 1011.

(which we considered above) and which requires that a child who is capable of forming his own views has the right to express those views freely in all matters affecting him and to be taken seriously. Article 13 accords a child the right to freedom of expression. In light of the Court of Appeal's judgment it is more likely that older children will be allowed to act as a party without a guardian/next friend.

Reform in this area

Unlike in public law proceedings, a child in s 8 private law proceedings will only be a party to the proceedings and entitled to separate representation if an order is made by the court to join the child as a party. S 122 of the Adoption & Children Act 2002 amended the Children Act 1989 to allow court rules to be made to provide for a child to be separately represented in all s 8 private law proceedings by making such cases 'specified proceedings' in line with public law, but in its Consultation paper *Separate Representation of Children* published on 1 September 2006 by the Department of Constitutional Affairs, the then Government stated that it did not support the extension of separate representation to all children in all s 8 private law proceedings.

What the Government did propose was to establish new rules so that where separate representation is needed it is provided in a timely and appropriate way. It proposed that all levels of court would have authority both to decide if a child is to be made a party and to hear applications by a child rather than refer them to the High Court thereby reducing stress, delay and promoting continuity. With the introduction of the Family Procedure Rules 2010, which uses the words 'the court' and therefore makes no distinction between the tiers of courts, this is now possible.

While it is agreed and accepted that giving the child party status and separate representation is most beneficial in intractable cases because it enables parents to refocus attention on the child, there is also concern that bringing a child into proceedings can be stressful and puts too much responsibility on the child.

Chapter 15
Litigants in person

Self-representation

A father may find that he has insufficient funds to pay legal fees but is still ineligible for public funding and has no alternative but to act as a litigant in person. In fact, as a result of dramatic cuts to legal aid and the virtual removal of public funding for private law Children Act cases (see Chapter 7) it is evident that there will be a rise in the already increasing numbers of litigants in person, and therefore more fathers representing themselves.

In any event, fathers often start out with legal representation but end up as litigants in person due to prohibitive legal costs. Some fathers may even decide that they are better off presenting their own case so might as well act in person. As one father put it 'why should I pay my lawyers thousands of pounds to put my case a tenth as well as I could put it myself?' His representatives would no doubt disagree, but whatever the reason for becoming a litigant in person it is clear that with more and more fathers representing themselves and with that number liable to continue rising, the courts will have to accommodate them. It is expected that judges will need to be exceptionally pro-active in managing cases where litigants in person are involved especially where the other party has legal representation to ensure that they are not disadvantaged in the proceedings. With increasing numbers of fathers acting in person the likelihood is that more of them will be exercising their right to reasonable assistance from a McKenzie Friend.

What is a McKenzie Friend?

The title McKenzie Friend comes from a 1970 case of that name, but the role a McKenzie Friend has to play was recognised as far back as 1831 in a case where it was noted that any person may:
- Attend as a friend of either party.
- Take notes.
- Quietly make suggestions.
- Give advice.

Litigants in person can often find the whole court process daunting and overwhelming especially when dealing with legal professionals. The presence of a McKenzie Friend is therefore an invaluable support, but in order for a McKenzie Friend to sit in on court proceedings the judge has to permit him/her to do so. This has caused problems in the past due to the inconsistent approach taken by judges about whether to permit a McKenzie Friend to sit in or not, a fact which was recognised by the Court of Appeal in a case several years ago.[160] The court considered the circumstances where a McKenzie Friend should be permitted to sit in on the proceedings, and the documents which can be disclosed to a McKenzie Friend and offered guidance on both. Guidance on McKenzie Friends was first issued by the Office of the President of the Family Division in May 2005, further guidance was issued in April 2008 and this was superseded by the latest guidance issued in July 2010.[161] The current position may be summarized as follows:

McKenzie Friends and court proceedings

- A litigant in person has a right to reasonable assistance from a McKenzie Friend and there is in fact a presumption in favour of allowing a McKenzie Friend to sit in on court proceedings so as to be able to provide that reasonable assistance.
- If the court permits the McKenzie Friend to assist (see below) then he/she may assist the litigant in person by offering moral support, taking notes, helping with case papers and quietly giving advice on any aspect of the conduct of the case.
- This ties in with Article 6 of the European Convention on Human Rights which directs that those who need assistance with the presentation of their case should receive it.
- The assistance does not extend to conducting litigation or acting as an advocate and they do not have rights of audience in court, although in exceptional cases, for example, where a litigant in person is inarticulate or has severe health problems and is and unable to present his case, some judges have allowed McKenzie Friends to address the court directly. In such circumstances the onus is on the litigant to persuade the court that it is in the interests of justice for the McKenzie Friend to be granted a right of audience or a right to conduct litigation, each of which have to be applied for individually as they are separate rights.
- McKenzie Friends are not entitled to act as the litigant in person's agent in relation to proceedings or to manage cases outside court by signing court documents.
- A McKenzie Friend has no independent right to provide assistance and the appointment is dependent on the court. If a litigant in person requires the assistance of a McKenzie Friend he should raise the issue as soon as possible with the court and provide details of the person he wishes to be his McKenzie Friend. The sooner he does so the quicker he can obtain the approval of the court for that assistance.

---

[160] O'Connell & Ors (Children) Rev 2 [2005] EWCA Civ 759.
[161] Practice Guidance: McKenzie Friends (Civil and Family Courts) Lord Neuberger of Abbotsbury, Master of the Rolls, Sir Nicholas Wall, President of the Family Division 12 July 2010.

- The McKenzie Friend should produce a short statement or CV about him/herself confirming that he/she has no personal interest in the case and that he/she understands the role of a McKenzie Friend and the court's rules as to confidentiality.
- While the application is made to the court to request the McKenzie Friend's assistance, it is good practice for him/her to be present in court. He/she may need to be there anyway to assist the litigant in person with the application. Also from the judge's point of view he can satisfy himself that the McKenzie Friend understands his/her role and the requirement to maintain confidentiality.
- The court may refuse permission on the grounds that he does not require the assistance as it is not in the interests of justice and fairness but if the court refuses or the other party object for that matter sufficient reasons have to be provided as to why he should not have assistance.
- The court cannot refuse to give permission just because the case is simple or straightforward; the litigant seems capable of conducting the case himself; the litigant is unrepresented through choice (that would make most fathers ineligible otherwise!); the other party is unrepresented; the litigant belongs to an organisation that promotes a particular cause; the proceedings are confidential and the court papers contain sensitive family information.
- Once the judge has given his approval, the McKenzie Friend will be able to offer the litigant in person assistance. The court should also consider permitting the McKenzie Friend to attend any meetings with advocates directed by the court.
- The court has the power to curtail assistance, however, if it feels that the McKenzie Friend's continuing presence will impede the efficient administration of justice. Examples of this would be where the McKenzie Friend is using the litigant as a puppet, directly or indirectly conducting the litigation or he/she has failed to understand the duty of confidentiality. The McKenzie Friend should also bear in mind that if he/she wastes time by unnecessary prompting or delay he/she may be warned by the court and if he/she persists his/her permission to assist may be revoked. If his/her behaviour becomes disruptive in court then he/she may be excluded from the proceedings.
- Remuneration. This has now been specifically mentioned in the latest guidance and permits litigants in person to enter into agreements to pay fees to McKenzie Friends for the provision of reasonable administrative assistance in or out of court. This includes photocopying or preparing bundles for example. Fees can also be recovered for the conduct of litigation but only where the court has granted a right for the McKenzie Friend to carry out the conduct of litigation. Fees cannot be recovered from the opposing party at all.

The documents which may be disclosed to a McKenzie Friend

We look at the prohibition on disclosure of documents to third parties generally in the next chapter. So far as McKenzie Friends are concerned the following considerations apply:

- S 12 of the Administration of Justice Act 1960 stipulates that it will be contempt of court to publish any information relating to the proceedings if the proceedings relate to children. There is specific reference in that Act to proceedings issued under the Children Act, brought under the High Court's inherent jurisdication and generally where there is an issue relating 'wholly or mainly to the maintenance or upbringing of a minor.' However, disclosure to an approved McKenzie Friend does not fall foul of the statute and is therefore not prohibited.
- Although it is good practice for a litigant in person to obtain the court's permission before enlisting the assistance of the McKenzie Friend, it should not be contempt of court for the litigant in person to seek the McKenzie Friend's assistance or to show him/her court papers before the court has given approval for that particular McKenzie Friend to assist. The reality is that the McKenzie friend is going to require knowledge of the case and access to the court documents to be able to assist. There is no special provision for litigants in person in the Family Procedure Rules 2010 save that litigants are permitted to disclose any information, including filed evidence, relating to the proceedings to a lay advisor or McKenzie Friend for the purpose of obtaining advice or assistance in relation to those proceedings.
- The McKenzie Friend should be aware that access to court documents brings with it the responsibility not to disclose them or to publish the information they contain to any third party without the permission of the court. The word 'publish' is used in the legal sense which includes giving information to friends or relatives as well as to the press.

Other considerations

In Chapter 12 we looked at notice of proceedings and preparation of court bundles where special considerations are given to litigants in person. The Court of Appeal has made it clear that litigants in person are entitled to as fair a hearing as any other litigant and as much courtesy! *Access to Justice for Litigants in Person* is a report prepared by the Civil Justice Council in 2011.[162] It makes recommendations to make justice fairer and simpler for those who represent themselves. It recognised that there are difficulties when one or both parents are unrepresented.

If you are acting as a litigant in person bear in mind that if you are not given adequate notice of all applications being made and/or do not receive copies of all relevant documents in time to be able to prepare for the hearing and seek assistance from a McKenzie Friend well before any court hearing or advocates meeting, this might well breach the right to a fair trial. In such circumstances it may well justify any order made being set aside on appeal.

---

[162] A Report and Series of Recommendations to the Lord Chancellor and Lord Chief Justice – November 2011.

Recent developments

In its Final Report, The Family Justice Review stated that it was concerned that due to the proposed changes in legal aid there would be a rise in the number of litigants in person appearing before the family courts.[163] What the review pointed out is that in the USA it is very common for parties to represent themselves and various forms of support are offered. In New York, for example, there is an online service for filling in forms – people are asked questions and the programme fills in the legal forms automatically based on their responses.

HMCTS are producing a *Guide for parents without a solicitor – Children and Family Courts* which offers advice and information for parents without a solicitor.

---

[163] Family Justice Review Final Report – November 2011, p.177, para. 4.180.

Chapter 16
Disclosure, Confidentiality, Publicity & Media Access

Disclosure & Confidentiality

The rules relating to what must be disclosed to the court by the parties to proceedings involving *children* and what may not be disclosed and to whom, have caused problems for fathers. Some have found themselves in contempt of court for revealing details or documents relating to their case to third parties. We looked specifically at what might be disclosed to McKenzie Friends in Chapter 15. Now we look at the issue more generally.

When disclosure must be made

Where the welfare of a child is the court's paramount consideration, the parties are under a duty to make full and frank disclosure of all matters relevant to the child's welfare and the issues the court must decide. This is so even if what they must disclose could be adverse to their case. For example, where the court has given permission for a report to be obtained that report must be disclosed even if it is disadvantageous. We looked at this in relation to expert reports in Chapter 12.

If a party who is legally represented has lied when giving evidence or failed to make proper disclosure and the lawyer representing him/her becomes aware of this, then that lawyer is under a duty to cease acting for that client unless matters are resolved. The difficulty for a lawyer is where a serious breach of disclosure comes to light but the client refuses to permit the lawyer to make full disclosure. Is the lawyer under a positive duty to make that disclosure? After all the lawyer has a duty not to mislead the court. The situation is not entirely clear, but since a lawyer owes a duty of confidentiality to the client, he/she must consider whether the circumstances are sufficiently serious to justify a breach of the duty of confidentiality – for example, in a case of physical or sexual abuse – and make the necessary disclosure.

Rules about what may be disclosed

The general rule in proceedings involving *children*, as per s 12 of the Administration of Justice Act 1960, is that the proceedings are confidential and it is a contempt of court or an offence to disclose them to the public. This covers disclosing details relating to the actual court proceedings and documents forming part of those proceedings which, for example, include witness statements and court reports. The reasoning behind the restrictions is that the child's welfare must come first and that the child must not be put at risk of being identified. However, once a case goes to appeal, although anonymised, public reporting of judgments that reveal many identifying features is permitted so the child's identity may be compromised anyway.

Restrictions on disclosure and the secrecy of the family courts have come under heavy criticism in recent years, particularly by fathers. Consequently both s 12 of the Administration of Justice Act 1960 and the Family Proceedings Rules 1991, the latter of which has been superseded by the FPR 2010, were amended to change the rules as to disclosure. There are now a number of exceptions to the s 12 general rule depending on whether the proceedings are held in private; the person who is making the disclosure; the person to whom the disclosure is being made; and the purpose of the disclosure.

Changes to the rules of disclosure in proceedings held in private

Where Chapter 7 of Part 12 of the FPR 2010 and Practice Direction 12G applies
These deal with the communication of information in proceedings relating to children which are held in private (whether or not that information is contained in a document filed with the court).

It is permitted to disclose information without the permission of the court for any purpose to:
- A party.
- A legal representative of a party.
- A professional legal advisor.
- A CAFCASS or CAFCASS Cymru officer.
- A welfare officer.
- The Legal Services Commission.
- An expert authorised by the court.
- A child protection professional.
- An independent reviewing officer who has been appointed in respect of a child who is or has been the subject of proceedings.[164]

Each of these parties owes a duty of confidentiality to the court and the information is to go no further. It is also permitted to disclose information where the court gives permission[165] or, subject to any direction the court might make in accordance with the rules, about the disclosure of information being made to a specified person for a specific purpose.[166] We look at specific purposes and specified persons below.

It is not permitted to disclose information relating to the proceedings to the public at large or any section of the public.[167]

---

[164] FPR 2010, Rule 12.73(1)(a).
[165] Ibid, Rule 12.73(1)(b).
[166] Ibid, Rule 12.73(1)(c).
[167] Ibid, Rule 12.73(2).

This means that s 12 of the Administration of Justice Act 1960 will apply unless the court grants permission for disclosure to be made. Disclosure of an unapproved draft judgment handed down by the court is not permitted either.[168] As we saw in Chapter 12 in relation to the instruction of experts, in children's proceedings the rule is that nobody may instruct an expert for any purpose relating to the proceedings without the permission of the court.[169] If an unauthorised expert is instructed then no evidence from that expert may be introduced without the permission of the court.[170]

The *specific purposes* connected with the proceedings where a party or his/her legal representative is permitted to communicate information are:
- Such communication is necessary to enable the party in question to obtain support, advice or assistance.
- To engage in mediation or ADR (now DRS and see Chapter 2).
- To make and pursue a complaint against a person or body concerned in the proceedings.
- To make and pursue a complaint regarding the law, policy or procedure in relation to these disclosure rules.[171]

Where the disclosure is for the purpose of support, advice or assistance then the recipient of that information cannot pass it on.[172] In all other cases the recipient may pass on the information so long as the person who initially disclosed it consents and passing on that information is for the same purpose for which it was disclosed in the first place.[173] Further disclosure is then permitted on the same terms.[174]

The *specified persons* to whom information may be disclosed by a party for a specific purpose are set out in PD 12G. They *include*:
- To a lay adviser, a McKenzie Friend, or a person providing pro bono legal services. What can be disclosed is any information relating to the proceedings for the purpose of enabling the party to obtain advice or assistance in relation to the proceedings. Note, and as explained above, that if you are acting in person and have a McKenzie Friend the information provided to that McKenzie Friend cannot be passed on.
- To a health care professional or a person or body providing counselling services for children or families to enable the party or any child of the party to obtain health care or counselling.

---

[168] Ibid, Rule 12.73(3).
[169] Ibid, Rule 12.74(1).
[170] Ibid, Rule 12.74(2).
[171] Ibid, 12.75(1).
[172] Ibid, 12.75(2).
[173] Ibid, 12.75(3)(a).
[174] Ibid, 12.75(3)(b).

- To the European Court of Human Rights for the purpose of making an application to the Court.
- Disclosing the text or summary of the whole or part of the judgment given in proceedings to a police officer for the purpose of a criminal investigation.

Practice Direction 12G lists the disclosure which may be communicated by legal representatives and CAFCASS but it also deals with communications to and by MPs.

What is important to note, however, is that it does not permit disclosure by a party to an MP, which means that it will be unlawful to give information to an MP without the permission of the court. This can be problematic. It does seem, however, that a party may communicate with his/her MP about the way he/she perceives he/she has been treated in proceedings, but the MP will not be able to publish that information. As we saw under litigants in person, the word 'publish' is used in the legal sense which includes giving information to friends or relatives as well as to the press.

So far as the media is concerned, a party has no right to communicate information relating to the children proceedings to anyone within the media without the permission of the court. There are a number of statutory provisions which restrict disclosure of information and documents to the media and a party may be able to provide information or documents from proceedings to representatives of the media if this is not prohibited by these restrictions. We consider these in detail below.

Publicity & Media Access

Background

In recent years the whole question of the 'secrecy' of court proceedings has been challenged more and more and there have been ongoing demands to make the courts more open and for the rules on disclosure to be relaxed.

There were a number of Government Consultations on the matter which received mixed views. Some felt that the public should have greater awareness of what happens in the family courts and the sort of situations children face. Others maintained that secrecy is sometimes justifiable to protect children's privacy, that children themselves shun and hate publicity and should be protected from public scrutiny. The previous Government decided that there should be no automatic right for the press or public to attend the family courts as this would jeopardise children's rights to privacy and anonymity which must be protected. It agreed that there should be more transparency and the information coming out of the courts should be improved but, since the interests of children are paramount, no step should be taken to increase that transparency unless it was clear the children's interests were protected.

Article 6(1) of the European Convention on Human Rights provides for the public hearing and public pronouncement of cases but with the proviso that the press and public may be excluded 'where the interest of juveniles or the protection of the private life of the parties so requires.' The application of Article 6(1) was considered by the European Court of Human Rights in two cases brought by fathers who had been refused permission to have their applications for residence orders held in open court.[175] The Court found that there had been no breach of each Applicant's right to a fair trial. The court made it clear that these children proceedings were prime examples of cases where exclusion of the press and the public were justified to protect the privacy of the child and the parties, and avoid prejudicing the interests of justice.

In any event, when making a decision the court has a difficult balancing exercise between competing Human Rights, but the court's paramount consideration remains the welfare of the child and generally the child's right to privacy will outweigh 'the right' of anyone else.

In terms of opening up the courts and, after a prolonged debate, it was decided to change the rules and from 27 April 2009 representatives of the media have been able to attend court hearings subject to the discretion of the court to exclude them!

Why all this secrecy in the family courts anyway when the starting point is open justice?

When it comes to considerations of publicity, the starting point in all courts is open justice. Open justice means that proceedings should be held in open court and the public and media may be admitted. It also includes allowing the publication to the wider public, that is those who were not in court, of fair and accurate reports of those court proceedings. The Human Rights Act 1998 has reinforced the principle of open justice through Articles 6 and 10 of the European Convention on Human Rights and Fundamental Freedoms. Then why the secrecy in family courts in the first place? It is partly down to the sensitive nature of the proceedings.

The principle of open justice can only be departed from to the extent that it is strictly necessary to do so – cases involving children which are considered to concern private matters will be an exception to the principle and will justify proceedings being held behind closed doors. It therefore follows that both access to family proceedings and the publication of information from family proceedings will be restricted.

Access to family court proceedings: the general public and the media

Part 27 of the FPR 2010 deals with hearings in private and attendance at them.[176] Hearings in the Court of Appeal are open to the public unless the court orders otherwise but most applications in the Family Proceedings Court, the County Court and the High Court (Family Division) will be heard in private. The general

---

[175] B v United Kingdom & P v United Kingdom (Applications 36337/97 and 35974/97) [2001] 2 FLR 261.
[176] It is supported by PD 27B which deals with hearings in the High Court and County Court and PD 27C which deals with hearings in the Family Proceedings Court.

public will be excluded under the FPR 2010 unless 'any enactment provides otherwise or the court directs otherwise.'[177] This means that if members of the public (as opposed to accredited media which we consider below) wish to attend a hearing then they will have to apply to the court and the court will undertake a balancing exercise of all the interested parties' Human Rights.

Where the proceedings are held in private, no one shall be present other than:

- An officer of the court.
- A party to proceedings.
- A litigation friend for any party, or legal representative instructed to act on that party's behalf.
- An officer of CAFCASS or Welsh family proceedings officer.
- A witness.
- Duly accredited representatives of news gathering and reporting organisations (subject to the power to exlude them on specified grounds – see below.) A media representative is accredited if he/she carries a press card issued by the UK Press Card Authority. What about foreign journalists? They are able to obtain UK Press Cards but it will be harder to enforce reporting restrictions against them and that will be a consideration for the court.
- Any other person whom the court permits to be present.[178]

At any stage of the proceedings the court may direct that the media may not attend the proceedings or any part of them if it is satisified that this is necessary for any of the following reasons:

- In the interests of any child concerned in, or connected with, the proceedings.
- For the safety or protection of a party, a witness in the proceedings, or a person connected with such party or witness.
- For the orderly conduct of the proceedings.
- Justice will otherwise be impeded or prejudiced.[179]

When applying the 'necessity test' the court must carry out a balancing exercise of all the competing rights in reaching its decision.[180] It is not simply an exercise of discretion. The court may exercise its power to exclude duly accredited representatives of its own initiative or where representations are made by:

- A party to the proceedings.
- Any witness in the proceedings.
- Where appointed, any children's guardian.
- Where appointed, an officer of CAFCASS or Welsh family proceedings officer, on behalf of the child who is the subject of the proceedings.
- The child, if of sufficient age and understanding.[181]

---

[177] FPR 2010, Rule 27.10.
[178] Ibid, Rule 27.11(2).
[179] Ibid, Rule 27.11(3).
[180] Re Child X (Residence and Contact: Rights of Media Attendance) [2009] EWHC 1728.
[181] FPR 2010, Rule 27.11(5).

Before it makes any decision it must allow the duly accredited representative who is present to make representations as to why he/she should not be excluded.[182] Also where a person wishes to exclude a duly accredited representative he/she must satisfy the court of the necessity of exclusion as it is not for that duly accredited representative to justify his/her attendance.

Access to court documents by the media

It makes sense that if a member of the media is attending court that he/she should be allowed access to at least some documentation so that he/she can follow what is taking place in court, but the FPR 2010 does not permit this and media representatives have no entitlement to receive or peruse court documents referred to in the course of evidence, submissions or judgment.[183] This means that the general rule under the Administration of Justice Act 1960 s 12 (which we looked at under disclosure above) continues to apply unless the court grants permissions for disclosure to be made. If a media representative wishes to see documents referred to in children's proceedings he/she will have to apply to the court. The court should consider the purpose of granting the request. Will it assist the media representative in following the proceedings? If so what documentation should be disclosed? The order will not extend to permitting the media representative to have access to the whole trial bundle.

Should the judgment be given in public?

Judgments in private law proceedings are normally given in private, but where issues of public interest arise the sensible approach is to give judgment in open court so long as appropriate directions are given to avoid identification of a child. Anonymised Family Court judgments may be made public where they involve some important principle of law which in the opinion of the judge makes the case of interest to law reporters.

In the case of Clayton v Clayton[184] a father appealed against an injunction restraining him from publishing various matters concerning his daughter until her eighteenth birthday, and the Court of Appeal considered the question of anonymity of children in family proceedings. The court agreed that although the prohibition on publication contained in the Children Act 1989 prevented identification of children involved in Children Act proceedings while those proceedings are continuing,[185] that prohibition ended once the proceedings were concluded. Any entitlement to anonymity after that was dependent on the court conducting a balancing exercise between the child's right to privacy and any competing right to freedom of expression under the European Convention on Human Rights.[186]

---

[182] Ibid, Rule 27.11(4).
[183] FPR Chapter 7, Rule12.73 (2) and (3).
[184] 2006 EWCA Civ 878.
[185] Children Act 1989, s 97(2).
[186] European Convention on Human Rights for the Protection of Human Rights & Fundamental Freedoms 1950.

However, the Court of Appeal made it clear that, even after the conclusion of proceedings, the court retains its welfare jurisdiction. In other words if the court is of the view that the child's welfare will be put at risk by the parent making public details of the case which identify the child, it can and will invoke its powers under the Children Act to grant injunctions to prevent that happening. The Court of Appeal also made it clear that while the decision in this case was a greater step towards transparency of court proceedings, it was not dealing with the broader question of whether or not family proceedings should be heard in private or open court. This case was of course in 2006 and the rules have been changed since then. Lord Justice Wall, who was one of the Appeal Judges in the case, said that giving judgments publicly assisted open justice by:

- Enabling informed and proper public scrutiny of the administration of family justice.
- Facilitating informed public knowledge, understanding and discussion of the important social, medical and ethical issues which are litigated in the family justice system.
- Facilitating the dissemination of information useful to other professions and organisations in the multi-disciplinary workings of family law.

Publication of the Judgment

Whether or not a judgment is handed down in private or public is primarily a matter for the judge's discretion. Senior members of the judiciary have encouraged the making of public judgments and these judgments may identify the parties and witnesses or may be anonymised and or redacted, that is edited for publication, so as to exclude sensitive information. A public judgment may be reported. A judgment handed down in private is however subject to restrictions applicable to reporting cases in general. In particular, the effect of the Administration of Justice Act s 12 is to prohibit the publication of much of the contents of the judgment in cases to which that section applies.

Reporting the proceedings

The fact that a case is heard in private does not in itself mean that it cannot be reported because, unless there are restrictions imposed by statute or court order, it can be. We have touched on the statutory restrictions that affect the reporting of children's proceedings. Here we consider them in more detail:

- Administration of Justice Act 1960 s 12(1)

It prohibits publication of information about children's proceedings in private and operates to prohibit dissemination of what went on in front of the judge and the documents filed for the proceedings, including written evidence, reports and written submissions. It also prohibits notes or transcripts of evidence and submissions, extracts from documents filed and summaries of them. The prohibition operates even if the documents are anonymised.

But it is not a contempt for a person to communicate information or to disseminate documents which he/she could have done if there had never been any legal proceedings, so long as that information (or those documents) is not linked to those proceedings. S 12 does not operate to prohibit publication of the contents of documents which are lodged at court, or used in the proceedings, which already existed (e.g. many exhibits to witness statements) or information of a similar nature. Therefore information in witness statements will not automatically fall within s 12 merely because it is included in a witness statement.

S 12 (2) provides that publication of the text or a summary of the whole or part of an order made by a court sitting in private shall not be a contempt of court unless prohibited by the court.

The court may disapply s 12 where the balance of the competing private and public interests favours disclosure, as opposed to continued confidentiality.

- Children Act 1989, s 97(2)

This prohibits the publication of material which identifies, or is likely to identify, a child involved in proceedings in which any power under the Children Act 1989 or the Adoption and Children Act 2002, may be exercised. The prohibition only lasts for the duration of the proceedings. The court has the power to dispense with the restriction where the welfare of the child requires it. When the proceedings conclude the court should consider whether it is necessary to continue such protection, although an injunction is unlikely to be justified in most cases. In any event the prohibition does not apply in the Court of Appeal.

- Judicial Proceedings (Restriction on Reports) Act 1926

S 1(b) imposes restrictions in relation to declarations of parentage and legitimacy where it would be unlawful to publish anything except the names, addresses and occupations of the parties and witnesses, a concise statement of the charges, defences and countercharges in support of which evidence has been given (or equivalent); submissions on any point of law arising in the course of the proceedings and the decision of the court thereon, the summing up of the judge and the findings of the jury (if any) and the judgment of the court and observations made by the judge in giving judgment.

- Magistrates Courts Act (MCA) 1980

In respect of the Family Proceedings Courts, MCA 1980 s 71 prescribes the matters which may be reported, namely: the names, addresses and occupations of the parties and witnesses; the grounds of the application, and a concise statement of the charges, defences and counter-charges in support of which evidence has been given; submissions on any point of law arising in the course of the proceedings and the decision of the court on the submissions; the decision of the court, and any observations made by the court giving it.

- Children and Young Persons Act 1933, s 39

It provides the court with jurisdiction to restrain the publication in newspaper reports of matters including photographs, which would lead to the identification of a child concerned in the proceedings.

- Contempt of Court Act 1981, s 11

Where a court allows a name or other matter to be withheld from the public in proceedings before the court, the court may give such directions prohibiting the publication of that name or matter in connection with the proceedings as appear to the court to be necessary for the purpose for which it was so withheld. It can only be invoked where the court allows a name or matter to be withheld from being mentioned in open court in the proceedings. It follows that it does not provide the court with a power to prohibit publication of any name or other matter which has been given in open court in the proceedings.

- Inherent jurisdiction of the High Court

We touched on this above. The High Court has jurisdiction, by virtue of the Human Rights Act and/or its inherent jurisdiction, to increase or relax the 'default position' in terms of access to court, to documents and to reporting of cases This is known as the disclosure and restraint jurisdictions. When considering whether to make such an order it must consider the competing Convention rights and undertake a balancing exercise between the competing rights. This encompasses the jurisdiction to grant injunctions *contra mundum* (against the world) including orders providing anonymity to anyone involved in the proceedings.

The benefits of open justice...

In another Court of Appeal case[187] Lord Justice Wall dismissed two separate applications for permission to appeal by two litigants in person - both fathers had been denied contact to their children. He said that it was in the interests of open justice to discuss these cases, not least to dispel the myth that there was a gender bias in the family court system which operated to deny contact to non-resident fathers. He also said that the press and some parents' pressure groups needed to understand that the reasons fathers in particular failed sometimes to remain in contact with their children was not due to gender bias in the system but to their own conduct. While contact did sometimes break down because of the implacable hostility of the mother, in the judge's experience it broke down more often because of the behaviour of the father.

Although Lord Justice Wall was speaking from his own experience, and not for the whole legal profession, his comments caused considerable debate and concern among devoted fathers whose children have no contact with them due to the implacable hostility of the mother. In Chapter 5 we looked at the issue of maternal gatekeeping and attempts by mothers to sabotage contact for no apparent reason and where the refusal had nothing to do with the behaviour of the father.

---

[187] Re B, Re O 2006 EWCA Civ 1199.

Part II of the Children, Schools and Families Act 2010

Part II of the Act, which is not currently in force, makes proposals to amend the restrictions in respect of the publication of information from family proceedings. Essentially there will be a general restriction on publication by any person unless it is an authorised publication of a court order or judgment, an authorised news publication or an authorisation made according to rules of court.

The authorised news publication relates to the reporting of information by an accredited media representative who has actually attended the proceedings which means that the press can report only information obtained from the media representative who was present in court. Moreover, there will be an automatic prohibition on reporting information which is particularly sensitive or which is likely to lead to identification of parties or witnesses (save professional witnesses) in the proceedings. This means that anonymity would be afforded to everyone in children proceedings save expert witnesses.

If a party breaches the provisions it will be a defence to a contempt of court if the person proves that at the time of the publication he/she did not know and had no reason to suspect that the information published was information relating to the proceedings.

There has been much criticism of the proposed changes as they are likely to reduce rather than increase the amount of information about children and other family proceedings which finds its way into the public domain. In its Final Report, the Family Justice Review, commenting on transparency and public confidence, stated that the question of media access to family courts was a complex area requiring further consideration by the Government but that they welcomed the Justice Select Committee's recommendation that the scheme to increase media access to the courts should *not* be implemented.[188]

---

[188] Family Justice Review Final Report – November 2011, p.13 para. 54 and p.90 para. 2.235.

Chapter 17
Residence

The question of residence

There is more and more emphasis on parents agreeing arrangements for their children between themselves post-separation and/or divorce, and this includes their living arrangements. Clearly it is in the interests of the children if parents can reach their own agreement without resorting to court proceedings and many do, but sometimes this is not possible and the question of residence must be determined by the court.

Generally, and I emphasize the word generally as it will depend upon the circumstances of a particular case, a mother is more inclined than a father to apply for a residence order to preserve the status quo. A father on the other hand is more likely to apply for a residence order in response to a mother repeatedly obstructing contact with the children or her announcing that she wishes to relocate abroad. In recent years more and more fathers have been applying for shared residence orders as is evidenced by the increased number of cases coming before the courts to decide the issue. We consider the court's power to make shared residence orders, their appropriateness, impact and effect and the highly contentious ongoing debate about making an order for shared residence the standard post-separation order later in this chapter.

The primary carer

In Chapter 1 we looked at the father's role and how it has changed. There are significantly higher numbers of 'hands-on' fathers who are involved in the day to day care of their children and these fathers are gaining greater recognition for their contribution in their children's lives. But fathers face a Catch 22 situation when it comes to their residence claims. Although a father might be more than capable of looking after his children and attending to their needs on a daily basis, the fact is that most fathers work full time and often very long hours, and this is used against them to defeat their claims. It is argued that, from a purely practical point of view, the children should remain with their mother and following a divorce or relationship breakdown in the majority of cases it is the mother who will be the primarily responsible parent and have residence of the children.

Although fathers generally have to work to continue to support the family whether the parties are together or apart, there are many mothers who work full-time and the children are cared for by nannies/child minders. What difference would it make if it were the other way round? Could it be argued that if a father does not have to work or could make arrangements for the children to be cared for while he is working that he could succeed in an application for a residence order? As we have seen, a father who is self-employed would be in a very good position to care for the children. What about the scenario where the father is a 'house husband?'

A few years ago a case – heavily reported in the media – related to a 'house husband' who for a considerable period of time had been the primary carer of the children and wanted residence of them. In this case the mother was the breadwinner and had a very lucrative career in the city. The mother decided she wanted to give up her career and take over the full-time care of the two children aged six and three until the younger of the two went to school. In addition to that she wanted to take the children out of their fee-paying London day schools and to move to Linlithgow sending the children to state schools there. By the time the matter came to court the child-care arrangements had changed to shared parenting. The judge at first instance ruled in favour of the mother and consequently the father sought leave to appeal to the Court of Appeal.

It was argued on behalf of the father that the judge had acted on gender discrimination. If the roles had been reversed and it was the father who wanted to give up his position in the City, with the direct consequence that this would create financial hardship for the family, it would certainly not have persuaded the judge to make an order in his favour. The Court of Appeal decided that, on balance, the mother's reasons for giving up work were genuine; she had based her proposals for residence and contact on an in depth consideration of what would be the best solution for the children and her proposals were actually better for the children than those of the father. The problem for the father was that he had based his proposals on the mother continuing to earn a lucrative wage in the City and when it was clear that that would no longer be the case, his proposals fell away. Lord Justice Thorpe, one of the Court of Appeal Judges, rejected the submissions made by the father's Counsel. Leave to Appeal was refused by the Court of Appeal.

Fathers' rights organizations were angered at the decision which they regarded as a regressive step for fathers. The case sparked a number of articles in the press about a father's role, and whether a father can be as good as a mother if their roles are reversed. In recent years the courts are finally recognising that many fathers are 'hands-on' fathers and are making more shared residence orders to reflect this.

The non-resident father

Fathers say that it is not just the fact that the children live with their mother that causes problems but the attitude that goes with the status of being 'the non-resident parent'. They assert that mothers believe they are more important than fathers, and that fathers are made to feel as if they are second class citizens, lucky even to be allowed to have contact with their children. The term 'non-resident' parent is seen as discriminatory. Because a father does not generally have residence, contact with his children becomes very precious and if the contact is restricted, then it is obvious that he will push for it and will be aggrieved if he is thwarted at every turn.

Current developments and reform

In Chapter 6 we looked at proposals to replace residence and contact orders with a child arrangements order. This would certainly remove the terms 'resident' and 'non-resident' parent but children have to live somewhere, and if that somewhere is with the mother then the effect of not being labelled a 'non-resident' parent is going to have very little practical significance for the father.

Applying for residence

There are many cases where the father could press for residence of the children but does not do so as it would mean dragging up undesirable details relating to the mother's past, and because he is advised that an application presented in such terms would not bode well with the court. One father told me he was advised in no uncertain terms by Counsel that dredging up these details would not put him in a favourable light with the court, and since he was unlikely to succeed in his application anyway then he was best to forget it.

In this case the mother was an alcoholic and regularly went off on drinking binges. She was not really capable of looking after the child, a boy aged twelve, whom the father had looked after since he was a baby. The father genuinely wanted his son to live with him because he feared for his safety and considered making a residence application. The father had his own business and was able to devote time to his son's upbringing. The divorce was particularly acrimonious. The father felt it would be in his son's best interests if he had residence, but he did not want his son to be caught in the crossfire and because he was strongly advised 'to forget any thoughts of applying for residence' he did not make the application. Furthermore, he knew his ex-wife would bitterly contest any application and their relationship would deteriorate further. He was in a very difficult position.

At the financial hearing an extremely unfavourable settlement was ordered on the basis that the son was to live with the mother. The assets in the case were tight and the father was effectively left high and dry. Subsequently the son moved in with his father anyway but the father spent years trying to unravel the financial settlement and still feels particularly dissatisfied with the way the legal process treated him. There are many fathers like him.

In the majority of cases the question of residence is therefore decided between the parties and no application for an order is made. Nearly all these cases result in the mother obtaining residence.

Considerations for the court

As a residence order is a s 8 order the court must consider the welfare principle and the checklist of welfare factors. The court must also consider, in accordance with the 'no-order' principle, whether it is better to make an order than no order at all. If an unmarried father who does not already have parental responsibility is applying for a residence order and the court grants that order, the court will also have to give him parental responsibility.

In situations where the children have been living with the mother since separation, fathers worry that this will go against them. It is true that courts do favour the status quo and for a court to alter a child's residence a father would have to provide clear evidence to demonstrate that the change in arrangements will be in the child's interests. A change of residence also has Human Rights implications. This is because a child's continuity of care comes under the umbrella of family life within Article 8 of the European Convention. If that continuity of care is disrupted it will impact upon family life and so any disruption has to be justifiable. In other words there has to be strong evidence that it is. Any judge who decides to transfer a child's residence will do so after due consideration of all the welfare factors and must explain his/her reasons for the decision. The judge will consider what impact any change of circumstances will have upon a child and ultimately whether the 'move' will be in that child's best interests.

It is generally considered in the children's interests for siblings to remain together although it does not mean that they will never be separated. For example they might already live apart, there might be a considerable age difference between them and/or not have a particularly strong relationship. There is also a preference for the children to be brought up by a parent rather than a non-parent. Again Article 8 is of relevance because the natural link between a parent and child is fundamentally important and is part of the 'respect for family life' underpinned by the European Convention. However, because the welfare test will govern any decisions about a child's future residence and, since the capabilities of parents are a relevant factor under the welfare list, the court might come to the conclusion that the welfare of the child will be best served by the residence order being made in favour of a non-parent. For example, this may be where the child has developed a deep bond with the non-parent – although, as we saw in Chapter 8, the court will be reluctant to separate the biological parent from his/her child.

The court can make an order for interim residence where it has not had time to fully investigate the issues or other matters remain outstanding. For example, until the financial position is resolved the parties living arrangements may be uncertain. Generally, although not always, the status quo will be maintained by an interim order.

Shared residence

Shared residence is not to be confused with shared parenting. Shared parenting means that both parents have responsibility for the children, whereas shared residence means that the children live some of the time with one parent and the rest of the time with the other parent.

The current legal position
The Children Act provides for shared residence.[189] It states that a residence order

---

[189] Children Act 1989, s 11(4).

may be made in favour of more than one person at the same time even though they do not live together and that it may specify the periods during which the child is to live in the different households concerned. It could be weekends with one parent and weekdays with the other parent; alternate weeks with each parent or term-time with one parent and holidays with the other, or other arrangements where the child is to spend large amounts of time with each parent. It follows on from this that a shared residence order does not mean that the children will automatically spend half their time with each parent. But where children spend considerable time with both parents it may be appropriate. We look at this below.

In 2002 the Sub-Committee of the Advisory Board on Family Law reviewed the question of shared residence in *Making Contact Work*. While in favour of parents sharing parental responsibility and maximising contact with the non-resident parent, it decided that a move towards shared residence was inappropriate. The justification for this is that where parties live a long way from each other it would be impractical; parents do not always behave rationally and reasonably in the context of parental separation; or one parent may need protection from the other and the child may need the same protection. Therefore recommendations were not made for it to be implemented at that time.

The issue was re-considered in *Parental Separation: Children's Needs and Parents Responsibilities: Next Steps 2005*. I myself submitted evidence to the Constitutional Affairs Committee on the point. Unfortunately, the Government was not persuaded that any legislative change to introduce a presumption of equal contact would benefit children, nor would it have any significance in practice.

The matter was revisited by the Family Justice Review. In its Final Report it recommended that there should be no legislative change – the welfare of the child is the paramount consideration under the Children Act and no change should be made which might compromise this. According to the Family Justice Review 'no legislation should be introduced that creates or risks creating the perception that there is a parental right to substantially shared or equal time for both parents.' For that reason they did not recommend 'a change canvassed in our interim report that legislation might state the importance to the child of a meaningful relationship with both parents after their separation where this is safe.'[190]

The argument against making any legislative change is that it is already accepted in law that it is in a child's best interests to have ongoing contact with both parents where it is safe and any further statement in legislation to this effect would risk confusion, misinterpretation and give rise to false expectations. The Review felt that people misunderstood the term 'shared parenting' and were more concerned about quantity of time rather than quality time. This is something I struggle with because there has to be a certain amount of time to build a quality relationship. To state otherwise is nonsensical; but then the problem becomes in deciding how much time. However, in the final analysis they decided against a statement being

---

[190] Full details of the comments made may be found in the Family Justice Review Final Report – November 2011, pp.21, 34, 138-142 paras. 4.23-4.40.

inserted into legislation to reinforce the importance of the child continuing to have a meaningful relationship with both parents because they felt it was a move towards a presumption of shared time.

They were also influenced by what has happened in Australia after the introduction of legislation in 2006 which included a similar provision.[191] As a result of that legislative change the courts in Australia have seen an increase in litigation over what this meaningful relationship denotes because it has come to be measured in terms of the quantity of time spent with each parent rather than the quality of the relationship with the child. The Family Justice Review was of the view that the focus 'should be on supporting and fostering a greater awareness of shared parental responsibility and on the duties and roles of both parents from birth onwards. Legislation is not the means through which to achieve this.'[192]

Proposed legislative change
In the Government Response to the Family Justice Review, the Government stated that 'there should be a legislative statement of the importance of children having an ongoing relationship with both their parents after family separation, where that is safe and in the child's best interests.'[193] Having indicated that legislation may have a role to play in supporting shared parenting (not to be confused with shared residence) the Government launched a Consultation Paper *Co-operative Parenting Following Family Separation: Proposed Legislation on the Involvement of Both Parents in a Child's Life*[194] setting out four legislative options. Essentially it proposed amending the Children Act 1989 to include a presumption in law or principle or starting point or addition to the welfare checklist emphasising the importance of both parents' involvement in their children's lives.

In *Co-operative parenting following family separation: proposed legislation on the involvement of parents in a child's life – Summary of consultation responses and the Government's response*[195] the Government has concluded that the best option is to introduce a presumption in law that a child's welfare is furthered by the involvement of both parents, where that is safe and in the child's best interests, and that both mothers and fathers will have more confidence knowing that the court has to consider fully the benefits of their involvement in their children's lives. We will consider the implications for fathers in depth in Part III, but bear in mind that this proposed legislative change, while giving legal recognition to the importance of both parents, does not amount to a legal presumption for the children's time to be shared between the parents *equally.*

---

[191] Family Law Amendment (Shared Parental Responsibility) Act 2006.
[192] Family Justice Review Final Report – November 2011, para. 4.28.
[193] The Government Response to the Family Justice Review: *A system with children and families at its heart* – Ministry of Justice & Department for Education, February 2012, Cm 8273, p.18 para. 61.
[194] Department for Education (DFE) 13 June 2012.
[195] Department for Education (DFE) 6 November 2012.

What fathers want

Fathers want equal treatment. Many fathers complain that while the parties were together the mother was more than happy for them to share equally in the child care duties and actively encouraged their relationship with the children, but that as soon as the relationship came to an end the rules were changed.

Although there are mothers who do actively encourage contact and who strive with the father to work together for the benefit of the children, this is not the same as having shared residence. Many fathers feel that the mother assumes she has superior rights to the father because she is the mother and may therefore resist the father's equal involvement. They say it's all about being in control. This is why fathers, fathers rights groups and many grandparents have been pressing for a presumption of shared care because they believe that such a presumption is necessary to ensure that they remain involved in a child's life.

The Family Justice Review and the Government have placed considerable emphasis on separating couples making their own arrangements and giving them more information so that they have a better understanding of parental responsibility and what it entails. The idea, or should I say the ideal, is for parents to work together and this is very admirable, but the fact is the parent-child relationship post-separation is very much dependent upon the inter-parental relationship (see Chapter 4). Co-operative parents tend to develop flexible shared care arrangements with positive outcomes for the children, but high conflict parents (if they are able to come to any agreement at all) are likely to develop rigid arrangements probably in the form of a court order which may have to be enforced leading to very negative outcomes for the children.

When mothers have residence fathers feel sidelined and forced to make contact applications and it is soul destroying even if, after months of battling to obtain a contact order, a mother still does not comply to allow the contact to proceed. It is argued that fathers would not need to make repeated applications for contact if a shared residence order was the standard post-separation order. In fact, many of the contact problems would fall away.

As we saw in Chapter 6, plans are afoot to replace residence and contact orders with a child arrangements order. Although the contentious term 'non-resident parent' will disappear, in the majority of cases the child will still be living with one parent for most of the time so what difference will this really make to the parent with whom the child is *not* living?

Attitude of the courts

Traditionally the courts were reluctant to make shared residence orders at all. It was recognized that in some circumstances a shared residence order could reduce the bitterness between the parties, but it was stressed that there would have to be unusual circumstances where it would be of positive benefit to the child. Therefore, the court could make a shared residence order in unusual but not unnecessarily exceptional circumstances. This could be where the child has a settled home with one parent and substantial contact with the other.

Fortunately, there has been a shift over the years towards more shared residence orders being made. In the case of Re D[196] in 2001 the Court of Appeal held that it is not necessary to demonstrate exceptional circumstances or a positive benefit to the child. It is sufficient to show that the order would be in his/her interests. This may be appropriate where, for example, there has been shared care for a period of time and during that time the child has coped well with the arrangements.

It was made clear though that if there are major unresolved disputes between the parents then a shared residence order would not be appropriate. Since that case however, objections of one parent to shared residence, the proximity between the parents' homes or even unresolved disputes between them have not been absolute bars to such an order being made. That makes sense because if the parents could agree everything between themselves the court would not need to intervene under the Children Act as they would fall within the no-order principle.

The Court may decide that the circumstances dictate that the child should make a settled home with one parent because two competing homes would lead to confusion and stress and the child needs the stability of a single home. On the other hand the court may feel that a shared residence order is necessary to reflect the reality of the father's involvement. The court needs to decide how best the child's time should be divided and whether that division of time is best expressed as a shared residence order or as a contact order.[197]

The bottom line is that the decision to make a shared residence order is at the discretion of the court on the specific facts of the particular case, and shared residence, as we have seen above, does not mean equal residence!

What are the implications of a residence order?

The court is given wide powers to attach directions, conditions, incidental and supplementary provisions to a residence order.[198] These might include directing that the non-resident parent be informed about where the child is to be educated, and any medical treatment the child requires where, for example, the parent with whom the child is living has religious objections to blood transfusions.

When a residence order has been made there are two aspects of parental responsibility which are automatically affected. They are name changes and removing a child from the jurisdiction.[199]

---

[196] Re D (Children) Shared Residence Order [2001] 1 FLR 495.
[197] Re P (Shared Residence Order) [2005] EWCA Civ 1639 [2006] 2 FLR 347.
[198] Children Act 1989, s 11(7).
[199] Ibid, s 13.

Name changes

When children are born it is convention that leads to them being known by the father's surname when the parents are married or living together, and by the mother's name when she is unmarried and living apart from the father. A child's surname may be changed by:

- The parents or those with parental responsibility.
- By the mature child him/herself.
- With leave of the court.
- By adoption of the child.

Where a residence order is in force a child cannot be called by a new surname without either the written consent of every person who has parental responsibility or the leave of the court.[200] Where there is joint parental responsibility the same conditions apply regardless of whether there is a residence order. For example, where one parent informs the school that the child's name should be changed on the school register, the school should not change it unless it has independent evidence that the other parent consents. If the mother wants to change the child's surname she has to obtain the father's permission and if he refuses it she will have to apply to the court. Name changes will involve Human Rights issues. This is because a change of name goes to the heart of a child's identity and falls within a person's right to a private life under Article 8 which also includes his or her personal development. See Chapter 25.

The court's decision will be based on the welfare principle, and once again the welfare of the child will be the paramount consideration. It has to be in the child's best interests. The court will want to be sure that the change of name will lead to an improvement in the child's life.[201] The court will therefore examine the family circumstances of the individual child very carefully. If the mother has remarried and wants to change her child's name to that of her new husband the court will have to consider the likely effect on the child if it grants her application and then that relationship subsequently fails. This is an area where the case law is changing all the time. However, there are some general principles to be followed:

- If the parents are married they both have a power and duty to register their child's name.
- If they are unmarried the mother has the sole duty and power to do so. (See Chapter 8 for how an unmarried father may register his name on the birth certificate.)
- After registration of a child's name, the grant of a residence order obliges any person wishing to change the surname to obtain the leave of the court or the written consent of all those who have parental responsibility.
- In the absence of a residence order, the person wishing to change the surname from that registered has to obtain the relevant written consent of all those who

---

[200] This also applies if a special guardianship order is in force for which see Chapter 21.
[201] Dawson v Wearmouth [1999] 1 FLR 1167.

have parental responsibility or the leave of the court by making an application for a specific issue order.

- On any application the welfare of the child is paramount.
- Among the factors to which the court should have regard is the registered surname of the child and the reasons for the registration; for instance, recognition of the biological link with the child's father. Registration is always a relevant and important consideration but it is not in itself decisive.
- Relevant considerations should include factors which could arise in the future as well as the present.
- Reasons given for changing or seeking to change a child's name based on the fact that the child's name is not the same as the parent making the application does not generally carry that much weight.
- The reasons for an earlier unilateral decision to change a child's name might be relevant.
- Any change of circumstances of the child since the original registration might be relevant.
- In the case of a child whose parents were married to each other the fact of the marriage is important and there would have to be strong reasons to change the name from the father's surname if the child was so registered.
- Where the child's parents were not married to each other the mother has control over registration. Consequently – on an application to change the surname of the child – the degree of commitment of the father to the child, the quality of contact if it occurred between father and child, and the existence or absence of parental responsibility are all relevant factors to be taken into account.
- The child's wishes are not decisive.

In terms of changing a child's forename is there any difference in the criteria to be followed from changing a child's surname? It would seem that if reasons can be shown why it might not be in the child's best interests to change the first name then that might prevent a change.

What is interesting to note is that under the Births & Deaths Registration Act 1953 a child's first name may be altered within 12 months of the initial registration. Sometimes this is because the name was changed when the baby was Christened or the parents decide to change it. However, the name initially registered remains the same.

Child arrangements order and name changes

In Chapter 6 we looked at proposals to replace residence and contact orders with a child arrangements order and, if it does, there are going to be practical implications. What will happen in respect of name changes? The Family Justice Review Panel recommended that the provision restricting those with parental responsibility from changing a child's surname without the agreement of all others with parental responsibility or a court order should remain, except that a residence order will be substituted by a child arrangements order.[202] The Government has drafted legislation to give effect to this. The introduction of a child arrangements order will impact on all situations where residence and contact orders are currently made and references in the Children Act 1989 to residence and contact will be substituted by a child arrangements order.

Removing a child from the jurisdiction

Where a residence order has been made no person may remove the child from the UK – except the person with the residence order and then only for a period of one month – without either the written consent of every person who has parental responsibility or leave of the court.

Holidays or short periods

As indicated above, the Children Act allows the person in whose favour a residence order has been made to take the child out of the UK for periods of less than one month without consent. So if the children live with their mother and she has a residence order she can take them abroad as many times as she likes provided each individual trip does not last more than one month.

The father, on the other hand, as the parent without the residence order, needs to seek consent every time he wants to take the children abroad for whatever period. To avoid him having to make repeated applications to the court, at the time the residence order is granted the court can add a direction allowing him to take the children out of the country. If he lives abroad this means that regular trips for his children to stay with him will be permitted, without having to go to the mother every time to request her consent to the trip.

If this proviso is not included and an application to obtain consent has to be made, the court will base its decision on the welfare principle. If a father wants to take his child on holiday abroad then it would not be difficult to persuade the court that this would be in the child's best interests, unless the mother can show that the holiday is being used as a cover for abduction. He would need to make an application with a statement in support to get leave for those dates.

If there is no residence order in force then in theory either party can take their children abroad without any restriction or need for consent. However, the parent proposing the trip could be prevented from taking the children by the other parent obtaining a prohibited steps order forbidding the children being taken abroad if there is a real threat that the other parent does not intend to return them. Additionally, a criminal offence will be committed by the parent or any other person removing the children if the permission of the other parent or the court is not obtained. The offences will be committed under the Child Abduction Act 1984. If there are concerns then the court could require the father to enter a bond – surety from the bank or another financial institution – on removal from the jurisdiction.

---

[202] Family Justice Review Final Report – November 2011, pp.22, 34, 149, 150.

Leaving the country permanently

This is one of the possibilities that fathers dread. Many of the cases involve mothers who have remarried and wish to relocate with their new husband or where the new husband is a foreign national. There are also cases where the mother is a foreign national and after the parties split she wishes to return 'home' to her family. For the mother to do this she will require the consent of all persons holding parental responsibility otherwise she will need to apply for leave to remove the children, in which event she will need to convince the court of the merits of her application.

In Chapter 11 we considered how guidance handed down by the Court of Appeal is followed by judges in the lower courts when determining cases before them, and how that guidance is useful in ensuring continuity of decision making across the courts. Until very recently the approach taken in respect of relocation cases has been dictated by guidance given by the Court of Appeal in two leading cases, that of Poel v Poel[203] in 1970 and Payne v Payne[204] in 2001.

These cases have caused controversy over the years because they placed considerable emphasis on the likely or possible negative effect on the resident parent if permission to relocate was not granted. This meant that in most cases the resident parent, generally the mother, was likely to succeed in her application with devasting consequences for the father and many children. In the Payne case it was stated that refusing the mother's request to relocate was likely to have a detrimental effect on her psychological well-being which would consequently have a negative effect on the child and so in that case the application was granted in the interests of the child.

The matter was revisited by the Court of Appeal in the case of MK v CK[205] in 2011 in which it was stated that the only principle of law enunciated in the case of Payne is that the welfare of the child is the paramount consideration and all the rest is guidance. The problem with the guidance given in Payne is that it had been elevated to principle of law status which meant it was being applied too rigidly in every case, whereas in fact it did not have principle of law status at all. There is no question that the guidance is invaluable because it identifies what are likely to be the most important factors the court needs to take into account in a relocation case and the weight that should be attached to them. Also it plays a vital role in promoting consistency in decision making. Ultimately though, the weight given to these factors will vary depending on the facts of the particular case.

The court considers the following factors on such an application:
- The test to be applied will be the welfare test and the court will review the welfare checklist. The court does not have to go through every factor but it must direct itself to the list. It will want to know the children's thoughts and feelings on the matter. What have they been told? Do they understand the

---

[203] [1970] 1 WLR 1469.
[204] [2001] EWCA Civ 166 [2001] 1 FLR 1052.
[205] (Relocation: Shared Care Arrangement) [2011] EWCA Civ 793.

implications of moving so far away in terms of the impact on contact with their father? Have they been able to talk to him about it? Will they suffer harm as a result of losing contact and, if so, is that sufficient reason to refuse the application? The older the child, or the greater the child's special needs at any age, the harder it may be to persuade the court that the child will be better off being uprooted than left in the jurisdiction with the other parent, provided that parent had played a full role in the child's care since separation.

- As we have seen, previously the courts held that the mother should be allowed to relocate because she might become unhappy if not allowed to do so and that this might adversely affect the child. Leave should only be granted if it is of positive benefit to the child and, where the child has a strong relationship with his or her father, and enjoys regular and quality contact with him, the mother will need to present a strong case before permission is granted. In the case of Payne, Dame Elizabeth Butler-Sloss stated that there is no presumption under the Children Act in favour of the Applicant parent. The court will consider the parties' respective Human Rights. It will need to take account of the mother's right to free movement but also the father's right to a fair trial.

- Contact. Are the current contact arrangements good or not and will the mother help maintain the contact? How is this going to be maintained? When direct contact cannot take place, what about indirect contact and how much will all this cost? This is a supremely important consideration. Fathers argue that on paper mothers' proposals may seem feasible and workable but that in reality, once the children are abroad, particularly if they are thousands of miles away, those proposals will go out the window. What will be the effect on the child if contact is denied?

- Checklist of matters. Has the mother really thought this all through and made proper arrangements for the children? She must give convincing and genuine reasons for uprooting the children. The court will consider her motives and want to ensure that she is not using the move as a means to cut the father out of the children's lives. Her proposals must be realistic. The court will scrutinize her plans. Has she considered:
  - Schooling. Availability? Suitability?
  - School holidays. These may be completely different in the country she is moving to and contact could be limited on that basis alone.
  - Child care arrangements if the mother is going to work full time.
  - Housing. Availability? Suitability? Location?
  - Her contact proposals. Realistic?
  - Employment. Is she working and if so, what will she be doing?
  - Language problems.
  - Her new partner/husband. What is his relationship like with the children?
  - Degree of commitment? How solid is the new relationship? What is his attitude? This may have an effect on the contact. The welfare of the children is best served by being brought up in a happy, secure family atmosphere.
  - The court will consider the father's opposition to the move. The court will

want to be sure that it is motivated out of genuine concern and that there is no hidden agenda.

- The court will also need to decide whether a transfer of residence to the father is appropriate in the given circumstances of the case.

Consequently, if the mother's plans are ill conceived, her application for leave will be refused, even if those plans are genuine. In one case the mother planned to relocate to Jamaica with her son and her maternal grandfather. The court refused her application because her plans were poorly thought through, there was no benefit to her son in relocating and the close bond with his father would most likely be severed as the father could not afford to fly out to Jamaica for contact. Also, as Jamaica is a non-convention country, the father might have difficulties enforcing any order for contact.

The court might allow the mother to relocate but attach stiff conditions to the grant of leave, such as requiring mirror orders to be obtained in the country to which she is relocating and appropriate undertakings from her so as to ensure contact takes place. She might, for example, be required to help with the cost of funding contact visits. In a recent case money from the sale of the mother's English property was held to the order of the court to provide the father with reassurances as to contact.

Relocation and shared residence

Payne was a case where the children lived with the mother and the father had contact, but what about where the parties have shared residence? In one case where the mother was granted leave to remove the children to the USA and where the children had been dividing their time between the parents equally, the judge ordered that there was no reason why a joint residence order should not be made spanning both jurisdictions.[206] On the basis the children would be spending significant amounts of time in both the UK and USA this was the appropriate order to be made.

It is clear from this case that the court's decision depends very much upon the circumstances of the particular case before it; it will consider all factors that affect the welfare of the child and no one factor outweighs another. The welfare of the child will be the paramount consideration. The court will need to determine if it is in the best interests of the child to relocate. Depending upon what it decides it will then have to determine whether the shared care arrangements should continue or whether the parent relocating should be granted sole residence, or whether that should in fact be be granted to the remaining parent.

---

[206] Re Y (Leave to Remove From Jurisdiction) [2004] 2 FLR 330.

Recent developments and reform

The Washington Declaration on International Family Relocation 2010.

This came about following an International Judicial Conference on Cross Border Family Relocation that took place in March 2010. It does not have the force of law but it makes a number of recommendations about the approach to be taken in international relocation cases and is worthy of mention as it may yet influence our law.

The essentials of it are that the primary consideration will be the best interests of the child; mediation and similar facilities should be encouraged and promoted to encourage agreement between the parties; reasonable notice should be given prior to relocation; and the court is required to take into account the impact on both the child and the parent who is left behind that making an order for relocation will have in terms of disrupting the frequency and amount of contact between them. What is most interesting is that it does not include, as a factor to be considered, the effect on the child of the negative impact upon the Applicant if the application is refused!

Child arrangements order and relocation

If the proposed child arrangements order is introduced and replaces a residence order then this will be relevant when it comes to removal from the jurisdiction applications. The Family Justice Review recommended retaining the facility to remove a child from the jurisdiction of England and Wales for up to 28 days without the agreement of all others with parental responsibility or a court order where a child arrangements order is in place, in the same way as a residence order, which the child arrangements order replaces.[207] Again the Government has drafted legislation to effect this.

Moving within the jurisdiction

There is another scenario where the mother does not emigrate but decides to move to another part of the country. At least in a situation where the mother is emigrating, the father has the opportunity to put his case when the mother makes her application for leave to remove the child from the jurisdiction. If she moves within the jurisdiction he does not have this opportunity. For example, a father might be further away or just as far away from his children in this country than a father whose children are in Northern Europe, but can do very little about it. What is more, if he does not have the money to pay for the cost of travel to see them, the contact will be severely limited. Is there anything he can do?

If a father wants to oppose the move and there is a residence order in force he could apply to the court for a variation of the residence order, or in exceptional circumstances he could apply under the Children Act for a prohibited steps order or for the court to impose conditions on any existing residence order. In a truly

---

[207] Family Justice Review Final Report - November 2011, pp.22, 34, 149, 150.

exceptional case a condition restricting the mother's own planned move could be contemplated. Courts are very reluctant to impose conditions. What would be an exceptional case? Where the child has serious health problems, for example. In one case the child had Downs Syndrome with a life shortening heart condition and respiratory problems and the judge imposed a condition on the order.[208] The mother appealed. The Court of Appeal decided that a move might cause severe emotional difficulties for the child and impede the father's contact and that the judge in his discretion was right to impose the condition.

The fact that contact with the father will be adversely affected will not be enough to prevent the mother's move in itself. In the final analysis the welfare of the child will be the paramount consideration and any decision must be made in accordance with that. However, this is a situation where making a shared residence order might be appropriate – to maintain that crucial link between father and child. In a case where a mother wanted to move to Edinburgh, a shared residence order was deemed the most appropriate way of ensuring the father's role in his child's life was maintained.[209]

---

[208] Re S (A Child) Residence Order: Condition [2001] EWCA Civ 847n [2001] 3 FCR 145 Civ 1795 [2003] 1 FCR 134.
[209] Re F (Shared Residence Order) [2003] EWCA Civ 592, [2003] 2 FLR 397.

Chapter 18
Contact

Reasonable contact

What is reasonable contact?

What one father may regard as reasonable contact may not be so to another father, but generally, whatever the level of contact it is not enough. Unfortunately, there is no definition of reasonable contact in the 1989 Children Act, nor anywhere else for that matter. The argument is that it cannot be defined since 'every case is different' and therefore there cannot be any legislation on it because we do not have a consensus on what it is. This makes for dissatisfaction all round and it is very easy to see how the system may be abused by a resident parent who wishes to deny the child's ongoing relationship with the other parent. As matters currently stand a father would be regarded as having very reasonable contact if he had contact every other weekend, telephone contact during the week and a couple of weeks holiday contact in the Summer and the rest of the holiday time split, although not necessarily equally. Reforms in relation to contact are inextricably linked with residence and we consider the reforms in detail in Part III.

It goes without saying that when the parent's relationship breaks down it is important to minimize disruption to the children but if they have a loving relationship with their father then the benefits of that to them, and the continuity of contact with him, will far outweigh any negative aspects. The reality is that after separation children's routines are going to be disrupted anyway, as instead of having one base they will have two, a direct consequence of their parents splitting up. But the disruption can be limited by the parents and, at the end of the day, what is important is to build healthy relationships. If a father does not have a sufficient degree of contact once he and the mother part, it is harder to build up the relationship with his children and they lose out. Again the parental relationship is a determining factor. A highly conflicted relationship between the parents does not bode well for contact.

Those advising fathers against the backdrop of contested divorce and/or financial proceedings, might recommend the father to 'back–off' and not press the mother on contact issues until the whole situation simmers down. But this approach places fathers in the unenviable position of having to wait to resolve matters, which in turn can cause frustration and encourage conflict and resentment because, once again, this leaves him in a no-win situation and subject to the whims of the mother. This is why there is such a push to direct parties away from the court process and to resolve matters between themselves with the use of dispute resolution services, if necessary, before contentious issues between them escalate. Having said that, the most difficult cases to resolve are the ones which were most conflicted to begin with. It follows that where there is less conflict there is more likely to be settlement between the parties.

Existing approach

The starting point is that the child has a right to know both parents and should have contact with the non-resident parent who in the majority of cases will be his/her father. It is not the other way round. There is a normal assumption that a child will benefit from continued contact with this parent, but that assumption can always be displaced if the child's interests indicate otherwise. The welfare of the child will always be the paramount consideration. Even though the courts must have regard to the parties Human Rights, that is respect for their private and family life under Article 8 of the European Convention, where there is conflict the welfare of the child will take precedence. The court is only concerned with the parents' interests insofar as they affect the welfare of the child and will refer to the welfare checklist of seven factors we looked at in detail in Chapter 11. Article 9 (3) of the United Nations Convention on the Rights of the Child makes it clear that States shall respect the right of the child, who is separated from one or both parents, to maintain personal relationships and direct contact with both parents on a regular basis, except if it is contrary to the child's best interests.

The problem for a non-resident parent seeking contact is that the onus is always on him/her to prove that more contact would be in the best interest of the child, whereas the resident parent is not obliged to show why contact should not take place. Because of the 'every case is different' approach and because there is no clear guidance on how much contact to recommend, it follows that any outcome can flow from any facts and contact can be stopped for any reason. A 'fit' parent has no presumptive entitlement to any time with the children.

Further, where the contact has stopped and there has been a period of no contact, the test to be applied is whether there are any cogent reasons why the child should be denied the opportunity of contact with the non-resident parent. Before ruling out the establishment or re-establishment of contact the court will wish to be satisfied that all avenues have been tested and so we venture into the realms of protracted litigation, delay, CAFCASS reports, investigation of allegations of abuse, violence etc.

The form of contact

The court has a wide and comprehensive jurisdiction to make contact orders. It can order for direct contact or indirect contact to take place and can attach conditions[210] to the contact. It may make it a condition of granting contact that a party undertakes a contact activity and may also direct a party to take part in a

---

[210] Children Act 1989, s 11(7).

contact activity. We consider both contact activity conditions and contact activity directions when we look at ways of facilitating contact below.

Direct contact

This means seeing and being with the children – face to face contact. The amount of contact can either be specified in the order or the order could be for 'reasonable' contact in which case the arrangements can be made between the parents. However, this can be unsatisfactory because, as we looked at above, the definition of 'reasonable' is in itself unclear and can be abused by a mother wishing to be awkward.

Where there is an order for direct contact there has to be a positive obligation on the parent who is to allow contact to take place. In other words it must state exactly what the resident parent is required to do. This is important from the point of view of enforcing the order. The order should state that the mother 'must make the children available for contact' with the father rather than to say that he is 'to have contact with the children'. The difference between the two is that the former is enforceable, in principle at least if not always in practice. The court must attach to the contact order a notice warning of the consequences of failure to comply. We look at this and the whole issue of enforcement below.

There is no set format for the order. It depends upon the case. It may set out times and dates and there may be conditions attached to the contact or to enable contact to take place.

Supported and supervised contact and Child Contact Centres

If a father has not seen his child for some time, or for example, in a situation where there has been domestic violence, the order may contain conditions and directions for the contact to be built up gradually. Depending on the circumstances of the case, the contact could be either supported or supervised.

There are several form of supported contact. It might be that the other parent is present during the contact visit; a friend or other relative is present; or the contact takes place at a contact centre. Where the supported contact does take place at a contact centre several families are in the room at any one time. Staff and volunteers observe the contact sessions and only step in if a child becomes distressed or a person behaves inappropriately.

Where the contact is to be supervised it will probably take place at a local contact centre. The contact is more likely to be supervised where there is a greater risk of harm and there needs to more formal supervision of the contact. Only one family will be present in the room at any one time and the person who monitors contact will observe it closely. Generally, supervised contact is only available if a fee is paid or if a family is referred to the centre by Social Services or CAFCASS and so this is dependent on available resources.

Where contact is ordered to take place at a contact centre there must be a contact referral which has to be delivered to the contact centre by the Applicant's solicitor. The National Association of Child Contact Centres (NACCC) has a protocol for referrals.[211] It is important to remember that NACCC is a charity and nearly all the staff are volunteers. Contact centres are a neutral and confidential setting and staff must remain impartial and not becoming embroiled in individual cases and wrangles between the parties. Their role is not to resolve disputes or to write reports or to attend family court proceedings but they will make a note of a party's attendance dates and times.

Contact centres are an invaluable resource because they make it possible for contact to take place in a comfortable and safe enviroment where there might not be any feasible alternative, and this is an exceptionally useful tool for a court proposing to make an order for contact where it meets objections from the resident parent to contact taking place without it being supported or supervised.

Indirect contact
This could be by telephone calls, letter, cards, e-mails, photographs, audiotapes, videos, DVDs for example. There might be a direction that the absent father should be sent school progress reports and any cards or letters he sends to the child be read to the child. An order of this nature would stipulate that the mother was to allow the father to have indirect contact with the father. Indirect contact can be used as a way of re-introducing a child to someone he/she does not know very well or at all – where there is no existing relationship to speak of there has to be a gradual re-introduction of contact. Unfortunately, all too often indirect contact can be easily eroded by the resident parent. This is because it is very much dependent upon that parent's co-operation and it can be difficult to monitor.

In one case the father was American and his wife was English but was working in America where they met. They married, and moved to the UK and had a daughter. The relationship broke down when their daughter was eighteen months old. The mother remained in the UK and went to live with her parents; the father's employment contract came to an end and he returned to the USA to work. The end of the relationship was very acrimonious and the mother and her family were hostile to contact and determined to limit contact as much as possible.

The father only had two weeks holiday a year and tried to organize his flights to the UK so that he would come over on a Friday and return home on a Monday, thereby carving out ten contact visits a year. He would book his flights well in advance and agree the dates with the mother but the mother would change the arrangements at the last minute. When he did see his daughter he had to go to her parents' house, was never left alone with her, the argument being that he was 'a stranger' to her as she had been so tiny when the parties had separated. The opportunity to develop a meaningful father/daughter relationship was denied. The problem was ongoing.

When the matter came to a head and the father made an application to the court the daughter was aged three. The father explained his predicament and how his attempts to see his daughter were constantly being thwarted by the mother. The District Judge said that the child was very young and that the father should

---

[211] 2 July 2010, for which see www.naccc.org.uk.

send her a card on her Birthday and that he could telephone his daughter even though it was evident to everyone that it was unlikely he would ever manage to speak with his daughter. The father was devastated. He indicated that, at the hearing, the District Judge was not interested in listening to his arguments about how hostile the mother was to contact, but took pains to accommodate her at every level and accepted her 'reasons' for limiting the contact. Unsurprisingly, he went away with no confidence in the system whatsoever.

Attaching conditions to contact

We looked at making the contact conditional upon it being supported or supervised above. Where there is indirect contact we also looked at the fact that the court can make a direction for the resident parent to provide the person having contact with progress reports and photos. There are other conditions which the court may attach to the order.[212] These are some examples:

- Relating to the 'pick-up' and return of the child – 'hand-over' conditions.
- Travel costs.
- Method of transportation.
- Where the child may go or whom the child may see during contact visits.
- What the child may eat during contact visits – the child might have a food allergy and particular care needs to be taken.
- That the party with contact does not drink alcohol during the contact visit.

The Children & Adoption Act 2006, which we look at in detail below under enforcement of contact, inserted new provisions into the Children Act 1989 giving the court power to attach a contact activity condition, requiring a person who has been granted contact to attend a specified contact activity.

Interim contact

An interim contact order might be made pending agreement or a final order. The court's approach depends on whether the dispute is about:

- Contact taking place at all, or
- How frequently or where it should happen.

If the dispute relates to contact taking place at all, interim contact will be ordered only if the court feels contact must take place so that the contact can be observed or assessed by a CAFCASS officer or other expert, or if the judge has heard enough evidence to decide whether interim contact is in the child's best interests.

If the dispute relates to the frequency and/or place of contact, then the court may try to decide what interim contact should take place without investigating all the evidence. The court will have to proceed with caution however, as without all the evidence the court will not have a complete picture of the facts of the case.

---

[212] Children Act 1989, s 11 (7) contains directions about how a contact order is to be carried out and the courts power to impose conditions on relevant parties.

No contact at all

A contact order can also be made preventing contact with someone. Another way of achieving this is to obtain a prohibited steps order, and we look at this in more detail in Chapter 20.

In deciding whether contact should cease or be reintroduced, the court will apply the principle that no court should deprive any child of contact to either parent unless it is wholly satisfied that it is in the interest of the child that contact should cease. This is a conclusion at which the court is extremely slow to arrive. In fact the court must not give up making an order until is it absolutely clear that contact would be of no benefit to the child. It would be a very drastic order because, as we have seen, it is usually deemed in the best interests of a child to have contact with the father.

There is no presumption that just because the non-resident parent is suffering from a medical condition like for example, Asperger Syndrome – a condition which affects the way a person communicates and relates to people who are around him/her – that this will be a bar to contact. In fact, the court will work on the assumption that it is in the best interests of any child concerned to have contact with that parent and the court will consider all the options available as to how best to effect that contact. Depending upon the age of the child, the court will want the child to gain an understanding of his/her parent's condition to obtain the most benefit out of any contact that takes place. Being in prison is no bar to contact either although arrangements for contact depend upon the prison. Some prisons have facilities for children to visit and also Prison Governors have discretion whether or not to permit contact visits to take place.

The court cannot make an order forcing someone to have contact with a child. Where the court is faced with an implacably irresponsible parent as opposed to an implacably hostile one, adjudicating on contact will be just as difficult. The court may also be faced with a situation where the child him/herself is unwilling for contact to take place and the court will want to investigate why before it makes a decision.

We look at ways the court deals with situations where the resident parent is intractable over contact and the various powers of the court in such situations under **Making contact work** below.

Making contact work

There are two aspects to this, and these are applying to the court to make or vary a contact order, where the father's contact is limited, and making an application to enforce a contact order. It has long been recognised that this is an extremely fraught area beset with difficulties and one where change is crucial – it has been all to easy for a recalcitrant resident parent to flout a contact order without suffering any adverse consequences or sanctions. There have been numerous Government Consultations over the years to debate what measures should be introduced to secure the resident parent's compliance with the order, while at the same time ensuring that any steps taken are in the best interests of the children involved.

Since the advent of the Human Rights Act courts are now under a duty to assist litigants in enforcing orders within a *reasonable* time, as it is essential that contact and residence cases are dealt with speedily. Reasonableness has to be considered in the light of the complexity and circumstances of the case. The Children & Adoption Act 2006 includes a range of powers to facilitate, monitor and enforce child contact orders which have now been incorporated into the Children Act 1989[213] and we look at these in detail below.

Applying to court to make or vary a contact order

For some, once the order is made, that is sufficient and the parties do manage to comply with it even though their own relationship is still very strained. However, it may be necessary to make further applications and to vary the order if other issues arise or there are changes in circumstances and the parties cannot agree these between themselves. The parties can of course vary a court order any time by agreement. The order for contact could contain a clause 'and any such further contact as may be agreed between the parties.'

Warning Notices
Whenever the court makes or varies a contact order it attaches to the order a notice warning of the consequences of failure to comply with it.[214] A party who fails to comply may be held in contempt of court (see below) and committed to prison or fined and/or the court may make an order requiring the party to undertake unpaid work (an enforcement order) and/or that he/she pay financial compensation. The warning notice acts as a deterrant and to encourage compliance with the order.

It is necessary for a warning notice to have been attached to the contact order and for a copy of that order to have been given to the relevant party (or for the relevant party to otherwise be informed of the terms of the contact order) in the event of non-compliance otherwise it will not be possible to apply for an enforcement order against him or her.

Applying to the court to enforce the contact order

A father faces a predicament where he has obtained a contact order but the mother still refuses to allow contact to proceed. He probably applied for an order for contact in the first place because the mother was seriously sabotaging contact. Unfortunately for some fathers, the sabotage does not cease merely by the fact that a court order is in existence and, despite warning notices attached to orders, the

---

[213] Children Act 1989, ss 11A-P.
[214] Children Act 1989, s 11I.

mother continues to disregard the authority of the court. These are situations where the mother is totally opposed to contact – implacable or hostile to contact.

In Chapter 5 we touched briefly on the subject of Parental Alienation Syndrome (PAS). This was the phrase given to it by the late US child psychiatrist Richard Gardner in the 1980s. According to Richard Gardner, where PAS exists the resident parent constantly undermines contact by programming the child to make it appear as if it is the child who is opposing contact while seemingly encouraging contact herself. Many child psychiatrists say PAS does not exist and certainly there has been reluctance on the part of the UK courts to investigate whether it does. There have been cases where the courts merely refer to 'parental alientation' and not the syndrome, but rather than state whether it exists or not the courts have concentrated on the circumstances of the parties and the facts of the particular case.

Children & Adoption Act 2006

This Act inserted new provisions into the Children Act 1989 as of December 2008 and provides the courts with more flexible powers to facilitate, promote and monitor child contact and enforce contact orders as follows:

- Measures to facilitate contact

Contact Activity Direction

Where there is a dispute about contact the court may direct a party to undertake a 'contact activity' before even making an order.[215] A contact activity direction is an activity that promotes contact with the child concerned. For example, to attend information sessions; meetings with a counsellor; parenting programmes or classes. A Separated Parents Information Programme (PIP), which we looked at in Chapter 2 under dispute resolution services, is an example of a contact activity programme. PIPs are currently carried out as part of the court process, but as we saw in Chapter 2, the Family Justice Review recommended that they should form part of the mediation assessment before court proceedings are issued.

The aim is to assist a parent in establishing, maintaining or improving contact which includes giving advice on organising arrangements for contact. Where there has been violent behaviour the purpose of the contact activity is to address that parent's behaviour to enable contact to take place. The parties could be directed to attend a mediation information session for the purpose of learning about the benefits of it but mediation itself is not obligatory. The contact activity direction must specify the activity and the person providing the activity.[216] It follows on from this that the activity proposed must be appropriate in the circumstances of the case and that the person providing the activity is suitable to provide it and, also the activity must take place in a location to which the party could reasonably

---

[215] Children Act 1989, ss 11A-B; E-F.
[216] Ibid, s 11A(4).

be expected to travel.[217] Additionally the court will want to ensure that the contact activity direction does not conflict with an individual's religious beliefs and does not interfere with that individual's hours of work or attendance at an educational establishment. The court would ask CAFCASS to check out these details and provide feedback for the court's consideration.

Contact Activity Condition

Similarly, on the making of the contact order the court will be able to attach conditions requiring a party to undertake a contact activity.[218] The court could make it a condition of granting contact that the parent undertakes a certain contact activity or activities. The court will use a contact activity condition as a way of resolving a dispute on a particular issue between the parties and as a means of stopping that dispute from continuing. The court can impose a condition for any of the following people to take part in an activity that promotes contact with the child concerned:

- The person with whom the child concerned lives or is to live.
- The person whose contact with the child is provided for in the order.
- A person upon whom that order imposes a condition under s 11(7)(b) – we looked at examples of the conditions the court might attach above.

When the court is considering making a contact activity condition, as with contact activity directions, the court will wish to ensure that the contact activity condition does not conflict with an individual's religious beliefs and does not interfere with that individual's hours of work or attendance at an educational establishment. Again the court would ask CAFCASS to check out these details and provide feedback for the court's consideration.

- Measures to promote contact

Monitoring by CAFCASS

The Act enables the court to require a CAFCASS officer (or CAFCASS Cymru) to monitor compliance with a contact order, monitor contact activity directions or conditions and enforcement orders and report to the court on compliance with the order concerned.[219] They can do this for up to one year without the parents' consent.

Family Assistance Order

Under the Children Act 1989 the court was able to make a Family Assistance Order (FAO) requiring a CAFCASS officer or Local Authority officer to advise, assist and generally help with the smooth running of the order, but the order could only be made in exceptional circumstances and run for six months. Under the

---

[217] Family Procedure Rules 2010 PD 12G, para. 2.1
[218] Children Act 1989, ss 11C-F.
[219] Ibid, s 11H.

Children & Adoption Act 2006 the exceptional circumstances requirement was removed and the order extended to twelve months.[220] They will only be used with the consent of the parent named in the FAO as it would be pointless to attempt to advise, assist or befriend a parent against their will – it simply would not work. We look at FAOs and the involvement of CAFCASS in detail in Chapter 21.

- Measures to enforce contact

Where a contact order is in place and the other party has failed to comply with it and it contains a warning notice, it is possible to apply to the court for an enforcement order (unpaid work) or an order for compensation for financial loss. We look at both these orders in detail below. It may be that the court has already made an enforcement order and it has been breached and so the application will be for the court to make an order in relation to that. A contact order made after 8 December 2008 will contain a warning notice, which means that if the order is prior to that date it will be necessary to make an application for a warning notice to be attached to the order before making any application for its enforcement. The application will be made on form C78.

Form C79 will be used for the enforcement application itself. All Respondents must be served, and also CAFCASS if they are monitoring the contact order.

Enforcement Orders

Where a contact order has been breached, the court has power to make an enforcement order imposing an unpaid work requirement for not more than 200 hours and to be performed during a period of 12 months.[221] The court has to be satisfied beyond reasonable doubt that a contact order (including failing to attend a contact activity that is a condition of contact) has been breached. There is nothing to prevent the court from making more than one enforcement order in relation to the same person on the same occasion.

Enforcement orders will not be made where a parent has reasonable excuse for any breach. It will be for the parent who is claiming a reasonable excuse to prove it on the balance of probabilities. Reasonable excuse relates to situations where it is within the parent's control to comply but for good reason cannot. An example would be where the child becomes genuinely ill so that contact cannot take place. It is to be distinguished from events beyond someone's control where there is no breach at all. For example, if all planes have been grounded due to severe weather conditions it would not be possible for the child to take a flight at a certain time.

The type of unpaid work to be undertaken will be determined by taking into account details of the breach of the order and the personal circumstances of the parent. For example, does it conflict with religious beliefs or does it interfere with the times at which the party normally works? Before it makes an enforcement order the court must be satisfied that the measures being taken are necessary and

---

[220] Ibid, s 16.
[221] Children Act 1989, ss 11J-N and Schedule A1.

proportionate to secure future compliance with the order. When the court makes an enforcement order a notice warning of the consequences of non-compliance must be attached to the order. The court will also ask for an officer from CAFCASS or CAFCASS Cymru to monitor, or arrange for monitoring of the person's compliance with the unpaid work requirement and report back to the court on the compliance: for example, if there is a breach or if the situation changes and performing the unpaid work requirement is no longer possible due to a change in personal circumstances.

The enforcement order may be varied but the court cannot reduce the number of hours below 40, and it may also be revoked. On revoking the order the court will take into account the extent to which there has been compliance with the order and what the likelihood is of the party complying with the contact order or any contact order put in place in the absence of the enforcement order. If the enforcement order is breached the CAFCASS officer must give the party a specified warning unless a warning has already been given in the previous 12 months. The court has to be satisifed that all appropriate warnings have been given and that it is proven beyond reasonable doubt that there has been non-compliance. The court might amend the first order and make the work requirement more onerous or make a second order in substitution of or in addition to the first order. Again the court will consider whether there is a reasonable excuse for failure to comply.

Financial Compensation

The court could also order one person to pay compensation to another where financial losses have been incurred as a result of the breach.[222] For example, where the cost of a holiday has been lost due to the resident parent refusing to allow the children to go at the last moment for no valid reason. Again, if the court finds that the parent in breach had a reasonable excuse for non-compliance no order will be made. If there is no reasonable excuse, in making an order the court will have to take into account the individual's financial circumstances and the welfare of the child concerned.

The amount awarded cannot exceed the amount of the Applicant's financial loss. The problem is if the resident parent, generally the mother, does not have the money to pay compensation and this order might leave her with insuffient monies for the children so, in the majority of cases, this type of order has been of limited application. If an order is made compensation can be recovered as a civil debt.

Other enforcement powers of the court

The powers provided by the Children & Adoption Act 2006 are in addition to the courts existing powers as follows:

- Enforcement by Officer of the Court

If the court is satisfied that the mother has not given the child up for contact, it could make an order authorizing an Officer of the court or a constable to take

---

[222] Ibid, ss 110-P.

charge of the child and deliver the child to the father. The whole scenario is very unsatisfactory from a practical point of view and could cause more harm than good for the child. This is why mothers who are determined to block contact are able to do so effectively, because judges are very reluctant to make an order which could be detrimental to a child.

- Imprisonment, committal and fines

The breaking of a court order is known as a 'contempt of court'. The penalty for this can be imprisonment, committal or a fine. Before any committal order can be made the court has to be satisfied beyond reasonable doubt that the defendant knowingly broke the order. Furthermore, the requirement is that a penal notice must have been attached to the order in question. A penal notice is a notice informing the person against whom the order is made that a failure to obey it constitutes a contempt of court for which the offender may be sent to prison. The order must be served personally, although both the High Court and County Court may dispense with service in certain circumstances, for example, if the party is present in court at the time the order is made and the consequences of non-compliance have been made clear to him/her. Good practice however, dictates that papers are served!

Because of the nature of committal proceedings, which are essentially criminal in nature, it is important that a Respondent has the opportunity of being represented and, if necessary committal proceedings should be adjourned for representation to be obtained.

Committal is only appropriate where the party repeatedly and wilfully refuses to comply with the court order and all other avenues have been exhausted. It is important not to lose sight of the child's welfare in these circumstances although it is *not* the paramount consideration. If the mother is totally hostile to contact the court must look carefully at her reasons. Traditionally the courts have regarded this as a remedy of last resort. Committal proceedings are provocative and emotional applications and could be very damaging.

However, over recent years there has been a shift towards making an order for committal if it can be justified in the circumstances. Even so, the court will give the 'offending' party every opportunity to comply and it is more usual, initially anyway, for a party to be given a warning, to return to court within the space of a week to monitor compliance and then to be given a suspended sentence before a committal order is made. So there is no immediacy about these proceedings at all.

In terms of the maximum sentence that can be passed in the High Court and County Court, it is 2 years imprisonment for breaches of injunctions or failure to comply with an order where there is a penal notice attached and in family proceedings courts it is 1 month or a fine not exceeding £2,500 or both.[223] The court might still make a suspended sentence and not send the party to prison at

---

[223] Contempt of Court Act 1981, s 14.

all. If the person is committed to prison the court can permit an early discharge from prison if there is legal justification, and it is for the contemnor (that is the one in contempt) to demonstrate and advance reasons for discharge – this is known as purging contempt.

Now that the court has the powers to make an enforcement order, and given the draconian nature of a committal order, it is important that the court considers whether making an enforcement order is more appropriate in the circumstances. If it decides that an enforcement order is unsuitable then it must give sound reasons for that decision and explain why it is both necessary and proportionate to make a committal order in the particular case.

- Sequestration of assets

If the contemnor's assets are sequestrated this means that they are frozen. Applications to sequestrate assets are brought in the High Court. The application must be made in accordance with the Civil Procedure Rules.[224] The notice of application must state the grounds of the application and must be accompanied by a copy of the witness statement in support. The court may grant permission to issue a writ of sequestration where a committal order has already been made against a party for non-compliance with a judgment or order and which required that party to deliver something to another person or to deposit it in court. The sequestration is used as a means of enforcing that judgment or order.

Where there are available assets and/or funds sequestration is a useful tool in child abduction cases where one parent has removed the child from the jurisdiction and has failed to return him/her in contravention of a court order. In such cases, if the abductor is found to be in contempt of court then the court may grant permission for leave to issue a writ of sequestration. There have been cases where an order has then been made directing the sequestrators to pay the other parent sufficient funds from those sequestrated assets to fund all the costs of recovering the abducted child.

- Transfer of residence

Should transfer of residence be used as a punishment for contempt? The general concensus has been that the threat of making a residence order should not be used as a means of enforcing contact. However, where it is justified on welfare grounds then the court should use its powers to transfer it. Of course if residence is transferred the court then has to consider contact arrangements for the child with the former resident parent!

Current Developments & Proposed Reform

The whole area of enforcement of contact orders is highly contentious and the existing methods of enforcement have been heavily criticised as being totally

---

[224] CPR, Part 23.

unsatisfactory and that includes methods introduced by the Children & Adoption Act 2006. Consider enforcement orders, for example. By nature of the fact that the work requirement is to be carried out over 12 months it is not going to be an immediate fix or, as the then Mr Justice Munby pointed out, it does not give what is required, namely 'swift, efficient enforcement.'[225] Certainly, critics of the current system for enforcement point out that it is not tough enough on those in breach of court orders enabling them to disregard the authority of the court. The system is also too slow in progressing cases and this delay gives a manipulative parent the opportunity to influence the views of children and to score points against the other parent.

In its Final Report the Family Justice Review recommended that where an order is breached within the first year the case should go straight back to court to the same judge to resolve matters swiftly; that the current powers of enforcement should be available; that a case should be heard within a fixed number of days and with the dispute resolved at a single hearing. In the case of orders breached after 12 months, the Review recommended that the parties should be directed to Dispute Resolution Services (we looked at these in Chapter 2) before returning to court to seek enforcement and that there should be no link between contact and maintenance.[226]

In the Government Response to the Family Justice Review,[227] the Government agreed with these recommendations save in relation to the range of enforcement methods currently available.[228] While the Government recognises that the ideal solution is to steer parties away from court proceedings and for them to make workable contact arrangements themselves, it also recognises that there are parties who cannot agree and believes that the key to dealing with a cycle of repeated litigation and non-compliance is to break that cycle. The Government has stated that a tougher stance needs to be taken when it comes to enforcing court orders. In its Consultation Paper *Co-operative Parenting Following Family Separation: Proposed Legislation on the Involvement of Both Parents in a Child's Life*[229] it sought views on the feasibility and appropriateness of widening the court's enforcement powers. While there is to be no link between contact and maintenance it is considering extending the enforcement powers that are currently used for enforcing child maintenance to contact orders. These powers permit the withholding of passports and driving licences as well as the imposition of a curfew order requiring the parent concerned to remain at a specified address between specified hours. Parents need to understand that both maintenance and contact are important and enforcement action will be taken to secure either where it is for the benefit of the child.

---

[225] Re D (Intractable Contact Dispute: Publicity [2004] EWHC 727 (Fam), [2004] 1 FLR 1226.

[226] Family Justice Review Final Report - November 2011, pp.36, 169-170 paras. 4.152-4.155.

[227] Government Response to the Family Justice Review *A system with children and families at heart* – Ministry of Justice & Department for Education, February 2012, Cm8273.

[228] Ibid, pp.79-80.

[229] Department for Education (DFE) 13 June 2012.

In his speech to the Association of Lawers for Children on 26 November 2010, Mr Justice Coleridge said that the family courts need to reassert their authority and that one of the ways this could be done would be by introducing a three strikes system whereby if a parent disobeys a court order three times the residence of the child should be transferred to the other parent. The problem is that sometimes balancing the welfare of any child concerned with the enforcement of a contact order is simply impossible. In a recent case the mother was totally implacable to contact and as a last resort the court transferred residence to the father, but it was so distressing for the child that the father conceded the child should live with the mother.[230] There was certainly no happy outcome to that case.

Changes to contact – child arrangements order

As we have seen, the Government intends to introduce legislation to replace residence and contact orders by a new form of order: a child arrangements order. This will deal with arrangements concerning who a child should live with, who the child should spend time with and who the child should have other types of contact with. To me, this seems like residence and contact by any other name, but instead of having two separate orders for residence and contact there will be one single order dealing with both. It will be interesting to see how this is applied in practice.

In terms of contact activity directions and contact activity conditions, which we considered when we looked at ways of **Making contact work** above, under the new legislation these will be referred to as 'activity directions' and 'activity conditions.' The idea is to emphasize that the activities are to help establish, maintain and/or improve the involvement of a person in a child's life. This is in line with the Government's policy on shared parenting.

Finally, so far as enforcement is concerned, amendments to the Children Act 1989 are being made so that it is clear, when a party is in breach of an order, what sanctions are available against the person with whom the child is living for breaches of that child arrangements order.

---

[230] Re S (Transfer of Residence) [2011] 1 FLR 1789.

Chapter 19
Domestic violence & contact

What happens where there has been domestic violence?

Where there has been a history of domestic violence between the parents this will impact on the court's decision on the level of contact granted. This is the case even though the child has not been physically harmed. Domestic violence is recognised as including not only any incident of threatening behaviour, physical violence or abuse but also psychological, sexual, financial or emotional abuse[231] and, as we will see below, in family proceedings the court takes into consideration the harm caused to a child by witnessing and/or hearing violence. If one parent is violent to another, a child will be caught up in that violence. It is important to recognize that domestic violence is not gender specific and there are many men who are themselves the victims of domestic violence. The fact is violence, whether it is perpetrated by a man against a woman or a woman against a man, is a very serious issue and its consequences have a devasting impact on people's lives.

Domestic violence is one of the most common reasons why a mother refuses to comply with a contact order. It may be that after the parties split the mother argues she is concerned that on contact visits the father might be violent towards the children. Furthermore, she may also be afraid that if he has been violent towards her in the past he may be violent again if she is not compliant over contact. It is therefore crucial that any allegations of domestic violence made are dealt with as soon as possible. The earliest opportunity for the court to consider the matter will generally be at the First Hearing Dispute Resolution Appointment (FHDRA). We considered mediation and Mediation Information Assessment Meetings (MIAMs) in Chapter 2 and the inappropriateness of a party attending both mediation and a MIAM where domestic violence is involved. Indeed, when there has been an allegation of violence against another party which has resulted in the issuing of court proceedings within the past 12 months attendance at a MIAM would not be expected.

It is a sad fact that each year thousands of fathers are falsely accused of child abuse. Mothers use this as a means by which contact can be prevented. However, proof of the child abuse must be shown. The problem is that it is all too easy to make allegations and once allegations have been raised the court must err on the side of caution and investigate them fully. Time wasted on cases where false allegations are made means less time devoted to genuine cases where children really need protection and that point cannot be emphasized enough, particularly in light of a report by Women's Aid on child homicide during contact, Twenty nine child homicides (2005).

---

[231] As defined by the Home Office in 2004. It is not a statutory definition but is used to help identify cases of domestic violence.

Background to domestic violence

The whole issue of domestic violence has been a driving force in relation to proposals for reform in relation to contact. In April 2000 the then Lord Chancellor's Department issued a Report on the matter of contact between children and violent parents.[232] It set out proposed Good Practice Guidelines for courts dealing with cases in which domestic violence is raised as a reason for the refusal of contact or for that contact to be limited. The then Government accepted the Guidelines. The Report was based upon the responses to a Consultation Paper issued the previous year. The definition of 'domestic violence' used by the Paper covered physical, sexual or emotional abuse, which has subsequently been widened. Although there is no presumption against contact, where domestic violence is proven to have taken place the court has historically exercised its discretion as to the level of contact awarded. The court has always considered negative factors. These are the seriousness of the violence, the risks involved, the impact on the child (that is the effect that exposure to domestic violence between the parents has had on the child), the impact on the residential parent and the motivation of the parent seeking contact. These negative factors have been balanced against positive factors and consideration given to the recognition by the violent parent of past conduct and that parent's commitment to change. Careful consideration has to be given to the motivation of the parent pursuing contact. Does the parent genuinely believe it is in the best interests of the child for contact to take place, or is it just a way to continue the campaign of harassment, intimidation or violence against the other parent?

Having made an order that there should be contact even though domestic violence has taken place, the court then has to decide on the form of contact. For example, the court may decide that direct contact is in the best interests of the child but that it should be supervised. Conditions may be attached to the order. If a father is violent because he is an alcoholic, one of the conditions may be that he seeks treatment for his alcoholism. Contact may be for a set period and a date given for the order to be reassessed. On an application for interim contact where the allegations of domestic violence have not been decided upon as yet, the court should give particular consideration to the likely risk of harm to the child. This applies whether contact is granted or refused. The court should ensure, so far as it can, that any risk of harm to the child is minimized and that the safety of the child and the residential parent is secured before, during and after any such contact.

The 2000 Guidelines were tested in four appeals in the Court of Appeal later that year where the approach suggested was followed.[233] In guidance to the judiciary in December 2001 the President of the Family Division expanded upon

---

[232] The Advisory Board on Family Law: Children Act Sub-Committee: Report on Contact and Domestic Violence (Lord Chancellor's Department 2000).

[233] Re L, V, M, H (Contact: Domestic Violence) [2000] 2 FLR 334.

these Guidelines and stressed that it was crucial for any allegations of domestic violence to be dealt with as early as possible in the proceedings and for the court to decide what affect the alleged domestic violence, if proved, would have in relation to any order for contact. The Court of Appeal has confirmed this approach.[234] The 2000 Guidelines and those of the President have formed the basis for all subsequent guidance from the Court of Appeal. This includes the May 2008 *Practice Direction: Residence and Contact Orders, Domestic Violence and Harm* which was revised in January 2009 and then incorporated into the Family Procedure Rules (FPR) 2010 Practice Direction 12J.

As indicated above, the definition of domestic violence in so far as it relates to family proceedings has been expanded over the years and continues to change. The Adoption & Children Act 2002 amended the Children Act[235] to include the recognition of the harm that children can suffer by actually witnessing domestic violence. As we have seen, in all cases where the court considers the welfare checklist the courts will have to decide if domestic abuse, violence or harm has taken place and if so, what the likely harm is to the child at the present time and in the future. Harm is defined as including impairment from seeing or overhearing the ill treatment of another. In its 2010 paper *Working Together to Safeguard Children*, the then Department for Children, Schools and Families considered the effect on children not only of direct domestic violence but also of witnessing it. In fact the paper emphasized that prolonged and/or regular exposure to domestic violence can have a serious impact on children's safety and welfare. Children may be hurt physically but they may also suffer psychological and emotional trauma from witnessing domestic violence.

Family Procedure Rules (FPR) 2010 Practice Direction 12J

As indicated above these are an amalgam of all the guidance from 2000 onwards. What is emphasized though is that the court must consider whether domestic violence is raised as an issue at *every* stage of the proceedings. It is also important to note that the court must give directions to enable any relevant evidential and welfare issues to be determined as quickly as possible and it is for the court and not the parties to decide whether any allegation made might be relevant. In terms of investigating the allegations the court must consider whether to have a preliminary hearing to decide the matter.

Investigating allegations of domestic violence and abuse

We considered procedure in Chapter 12. When a party commences proceedings, he/she must complete form C1A if he/she sets out allegations of domestic violence

---

[234] Re H (Contact: Domestic Violence) [2005] EWCA Civ 1404.
[235] Children Act, s 31(9) inserted by the Adoption & Children Act 2002, S 120.

and abuse in the application form. We also considered safeguarding issues, any risk assessment which CAFCASS is under a duty to carry out once an application has been made, but before the FHDRA takes place, and the approach of the court at the FHDRA.

When should there be a fact-finding hearing?

Practice Direction 12J states that the court should determine as soon as possible whether it is necessary to conduct a fact-finding hearing in relation to any disputed allegation of domestic violence before it can consider any final order for residence or contact. If the court decides that a fact-finding hearing is not necessary, the order must record the reasons for that decision. If it decides that a fact-finding hearing is necessary then it is important this takes place as soon as possible because to delay is detrimental to the case proceeding or settling. It is more difficult to make reliable findings the longer the time that has passed since allegations were made, and the quicker the case is dealt with the harder it is for a parent who is trying to obstruct contact to make more allegations before the matter has been decided. Also the court cannot apply the welfare checklist properly while these issues are unresolved.

Once the court has decided a fact-finding hearing is necessary it should consider:

- Making a direction for the parties to file written statements setting out full details of the allegations made, and of any response to them, in such as way as to identify clearly the issues that need to be decided by the court.
- Whether any evidence is required from third parties such as the police or health services. If so the court will need to make a direction for it.
- Whether there is any other evidence that the court requires in the particular circumstances of the case or any other directions the court needs to make. The court should consider whether it is appropriate to make an interim order for residence or contact. More particularly, is it in the interests of the child and can the safety of both the child and residential parent be secured during and after any contact? Is direct contact possible and if so should it be supported or supervised? If direct contact is unsuitable will indirect contact be more appropriate?

Once the court fixes a date for the fact-finding hearing it must also arrange a further hearing in order to make a decision on the application. It is important that the same judge conducts both hearings.

What is a split hearing?

A split hearing, as the name suggests, is a hearing divided into two parts. During the first part the court makes findings of fact on issues either raised by the parties or identified by the court and during the second part the court will decide the case based on the findings it has made in the first part.

In 2010 the then President of the Family Division issued new practice guidance for judges and magistrates on when it is suitable to direct a split hearing or to conduct a fact-finding hearing.[236] The concern was that there seemed to be a very large increase in the number of split hearings being directed by the courts, which in turn were using up too much of the court's time and resources. The President made the point that the decision to direct a split hearing is one for the judge to decide and not a decision for CAFCASS or for the parties. He also gave the specific example of allegations of domestic abuse in a child contact case not being a reason automatically to have a split hearing with a preliminary fact-finding hearing. The whole point is that if the allegations are unlikely to have any impact on the court's order, there is no need for a separate fact-finding hearing. In other words, is the nature and effect of the domestic violence alleged such that, if proved, the decision of the court is likely to be affected?[237]

What happens if allegations are withdrawn before the hearing?

It may be that even though the resident parent seeks to withdraw the allegations the court will still proceed with the investigations if the court has any doubt about the child being at risk of harm. The court will also want to be sure about the reasons for withdrawing the allegations. Are they being withdrawn because they are not genuine or has pressure been placed on the parent to withdraw those allegations? The court will be very sceptical if allegations are withdrawn and then subsequently a party wants to reinstate them. Consequently, where a fact-finding hearing has already been listed the court will proceed with caution before dispensing with the hearing.

The fact-finding hearing

The standard of proof is the same in Children Act proceedings as in other civil proceedings, that is the balance of probabilities. The court must therefore be satisfied that on the evidence it is more likely than not that the event occurred. In a case where allegations are made the court will need to hear evidence from all the parties. The court must make findings of fact as to the nature and degree of any violence and/or abuse which is proved and the effect on the child, parents and any other relevant person. Findings must be recorded in writing and a copy of the record must be served on the parties. If any admissions are made at the hearing then these should also be recorded in writing and retained on the court file.

Orders to be made

Obviously this will depend upon what findings the court makes. There may be no case to answer. If there is, then the steps the court takes will be dependent upon the nature and extent of the domestic violence that has occurred. The court might decide that contact may take place but attach conditions. We looked at contact activity conditions and contact activity directions in the last chapter. If a s 7 report has not been ordered the court might make a direction for one and if one is already

---

[236] The President's Guidance In Relation to Split Hearings May 2010 [2010] 2 FLR 1897.
[237] PD 12J.

underway the court may vary the order in terms of what the s 7 report needs to deal with. Is any psychiatric, psychological or other assessment required of any of the parties or the child? Are there are any facilities locally to assist any party or child where domestic violence has taken place?

Deciding issues of residence and contact where there has been domestic violence

As the Court of Appeal has made clear, domestic violence does not itself constitute a bar to contact but is one factor in the difficult and balancing exercise of the court's discretion.[238] Essentially the court must look at the facts of the specific case and the degree of violence, taking into account the seriousness of the impact of this violence on both the child and the resident parent.

When considering the impact of the violence this covers not only harm the child has suffered already, but also any harm the child is at risk of suffering if an order for residence or contact is made. It follows from this that the court can only make an order if it can be satisfied, so far as possible – something which is not always easy to assess – that the physical and psychological safety of the child and parent may be secured before, during and after contact. We considered the court's criteria when we looked at the background to domestic violence earlier in this chapter.

Recent developments and reform

The Government is planning to change the 'official' definition of domestic violence from March 2013. The definition updates the statutory definition used by the Home Office since 2004 to identify cases of domestic violence and abuse and recognises domestic violence and abuse to those aged 16 and 17.[239] It will now state: 'Any incident or pattern of incidents of controlling, coercive or threatening behaviour, violence or abuse between those aged 16 or over who are or who have been intimate partners or family members regardless of gender or sexuality. This can encompass but is not limited to the following types of abuse:
- Psychological.
- Physical.
- Sexual.
- Financial.
- Emotional.'

Controlling behaviour is 'a range of acts designed to make a person subordinate and/or dependent by isolating them from sources of support, exploiting their resources and capacities for personal gain, depriving them of the means needed for independence, resistance and escape and regulating their everyday behaviour.'

---

[238] Re L, V, M, H (Contact: Domestic Violence) [2000] 2 FLR 334.
[239] See http://www.homeoffice.gov.uk/media-centre/domestic-violence.

Coercive behaviour is 'an act or a pattern of acts of assault, threats, humiliation and intimidation or other abuse that is used to harm, punish or frighten their victim.' The definition also includes 'honour' based violence and female genital mutilation and forced marriage. Victims under this definition are not confined to one gender or ethnic group.

A Young People's panel has been set up by the NSPCC. Children and those supporting them need to know what constitutes abuse so that they can seek the support they require early on and do not suffer in silence.

Chapter 20
Emergency procedures

Prohibited steps order

We looked at the definition of a prohibited steps order in Chapter 6. The first point to note is that the court cannot make a prohibited steps order if the purpose behind it is to achieve a result that could be achieved by a residence or contact order.[240] Essentially a prohibited steps order (and a specific issue order which we consider below) is used by the court to resolve disputes which relate to the exercise of parental responsibility. It is easier to demonstrate by example exactly what can be achieved by this order.

Where a prohibited steps order would be appropriate

- In an abduction case, if the father has abducted the child and the result required is for the abducted child to be returned to the mother, the correct order for her to seek is a residence order with appropriate conditions and directions preventing unauthorized removal.
- If the child is living with the mother and she abducts the child and the required result is to obtain the return of the child to the UK and to prevent further removal of the child, then a prohibited steps order is the correct order to obtain. The child will nevertheless remain living with the mother.
- If no residence order were in force, a prohibited steps order could be used to prohibit the removal of the child from the country or prevent a change of surname. We looked at changes of name and relocation matters such as removal from the jurisdiction in Chapter 17.
- If a father wants to obtain an order preventing a child from living with someone else, the correct order would be a residence order.
- A prohibited steps order could be used to prevent another party from registering or enrolling a child at school or from permitting or preventing a child from having medical treatment.
- Sometimes it is difficult to know which would be the most appropriate order and it really does depend on circumstances. In one case where the mother's cohabitee had abused the children, the court decided that a 'negative' contact order preventing the mother from allowing contact would only afford partial protection. The court made a prohibited steps order against the cohabitee instead.
- If an order is needed to restrict publicity, a prohibited steps order is not the appropriate order. This is because a prohibited steps order can only relate to

---

[240] Children Act 1989, s 9(5).

matters which are included within parental responsibility and publicity is not one of these matters. This would be covered by the wider powers of wardship and dealt with by the High Court. We looked at this in Chapter 16.

Specific issue order

We looked briefly at specific issue orders in Chapter 6. A father would need to apply for a specific issue order where he disagrees with a decision the mother has made in relation to a specific issue and which they cannot resolve between themselves. In the same way as a prohibited steps order, a specific issue order cannot be used to achieve 'back door' residence or contact orders.

Where a specific issue order would be appropriate

The following are examples of specific issue orders:
- For the court to decide which school the child should attend because the parents cannot agree. The non-resident father with parental responsibility is entitled to be consulted about a change of school. Failure to consult and to involve the father will not be looked on favourably if he decided to take the matter to court.
- For the court to decide whether the child should have a particular operation or course of treatment such as, for example, a blood transfusion or vaccination.
- The religion the child should adopt and also religious issues such as male circumcision, for example, which while a medical intervention, has religious implications. The court will consider the welfare test and consider all the factors in the welfare checklist. The court will also be conscious of parties' rights under Article 9 of the European Convention on Human Rights which covers freedom of thought, conscience and religion.
- If it is desired to prevent anyone having contact with the child, this seems to be the appropriate order to obtain as it is accepted that a contact order can only authorize contact and not prevent it. However, it has been held that the court could make a contact order providing for no contact. The person with whom the child lives could be prevented therefore from allowing contact with an abusing parent or someone else the court considered was harming the child in any way.

Making an application for a prohibited steps order or specific issue order

As these are s 8 orders they will be made on Form C100 in the same way as residence and contact orders. But if there are already existing proceedings under the Children Act then the application should be made on Form C2. As a parent, a father will not need leave to apply for either of these orders as he has an automatic entitlement to apply for any of the s 8 orders, unlike a grandparent, as we have seen in Chapter 12. It is worth bearing in mind that courts sometimes use both a prohibited steps order and specific issue order together. For example, one parent might apply to the court for a name change. The court may decide to make a specific issue order that a child will be known by a particular name and also a prohibited steps order forbidding a parent from changing the name. We considered the whole issue of name changes in Chapter 17.

Child abduction

Basics

In Chapter 17 we looked at residence orders and the effect of a residence order where a party wants to take a child abroad as well as applications for leave to remove a child from the jurisdiction, but the important issue is when the removal of a child becomes an abduction matter. The law relating to parental child abduction is complex and this chapter provides only an overview. I would urge anybody reading this book, who has concerns over an imminent child abduction, to seek immediate advice on their particular circumstances and to contact the International Child Abduction and Contact Unit, referred to at the end of this chapter.

Authorized removal or abduction?

- If a residence order is in force, it may have conditions attached to it about removing the child. The court can enforce the conditions by an order that the child be handed over to the parent with the residence order.
- If there is no residence order in force, a without notice application for a residence order or prohibited steps order could be applied for and then enforced by the court. The court has power to order anyone who may have information as to a child's whereabouts to disclose it to the court.
- If the child is removed from England to another part of the UK, this enables a s 8 order to be recognized and enforced by a local court. The order has to be registered.
- If a mother has a residence order, the father will commit an offence if he does not have her consent or the permission of the court to remove the child. This would be 'wrongful removal'. She will not commit an offence if she removes the child unless they are away for more than one month and it is clear they are not on their way back. This would be 'wrongful retention'.
- Where there is no residence order in force and the father removes the child no offence is committed 'initially' but this will become a criminal offence if he refuses to return the child. In any event, it is a criminal offence for any person except a person with parental responsibility to take a child from any person without lawful authority or reasonable excuse.

Following on from this, and in light of a case in 2011 where the mother with sole parental responsibility was able to remove the child without any recourse for the natural father,[241] I cannot stress enough how important it is for an unmarried father to acquire parental responsibility or take steps to acquire it if he thinks the mother with sole parental responsibility might abduct the child.

Isn't child abduction kidnapping?

Currently the offence of child abduction carries a seven year prison sentence under the Child Abduction Act 1984 but it is not classified as kidnapping for which the maximum sentence could be life imprisonment. The question is whether parental child abduction should be classified as kidnapping. In two recent cases the Court of Appeal dismissed the appeals of two fathers who were appealing against their sentences for child abduction.[242] The first father had been sentenced to ten years imprisonment for two counts of child abduction and the second father to nine years imprisonment for three counts of child abduction, but the Court of Appeal decided that the sentences were not disproportionate in terms of the offences committed.

The Court of Appeal felt that the question of whether parental child abduction should be treated as kidnapping should be addressed, but that in any event the sentences for child abduction should be increased.

Preventative measures

Port alert procedures

If there is an imminent threat of abduction (that is within the next 24 to 48 hours) then the port alert procedure can be used. There has to be a real threat that the child is going to be removed unlawfully.[243] The application should be made to the Applicant's local police station or, if it is urgent or a court order has just been made, to any police station. The authorities will need a full description of the child who is travelling, the likely abductor and time of travel, the place they are expected to leave from, probable destination, and photographs. Curiously enough, there is no need for a s 8 order to have been obtained if the child is under 16, although if there is an order in existence it should be produced to the police. On the other hand, the system is only available for children over 16 if a s 8 order exists.

The child's name will remain on the 'stop' list for four weeks and will then be removed unless another application is made to the police.

---

[241] Mercredi v Chaffe [2011] EWCA Civ 272.
[242] R v Kayani, R v Solliman [2011] EWCA Crim 2871.
[243] Child Abduction Act 1984.

Passports

If a father wants an order preventing the issue/surrender of a passport, he can only obtain it if there is already in existence an order prohibiting or restricting the removal of the child from the UK[244] – for example, a prohibited steps order forbidding removal; a residence order in his favour confirming that his consent is required to allow the removal to take place; an order confirming that the removal is contrary to the wishes of the court. As part of an order there may be a direction that the child's passport be lodged with the other party's solicitor if there is a threat of abduction. If any of those orders are in force a request may be made to the Passport Agency not to issue a passport for the child or children in question without the agreement of the other parent (generally the father) or the permission of the court.

If a child's details are registered with the Passport Agency so that no passport may be issued it is important to remember that the registration is only effective for twelve months and so must be re-registered.

Remedies

Although a criminal offence will be committed if a child is abducted abroad, it will not bring about the return of the child. The Hague Convention of Civil Aspects of Child Abduction 1980 and the European Convention of Recognition and Enforcement of Decisions Concerning Custody of Children 1980 provide procedures for tracing a child and for their return. If the other party has taken the child to another country it may be possible to obtain the child's return, but this depends upon the country. The Child Abduction Section of the Foreign Office website is in the course of preparing country-specific information for parents which provides details of the legal issues relating to parental child abduction in that particular country.[245] This will be added to in due course.

Convention countries

If the child has been removed unlawfully to a convention country without the other parent's consent and wrongfully retained there, the Convention will be able to help with the return of the child. The Hague Convention provides that the Central Authority of the country to which the child has been taken must help the parent find the child and protect the child once found. If a child is abducted, a parent must take immediate action and commence proceedings for the return of the child as after one year the return of the child becomes more difficult, although it does not mean that a return is impossible.

Where proceedings are commenced more than one year after the abduction one of the issues the court will need to consider is whether the child is settled in his/her new environment. This does not just mean by virtue of the fact that the

---

[244] Family Law Act 1987, s 37.
[245] http://www.fco.gov.uk/en/travel-and-living-abroad/when-things-go-wrong/child-abduction/country-specific-info/

child has physically been there for over a year, but also from an emotional and psychological point of view. The more deceitful and sly the abduction, the more difficult it will be to establish emotional and psychological settlement. Even if it is established, the court has a residual discretion under Article 18 of the Convention to order the return of the child.

Non-convention countries
Where a child is abducted to a non-convention country such as Saudi Arabia, for example, then the court is free to determine the case on its merits under the wardship jurisdiction, although it will commonly have regard to the factors specified in the Hague Convention in reaching its decision. The court may make the child/children wards of court and order the abductor to return the children to the jurisdiction. If the abductor fails to do so, the court may make an order that the abductor is in contempt of court and can then make an order freezing the abductor's assets in the UK, that is sequestrate them. If the abductor returned to the UK he would then be arrested.

Information on child abduction

Each of the signatory countries has an administrative body known as the Central Authority which is responsible for administering the operation of the Convention. In England and Wales the Central Authority is the Lord Chancellor who delegates the duties of the Central Authority to the International Child Abduction and Contact Unit (ICACU) of the Ministry of Justice.[246] The Justice website provides helpful information on the issue of child abduction.

My child has been abducted to England from another country. What do I do?

If it is a convention country then there will be a Central Authority. It will be necessary to contact the Central Authority in the country from where the child has been abducted. That Central Authority will contact the Central Authority in England which means that the matter will be dealt with by ICACU who will appoint a child lawyer who specializes in child abduction to represent you. Representation is free. In such a situation the English court has to decide whether the child should be returned to that country either under the Child Abduction & Custody Act 1985 if the other country is a signatory to the 1980 Hague Convention or the European Convention on the Recognition and Enforcement of Decisions Concerning Custody of Children 1980. Additionally, the court may use its inherent power to decline 'jurisdiction of the welfare of the child' which requires that any issue relating to the child should be determined in the court of his/her former residence.

---

[246] http://www.justice.gov.uk/protecting-the-vulnerable/official-solicitor/international-child-abduction-and-contact-unit.

If the child has been abducted from a non-convention country either contact a child lawyer specializing in child abduction in England directly or through a lawyer in the country from which the child has been abducted who will then deal with the necessary court proceedings.

Mediation in cases of international child abduction

In Chapter 2 we looked at mediation and the Pre-Application Protocol and the obligation for parties to see a mediator as part of a Mediation Information and Assessment Meeting (MIAM) to ascertain if mediation is suitable. But what is the situation in child abduction cases? We looked at exemptions from attending a MIAM and one of these is where the prospective application is urgent meaning:

- There is risk to the life, liberty or physical safety of the Applicant or his or her family or his or her home; or
- Any delay caused by attending a MIAM would cause a risk of significant harm to a child, a significant risk of a miscarriage of justice, unreasonable hardship to the Applicant or irretrievable problems in dealing with the dispute.

It would seem that child abduction proceedings will be covered by either of these exemptions. That does not mean to say mediation is automatically unsuitable in parental child abduction cases. As we saw in Chapter 2 in the case where the Saudi Arabian father had abducted the five children of the family from London to Riyadh four years earlier, the parties finally came to a judicially led mediated settlement. Mr Justice Thorpe in the Court of Appeal stated that there is, 'no case however conflicted which is not potentially open to successful mediation.'[247]

Other procedures

Missing children – Family Law Reform Act s 33

Where a child is missing the court may make an order requiring any person whom the court has reason to believe has relevant information about the whereabouts of a child to disclose that information to the court. This means that the order may be directed to persons who are not parties to the proceedings. An order cannot be made unless there are proceedings to which s 33 applies – for example proceedings for a s 8 order or under the Child Abduction and Custody Act 1985. The application is made on form C4 and there must be a statement in support of the application. It should normally be made on notice but may be made without notice in an emergency. We looked at without notice applications in Chapter 12.

---

[247] Al Khatib v Masry 2004 EWCA Civ 1353 [2005] 1 FLR 381.

Application for recovery of a child – Family Law Reform Act s 34

Under s 34 where a party has failed to comply with an order to give up a child, such as a s 8 order for example, any court may authorise 'an officer of the court or a constable' physically to take charge of the child, with the use of such force as necessary, and for the delivery of the child to the person entitled. The order will not be made unless it is in the interests of the child and use of the order is more likely to be appropriate for transfer of residence than for achieving contact.

The application is made on form C3 with a statement in support of the application. As with applications under s 33 it should normally be made on notice but may be made without notice in an emergency. What the court might do is make an 'unless' order which basically states that unless the party retaining the child hands over the child at a specified time and place, the power to take the child may be exercised. This allows that party to save face by delivering the child.

Recent developments and reform

On 1 November 2012 the 1996 Hague Convention on the Protection of Children[248] came into force. It will be relevant in most child care cases where there is a *foreign* element. Although it is dated 1996 it was only ratified by the UK in 2012. The existing 1980 Hague Convention continues to deal with child abduction. The 1996 Hague Convention deals, among other things, with the physical protection of children and matters such as parental responsibility, contact, residence, children's property, guardianship and foster parents.

It will usually be the country in which the child is habitually resident which will have jurisdiction in children's cases. We considered habitual residence in Chapter 6. The general rule is that each Contracting State will apply its own law and a decision of a court made in that Contracting State must be recognised in all other Contracting States. This new legislation enables a contact order in favour of the parent who has been left behind to be recognised without the need for proceedings for a mirror order. In terms of enforcement this remains to be determined by the particular Contracting State according to its national law. There are provisions for Contracting States to co-operate in order to protect children.

---

[248] The Hague Convention on Jurisdiction, Applicable Law, Recognition, Enforcement and Co-operation in respect of Parental Responsibility and Measures for the Protection of Children.

Chapter 21
Two further orders of relevance to fathers...

Special guardianship order

What is the difference between guardianship and special guardianship?

Special guardianship is not to be confused with guardianship. When parents think of the term guardian they generally think of it as someone who will look after their children were they to die while the children are still minors. Provided a parent has parental responsibility he/she may appoint a guardian for his/her children and can make provision for this eventuality in his/her Will. If that parent dies the appointment of a guardian will take effect unless there is another parent still living who has parental responsibility.

A special guardianship order (SGO) is made while the parents are still living. SGOs were introduced by the Adoption and Children Act 2002, which amended the 1989 Children Act by inserting a whole new section into the Act.[249] Essentially, an SGO is a 'type' of s 8 order. It is an order where the natural parent retains parental responsibility but the special guardian is given parental responsibility and can make most decisions about the child without consulting anyone else. An SGO might be made in a situation where adoption is too drastic a measure because it severs ties with the natural parents whereas an SGO does not, but the court wants to put in place more suitable long-term living arrangements for the child with someone other than the natural parents.

When would special guardianship be suitable?

As indicated above, adoption is a very drastic measure because of the fact it severs all ties with the birth family and is not always suitable for the children involved. The easiest way to explain is by way of examples where a special guardianship order might be made:
- Where the child is older, is keen to retain links with the birth family and does not wish to be adopted.
- Where the child has been cared for by members of the extended family and severing that connection by adoption would not be in the child's best interests. This is a situation therefore where an SGO could be made in favour of a grandparent or other close relatives such as an aunt or uncle.

---

[249] Children Act 1989, s 14 A-G, supported by the Special Guardianship Regulations (SI 2005/1109) and the Special Guardianship Guidance.

- Where there is a long-term placement which needs the greater security of an SGO, together with the extra local authority help that comes with it.
- For cultural or religious reasons depending upon the circumstances of the case.

How does special guardianship work?

The special guardian acquires parental responsibility[250] and can exercise it to the exclusion of anyone else except another special guardian unless the consent of more than one person is required.[251] The parents do retain parental responsibility but their ability to exercise it is curtailed, although in law the child remains theirs, unlike the position where an adoption order is made. The special guardian cannot change the child's surname or remove the child from the jurisdiction for more than three months without the consent of anyone else with parental responsibility or order of the court. It is worth remembering that when an SGO is in force an application for a residence order cannot be made without the leave of the court.[252] We looked at leave to apply in Chapter 12.

Who may apply to be a special guardian?

Those entitled to apply
- The child's guardian.
- A person in whose favour a residence order is in force.
- A local authority foster parent or relative with whom the child has lived for at least one year preceding the application.
- Anyone with whom the child has lived for three of the past five years.
- Anyone else with the consent of a person with a residence order, or, in the case of a child in care, the local authority, or otherwise all persons with parental responsibility.
- Anyone else not listed above who obtains the leave of the court to make the application. This will include the child him/herself.

It is clear that grandparents and members of the extended family may fall into a number of these categories.

Those not entitled to apply
- Anyone under the age of 18.
- A parent of the child.
- A local authority on behalf of someone else.

---

[250] Children Act 1989, s 14C.
[251] Ibid, s 14C(2)(a) relates to any legal enactment or Rules of law that would require another person's consent.
[252] Ibid, s 10(7A).

By order of the court

The court can impose an SGO on parties who have not applied for it, and may not even seek it, provided the court is satisfied that the welfare of the child requires it.[253]

Making the application

Notice to the local authority

The local authority must be given three months notice of an application being made. If the child is in care then notice must be given to the relevant local authority responsible for the child. If not, then notice must be given to the local authority where the Applicant lives. The local authority will use the three month period to write a report on the appropriateness of the SGO. The report must deal with the suitability of the Applicant to be a special guardian and all matters the local authority considers relevant and other matters, which may be prescribed by the Secretary of State![254] The court requires this report before it can make a decision. This means that if the court decides to make an SGO of its own accord it will have to order a report before it can do so.

The application itself

We looked at court forms in Chapter 6. The application will be made on form C1 (unless leave of the court to make the application is required or there are existing proceedings under the Children Act in which case the form to use will be form C2) supported by form C13A – Supplement for an application for a special guardianship order. On form C13A the Applicant will need to state his/her relationship to the child – in other words, which one of the categories listed under those entitled to apply above she/he falls into. Details of notification to the local authority must also be provided, as must reasons for the application and plans for the children.

If there are existing Children Act proceedings, then the application must be made to the court dealing with those proceedings. If not then the application may be made in the Family Proceedings Court, County Court or High Court. Once the application has been issued and a date fixed for a directions hearing, the papers must be served on all the Respondents and other interested parties (see below).

Who are the Respondents?

- Anyone who has parental responsibility for the child or children who are the subject of the application.
- Where there is a care order in place, all those who had parental responsibility before it was made.
- Where there is a care order in place and the child is separately represented by a guardian it is the guardian who must be served with all the papers.

---

[253] Ibid, s 14A(6)(b).
[254] Ibid, s 14A(8).

Which other interested parties must be notified?

- If the child is in local authority care the social services department of that local authority.
- If the child is not in local authority care, the social services department of the local authority where the Applicant lives.
- Anybody who is caring for the child.
- If the child is in a registered children's home or a refuge the person who provides that accommodation needs to be notified.
- Anybody the child has lived with for at least three years prior to the application.
- If there has been a court order then everybody named in that order.
- If there are existing proceedings and the parties to those proceedings are likely to be affected by the application they must all be notified.

The list is very extensive.

How does the court decide?

At the directions hearing the court will determine what steps need to be taken to progress the case, including whether a further directions hearing is necessary before the final hearing takes place. Once the local authority's report is filed at court this will form part of the evidence before the court upon which the court will base its decision. The court must decide whether to disclose the report to the parties and what, if anything, should be deleted from the report before disclosure is made.

The court will decide whether or not to make the SGO by applying the welfare checklist in the same way as for any other s 8 order. Because an SGO limits parental responsibility it will have to be justified in terms of respective parties' human rights. It must be necessary and proportionate. If the court decides to make an SGO and there are existing s 8 orders in place the court must consider what should happen to them. Should they be varied or discharged? If there is an enforcement order or a contact activity direction should they be discharged? Does the court need to make any directions or conditions to regulate the contact? And what arrangements are to be made for contact, for example, with the parents or a relative?

The court can also consider by what surname the child should be known. In one case a six-year old child had been living with his grandparents since he was six months old. The grandparents were granted an SGO and the judge allowed them to change the child's surname to theirs, although admittedly the parents had not opposed the change.[255] In another case the maternal grandparents had been made special guardians but the judge refused to grant permission to change the child's surname and the grandparents appealed. The court dismissed the appeal, making it clear that the question of identity was a significant feature of the child's welfare. The child needed to learn that she was being brought up by her grandparents and not her parents.[256]

---

[255] S v B and Newport City Council [2007] 1 FLR 1116.
[256] Re L (Special Guardianship: Surname) [2007] EWCA Civ 196.

If there was a care order in force the making of the SGO will discharge it. This is also a situation where the court will consider controlling further applications through the use of s 91(14) of the Children Act which we looked at in Chapter 12.

What are special guardianship support services?

After the order is made, irrespective of whether the child was in care or not, the local authority will have duties and these include making arrangements to provide special guardianship services such as counselling, advice and information and other services as are prescribed.[257] The assistance includes mediation and possibly family group conferences, which we looked at in Chapter 2. Special guardianship services include the provision of financial support. Financial assistance is crucial, as the special guardian will have more expenses as a result of being the day to day carer of a child. In terms of legal costs, if public funding is available then it is unlikely any legal case would be financially assisted by the local authority, but where it is unavailable the local authority can provide assistance towards legal costs not only for the application to obtain a special guardianship order, but for an application to vary or discharge the order as well as a s 8 order.[258]

How long does an SGO last for?

An SGO lasts until the child's 18th birthday, but it may be varied or discharged.[259]

Varying or discharging an SGO without leave
An application to vary or discharge an SGO may be made without leave by the special guardian, any individual in whose favour a residence order is in force, and a local authority with a care order in respect of the child.[260]

Varying or discharging an SGO with leave
Those requiring leave are the child him/herself, any parent or guardian, any step-parent who has acquired and not lost parental responsibility, and anyone else who is not the child's special guardian, parent or guardian or a person in whose favour a residence order is in force but who has, or immediately before the making of the SGO, had parental responsibility for the child.[261]

There is a high threshold for variation or discharge, reinforcing the intention of an SGO being regarded as a long-term secure order. In the case of a child, the court will only grant leave if it is satisfied the child has sufficient understanding to make the proposed application. Anyone else entitled to apply for leave must show a significant change in the circumstances since the making of the SGO before leave will be given.

---

[257] Children Act 1989, s 14F(1)(a) and (b).
[258] Special Guardianship Regulations 2005 Regulation 6(2)(c).
[259] Ibid, s 14D.
[260] Ibid, s 14D(2).
[261] Ibid, s 14(D)(3).

Varying or discharge of an SGO without an application

The court has the power to vary or discharge an SGO in any family proceedings in which a question arises as to the welfare of the child if it considers that it should be varied or discharged even though no application has been made.[262] It will apply the welfare test.

Special guardianship orders and Family assistance orders

When it makes an SGO in private proceedings the court may also make a family assistance order (FAO) for any period up to 12 months to help with the smooth running of the order. The order will be made to CAFCASS or to the local authority. We consider FAOs in the next section.

Family assistance orders

What is a family assistance order?

A family assistance order (FAO) is an order requiring a CAFCASS or local authority officer to advise, assist and generally help with the smooth running of a s 8 order, generally a contact order, as we saw when we looked at ways of making contact work in Chapter 18. The power to make an FAO exists under the Children Act s 16 as amended by the Children & Adoption Act 2006. Unless otherwise specified an FAO will last for twelve months. There is no provision for extending the order beyond twelve months, but it is possible to make a further order where proceedings are ongoing.

Who may be named in the order?

- Any parent, guardian or special guardian of the child.
- Any person with whom the child is living or in whose favour a contact order is in force with respect to the child.
- The child him/herself.[263]

Any person named in the FAO may be directed to take such steps as may be specified to enable the CAFCASS or local authority officer assigned to the case to be kept informed of his/her address and to be able to visit that person. An FAO will only be made with the consent of every person named in the FAO (except the child) as it would be pointless to attempt to advise, assist or befriend a parent against their will – it simply would not work.

---

[262] Ibid, s 14D(2).
[263] Ibid, s 16(2).

Where a s 8 order is in force...

If an FAO is made with respect to a child and is in force at the same time as a:

- S 8 order made with respect to the same child, the FAO may direct the CAFCASS or local authority officer to report to the court on such matters relating to the s 8 order as the court may require including the question whether the s 8 order ought to be varied or discharged.[264]
- A contact order made in respect of the same child, the FAO may direct the CAFCASS or local authority officer to give advice and assistance as regards establishing, improving and maintaining contact to any of the persons specifically named in the order as requiring this advice and assistance.[265]

Is an FAO suitable in the case?

The consent of CAFCASS or that of the local authority (provided the child lives or will live in the area) is not required before an order is made. However, the court must have obtained the written or oral opinion of the appropriate CAFCASS or local authority officer as to whether making an FAO is in the best interests of the child. It may form part of a s 7 welfare report. The court must also give any person who is to be named in the order an opportunity to comment upon the opinion given by any CAFCASS or local authority officer.

CAFCASS will probably recommend an FAO where there are welfare issues that are unlikely to be met without CAFCASS's assistance such as safeguarding matters. But in any event, and as we have seen above, for an FAO to work the adults named in the order must consent to that assistance. The court will want to be satisfied that CAFCASS or the local authority will be able to allocate a welfare officer otherwise there will be no practical benefit to the child or the parties involved. CAFCASS's policy will be to allocate a Family Court Advisor who will work as case manager.

What happens when the FAO comes to an end?

Before the FAO ends the case manager should organize a meeting with the parties and review what has been achieved by the FAO. Depending on the terms of the FAO it may be necessary to report back formally to the court and so it will be important to identify exactly what the benefits of the FAO have been. Are there any ongoing needs? If so, how may these be met? As we saw above, if the proceedings are continuing then it is possible to make a further FAO.

---

[264] Ibid, s 16(6).
[265] Ibid, s 16(4A).

Chapter 22
Grandparents and the extended family

Contact Scenarios

Contact subject to parental control

In the majority of cases when parties are together, the degree of contact that the children have with their grandparents will depend upon the parents because they control the contact. Should the parents not have a close relationship with the grandparents they will probably not promote the grandchild/grandparent relationship.

Post-separation contact

After separation, the amount of contact children have with the grandparents is governed by the parent with whom the children live. Since this is invariably the mother, generally the maternal grandparents retain a closer link because they form part of her extended family to whom she will turn for support. Unless the mother has a good relationship with the paternal grandparents their relationship with the grandchildren will suffer. Grandparents can help the children because if they have supporting roles they can reduce the disruption of the parent's separation. Grandparents provide the bulk of non-parental childcare in this country. It is estimated that this is at least 60%.

In one case the parties separated when their son was sixteen months old. The father remarried and moved far away. The mother had no alternative but to return to work full-time in order to make ends meet, so she entrusted the daily care of her son to her own parents since she could not afford child care. The maternal grandparents played a pivotal role in this child's upbringing. They cared for him every week day from 8am to 6pm until he went to school, and thereafter all the school holidays until he reached the age of fourteen.

Is promotion of contact generally dependent upon the mother or not?

A great deal depends upon the mother's relationship with the father's parents. Some mothers have amicable ongoing relationships with their in-laws and freely facilitate contact. In the case referred to above, the mother encouraged contact with the paternal grandparents, and she herself had an excellent relationship with the paternal grandmother. Unfortunately, not all cases are like this and in many cases the paternal grandparents will be limited to contact when the father has contact visits – and even that could be severely curtailed if the mother raises objections.

Additionally, if it was the mother who had previously encouraged contact with the father's parents and no longer does so, then the split will be detrimental to the paternal grandparent/grandchild relationship. Thus the loss/lack of contact with paternal grandparents might occur not because the mother prevents it, but because the father leaves the responsibility for maintaining contact with her, even though they are now apart.

There has been considerable debate about the importance of maintaining contact between grandchildren and their grandparents and the positive contribution which grandparents make to their grandchildren's lives. Grandparents are often key confidants for children facing enforced change as they represent stability and many children report having very close relationships with their grandparents.

Other family members

Children can feel torn when there are a number of other relatives pressing for contact. Usually children will have more contact with the relatives of the parent with whom they live. Contact may become more fragmented when parents remarry and step relations are introduced.

Parents see their relatives as important sources of support and turn to them in times of crisis. They may also be dependent on their family for emotional and financial support and this can be ongoing; and sometimes that puts a strain on those relationships too. Given the heavy reliance on the extended family during this period, it is difficult to imagine how a father who does not have an extended family copes alone at this time.

The current legal position for grandparents and members of the extended family

The legal position is set out in the Children Act 1989.[266] Grandparents are not specifically mentioned in the Act. They do not have an automatic right to apply for any s 8 order, but if they can show that their grandchild who is the subject of the application has lived with them for at least three years out of the last five years before they made the application or they have the consent of all those with parental responsibility, with a residence order or the local authority if the child is in care, then they will be entitled to apply for a residence or contact order without requesting leave from the court.[267] Also, as a 'relative' a grandparent is entitled to apply for a residence or special guardianship order (see Chapter 21 and below) without the court's leave provided the child has lived with him/her for a period of one year immediately proceeding the application.[268] 'Relative' will include other

---

[266] Children Act 1989, s 10(5).
[267] Ibid, s 10(5) b & c.
[268] Children Act 1989, s 10(5).

members of the extended family such as brothers, sisters, uncles or aunts (whether of the full blood or half-blood or by marriage or civil partnership) or step-parents. If a grandparent or member of the extended family does not fall within any of these categories then they will need the leave of the court to apply for a s 8 order. As we have seen, the welfare test does not apply where the court is considering an application for leave to apply for a s 8 order because the application is procedural and does not involve questions about the child's upbringing. However, the welfare of the child will be applicable if leave is granted and the s 8 application proceeds. The court will then apply the welfare factors.

What is frustrating for grandparents and members of the extended family is that the Children Act 1989 allows others who have no biological connection to a child to apply for any of the four s 8 orders without permission of the court when they, with their blood ties, usually have to seek leave to apply. An important example is the 'psychological' parent – we looked at this in Chapter 8.

Courts recognize the importance of grandparents and other relatives. However, every case must be decided on its own facts and courts are aware that an application for leave to apply for a s 8 order generally will have arisen where there are strained relations with ex in-laws and long-standing problems with grandparental contact where grandparents have been denied contact post-separation of the parents. The courts will be mindful not to disrupt a child's life and cause harm. The requirement of leave is intended as a filter to protect the child and family against unwarranted interference. There is no presumption that leave will be granted but grandparents are much more likely to find it easier to obtain leave than other members of the extended family and non-family members.

We looked at the application for leave to apply for a s 8 order in Chapter 12.

Special Guardianship Orders (SGOs)

We looked at SGOs in detail in Chapter 21. What is interesting to note is that where children are placed with 'relatives' following the making of an SGO they will most commonly be placed with grandparents, then aunts and uncles. There is no question that grandparents can be central in keeping the family together during difficult times. Their support, advice and experience is invaluable and, in the context of SGOs, they can offer stability to often very vulnerable children within a 'familial' setting. There is nothing to prevent a child being adopted by relatives, but this can cause more disruption for a child whose grandparents then also become his/her parents and his/her aunt or uncle siblings. Also adoption generally weighs against grandparents because of their age. An SGO might be considered more appropriate depending upon the circumstances.

Is there a case for changing the law to accommodate grandparents and the extended family?

There is no question that grandparents and members of the extended family can be a vital resource and this has been recognised by successive Governments, but none of them have seen fit to remove the requirement for a grandparent to apply for leave.

In 2005 the Constitutional Affairs Committee's inquiry *Family Justice: the operation of the family courts*, considered whether the requirement for grandparents to obtain leave should be removed. Families need Fathers gave oral evidence to the Committee that 'grandparents should have a legal right to apply for contact without permission.' In my view, which I also expressed to the Committee, where the resident parent does not encourage contact with the non-resident party's parents then in many cases it simply does not happen. The Committee recommended that a change should be made in the law to enable grandparents to apply to the court for contact without the need to apply for leave first.

The then Government indicated that it would consider simplifying the process but no promise was made to remove the need to apply even though the importance of grandparents and the extended family continued to be emphasised. For example in 2008 in the Ministerial Forward to its paper *Families in Britain: An Evidence Paper*[269] the then Department for Schools and Families stated that 'Extended family members provide one another with support thoughout life, especially in difficult times and during critical moments, such as when a child is born, when a couple is separating or when relatives need caring for. It is within families that a sense of identity develops, and cultural and social values are passed on from one generation to the next...'

When the Centre for Social Justice, the Think Tank set up by the Rt. Hon. Iain Duncan Smith MP when he was in Opposition, produced its report Breakthrough Britain, *Every Family Matters*, an in-depth review of family law in Britain in July 2009 it set out its recommendations on the rights of the extended family.[270] These were that:

- Grandparents should be placed in a distinctive legal position.
- To protect the child from multiple claims for contact, 'grandparents' should be defined for this legal purpose strictly in terms of a biological or adoptive relationship to the child.
- A single straightforward application for contact for grandparents should not require leave although other applications for s 8 orders would follow existing procedure.
- Subsequent judgments regarding contact should be based on well-understood relevant criteria, which should include a grandparent's prior interest and contact with the child.

---

[269] Ref: DCSF-01077-2008.
[270] Section 5.4 Rights of extended family, pp167-179.

- An early approach with mandatory attempts at mediation between grandparents should be encouraged before the issue of proceedings at court.
- The use of child care credits to be paid to grandparents who are not themselves registered child minders, when this would enable a parent to take up employment or training. The rate should be set at 70 per cent of the rate of the carer's allowance.
- Authorities responsible for housing allocation should be sensitive to the importance, except where there are contra-indications, to children's well-being of maintaining contact with their kinship network, especially their grandparents.

This was all very encouraging for grandparents. Unfortunately, these recommendations, although useful and persuasive, do *not* have the force of law.

Recent developments & reform

Leave to apply

The whole issue of whether grandparents should be required to apply for leave was revisited by the Family Justice Review. In its Final Report it recommended that the need for grandparents to apply for the leave of the court before making an application for contact should remain.[271] The Review's findings were that it was not over burdensome for grandparents to seek the leave of the court before making an application which is why that requirement should be retained. The point was made that contact is the right of the child not of the parents and thus not the right of the grandparents. By leaving the status quo unaltered this would prevent 'hopeless or vexatious applications' which are not in the interests of the child.

One of the other complaints raised by grandparents was that they should not have to pay two sets of fees: for the leave of the court to make a s 8 application and then for the substantive s 8 application itself. But under the Family Proceedings Fees (Amendment) Order 2010 when an application requires permission of the court, although the relevant Children Act 1989 fee is payable when permission is sought, no further fee will be charged if the permission is granted and a s 8 application is subsequently made.

The Government accepted these recommendations and, so far as leave is concerned, felt it should remain as it is an important safeguard for children and their families and is consistent with the principle that the court's paramount consideration must be the welfare of the child. 'However, the Government is committed to ensuring that children have meaningful relationships with family members who are important to them following family separation where it is in their best interests and safe. As a matter of good practice, supporting a child's ongoing relationships with their grandparents and wider family members should be considered when making arrangements for a child's future.'[272] The idea is that

---

[271] Family Justice Review Final Report – November 2011, pp.21, 34, 142-143 section 4.41-4.48.
[272] The Government's Response to the Family Justice Review: A system with children and families at its heart – Ministry of Justice & Department for Education, February 2012, Cm 8273, p.67.

the importance of the relationships children have with other family members should be emphasised in the process of making Parenting Agreements. We shall see how this pans out in due course.

Child arrangements orders and grandparents

The introduction of the proposed child arrangements order to replace residence and contact orders will also be relevant to grandparents. It was recommended by the Family Justice Review that a child arrangements order be available to a family member with the permission of the court and that where 'the order requires wider family members to exercise parental responsibility, the court would make an order that the person should have parental responsibility for the duration of the order.'[273] The Government in its response confirmed that where parental responsibility was necessary to fulfil the order it should only last for as long as the order was in existence and that, 'If PR were to be awarded on an ongoing basis, the child's care arrangements are likely to become unnecessarily complicated.'

Family Group Conferences

We considered these in Chapter 2 and how they promote the involvement of the extended family in decisions about the future plans concerning child arrangements.

---

[273] Family Justice Review Final Report – November 2011, p.22 para. 113. See also pp.34 and 150.

Chapter 23
Appeals under the Children Act 1989

Making an appeal

If deciding to lodge an appeal either against the making of any order under the Children Act or against a refusal to make an order, a father needs to know to which court to appeal, which rules cover that appeal, whether he has an automatic right to appeal or requires permission, the grounds of appeal, how to prepare the case for appeal and what orders can be made. We look at the appeals process in family proceedings below.

Family Proceedings Court

- Since 6 April 2009 appeals from the FPC are to the County Court. Prior to that date appeals from the FPC were to the High Court.
- Permission to appeal is required for Children Act 1989 orders.
- Issuing an appeal does not automatically stay the order, that is to stop the terms of the order being implemented, pending the appeal so it will be necessary to make any request for a stay to the County Court which will be dealing with the appeal or to the FPC which made the order. The request needs to be made during the time period available to lodge an appeal (see below under **The appeals procedure**).
- For appeals under the Children Act 1989 the procedure is set out in Part 30 of the Family Procedure Rules 2010 (FPR 2010).

County Court

- A party may appeal against an order made or given by a district judge to a circuit judge in the County Court.
- Permission to appeal is required unless the appeal is against a committal order or a secure accommodation order. (A secure accommodation order is essentially an order where a child in care is kept in secure accommodation for his/her own protection. For example, if the child has a history of running away or of self-harm.)
- Either the district judge who made the order or the circuit judge to whom the appeal is being made can stay the order pending the appeal. The request needs to be made during the time period available to lodge an appeal (see below under **The appeals procedure**).
- The procedure is set out in Part 30 of the Family Procedure Rules 2010 (FPR 2010).

High Court

- The appeal is from a district judge of the High Court or the Principal Registry of the Family Division to a judge of the High Court.
- Permission to appeal is required unless the appeal is against a committal order or a secure accommodation order. (For the definition of a secure accomodation order see under County Court above.)
- Either the district judge of the High Court, or the Principal Registry of the Family Division who made the order, or the High Court judge to whom the appeal is being made, can stay the order pending the appeal. The request needs to be made during the time period available to lodge an appeal (see below under **The appeals procedure**).
- The procedure is set out in the Family Procedure Rules 2010 Part 30, Practice Direction 30A.
- The appeal to the High Court must be filed in the Principal Registry of the Family Division or the District Registry nearest to the court from which the appeal lies.

Appeals to the Court of Appeal

- The appeal is from a circuit judge of the County Court or a judge of the High Court.
- Permission to appeal is required unless the appeal is against a committal order or secure accommodation order, or a refusal to grant habeas corpus. (For the definition of a secure accommodation order see under County Court above. Refusal to grant habeas corpus would be the scenario where the court refuses to issue a writ ordering a person to be brought before the court to ascertain whether that person's detention in custody is lawful.)
- Either the County Court or High Court or the Court of Appeal can stay the order pending appeal. The request needs to be made during the time period available to lodge an appeal (see below under **The appeals procedure**).
- The rules governing these appeals are the Civil Procedure Rules 1998 Part 52 and PD 52.

The appeals procedure

Filing a notice of appeal

A notice of appeal setting out the grounds of appeal including (if permission is required) a request for permission and an appeal bundle (see section below) must be filed at court within 21 days of the date of the hearing being appealed against or such time as the court directs.

Grounds of appeal

When setting out the grounds in the notice of appeal it is important to ensure that a father includes any matters upon which he wishes to rely otherwise he will not be able to rely on them unless the appeal court grants permission. If he believes the decision against which he is appealing was plainly wrong or unjust because of a serious procedural or other irregularity he must set out his reasons clearly and specify in respect of each ground whether it raises an appeal on a point of law or is an appeal against a finding of fact (see below under the section on Orders which may be made on appeal).

Permission to appeal

If a father decides he wishes to appeal against an order he has two choices. He can either ask for permission to appeal from the judge whose decision he wishes to appeal at the hearing or he can make the request in his notice of appeal. It may well be that the judge in the lower court may refuse permission and so he will have to make the application to the court where he is lodging his appeal. The appeal court may consider the request without there being a hearing, but if permission is refused then the father can within 7 days of that refusal request that the court reconsider his request at a court hearing.

For permission to be granted there has to be a real prospect of the appeal succeeding or there has to be some other compelling reason why it should be heard – to prevent a serious miscarriage of justice, for example, like in a case of alleged child abuse where fresh medical evidence has come to light about the child's injuries. If the case has already been appealed to the County Court or High Court, in other words this is the second appeal, then only the Court of Appeal can grant permission and it will not do so unless it considers the case raises an important point of principle or practice or there is some compelling reason for it to hear the case.

The Court of Appeal set out some useful pointers in a case of a father acting as a litigant in person who was seeking permission to appeal against an order for supervised contact with his two children.[274] The judge in the lower court concluded that the father was not seeing the children due to his own behaviour. The father asserted that lack of contact with the children was because of maternal manipulation, her deliberate alienation of the children from him, and a gullible and corrupt family justice system which had dishonestly and deliberately sided with the mother. The Court of Appeal stated that it was apparent from the father's submissions that he, like many other litigants in person, thought that the Court of Appeal possessed powers on an application for permission to appeal that it simply did not have and set out to clarify the position. The Court confirmed that when considering such an application, the issue the court had to decide was whether or not the original order was plainly wrong. In reviewing the judge's

---

[274] Re W (Permission to Appeal) [2007] EWCA Civ 786.

decision the court had to consider whether the judge had made any error of law in reaching his judgment, whether there was sufficient evidence on which the judge could properly have made the findings of fact and the assessments of witnesses that he made, and whether there was any error in the exercise of his discretion which would lead to the conclusion that his order was, arguably, plainly wrong. Only if the answer to any one of those questions was Yes could the Applicant be given permission to appeal. In this case the father failed on all points.

Serving the notice of appeal

The notice must be served by the Applicant as soon as possible after filing, but no later than 7 days after filing, on each Respondent to the proceedings. It must also be filed on any children's guardian (not applicable if appealing to the Court of Appeal) and on any local authority which has prepared a special guardianship report. If the appeal is from the FPC it must also be filed on the court officer.

The appeal bundle

This should include:
- A sealed or stamped copy of the Appellant's notice.
- A sealed or stamped copy of the order being appealed, or a copy of the notice of the making of the order.
- A copy of any order giving or refusing permission to appeal, together with a copy of the court's reasons for allowing or refusing permission.
- An affidavit or witness statement filed in support of any application included in the Appellant's notice.
- Where the appeal is against a Consent Order, a statement setting out the change in circumstances since the order was agreed or other circumstances justifying a review or re-hearing.
- A copy of the Appellant's skeleton arguments (see below).
- The transcript or note of judgment, or in a magistrate's court written reasons for the courts decision (see below).
- In cases where permission to appeal was given by the lower court those parts of any transcript of evidence which are directly relevant to any question at issue on appeal.
- The application form.
- Any application notice relevant to the subject of the appeal.
- Any other document which the Appellant reasonably deems necessary to enable the appeal court to reach its decision.
- Any other documents the court directs.

If it is not possible to file all the documents at the time the bundle is lodged the reason for not doing so must be explained to the court and the documents must be filed as soon as possible.

Skeleton argument

This is basically a document which sets out, clearly and succinctly, the areas in dispute point by point. It is prepared as a separate document and is lodged with the appeal notice. A litigant in person does not have to lodge the skeleton argument at the same time as the notice, but it must be filed at court and served on all Respondents within 14 days of the notice being filed at court. It is useful to provide a chronology of the events as well because this acts as a quick reference guide for the court.

Transcripts & notes of the judgment

If a transcript of the judgment is available, in other words it was officially recorded and can be transposed to text, then this must be obtained and included in the bundle. If there is no transcript then a written judgment endorsed with the judge's signature will suffice. If the hearing took place in the FPC then the magistrates written reasons are acceptable. There may be no transcript but where the parties have an agreed note of the judgment, they can submit it to the judge whose decision is being appealed against for his/her approval. If they cannot agree the note of the judgment they can submit both sides notes to the judge with an explanatory letter and ask him/her to sign off an approved version.

In a case where the Appellant is a litigant in person and the Respondent is represented and there is no transcript, there is a duty on the Respondent's barrister/solicitor to make his/her note of judgment available to the Appellant free of charge. Also, even if there is a transcript, if the Appellant is a litigant in person with limited funds, the court may certify that the cost of obtaining the transcript will be waived and borne at public expense.

Respondent's notice

The Respondent may seek permission to appeal or wish to appeal to a higher court to uphold the lower court's decision. The lower court may direct that the Respondent file a notice by a certain date. If the Respondent has been served with an Appellant's notice and no direction as to filing has been given by the lower court, then he/she has 14 days to file a Respondent's notice. This 14 days timescale also applies if the Respondent has been given permission to appeal by the Court of Appeal. The notice must be served as soon as possible and certainly not later than 7 days after filing.

Orders which may be made on appeal

On appeal, if the court decides that a case is totally without merit it might strike it out but if it does this it must set out its reasons as to why it believes the case to be unmeritorious. The court has the power to affirm, set aside or vary any order.

It might make a fresh order; decide that the case should be remitted for a rehearing to the original court who heard the case; or decide that the case should be remitted to a higher court.

If there was a problem because information was withheld for example, then the judge might set aside the original order, make another order or rehear the case. In children's cases rehearings are not desirable because of the delay this will cause in deciding arrangements for the children involved. The court also has discretion to consider whether to admit new evidence which has come to light.

When an appeal will be allowed

- Where a decision is plainly wrong because of an error or errors of law.
- The decision is unjust because of serious procedural or other irregularities.
- The judge's exercise of his/her wide discretion was wrong.

Procedure is very important and every hearing must be compliant with Article 6 and Article 8 of the European Convention on Human Rights. Judges must give reasons for their decisions otherwise they are in breach of the Article 6 right to a fair trial. The reasons must include a statement of the issues, the court's finding of fact on these issues, reasons for preferring one witness's evidence to another, reasons for not following the recommendation of a CAFCASS officer, guardian representing the child (which we considered in Chapter 14) or expert witness. The appeal court will need to be satisfied that the judge took into account all relevant matters and not irrelevant ones. The judge must reach a decision applying the welfare principle and having regard to all the circumstances of the case including the factors set out in the welfare checklist.

Discretion cases are the most difficult to succeed with because a judge has a wide discretion and an Appellant has to show that the judge when exercising that discretion in someway exceeded it. Findings of fact are a perfect example of this – this is because issues of fact and credibility as to what and who is to be believed (or not as the case may be) will be a matter for the judge to decide on the oral evidence given at the time. Even though an appeal court has the transcript of the hearing and can read the evidence, it will not have heard witnesses giving evidence or observed their demeanour and so it is harder for it to question the credibility of their oral evidence.

Case management decisions are discretionary decisions and include, for example, decisions about judges ordering disclosure of documents, filing of witness statements and experts reports. The judge might not order an expert report on the basis that it would add nothing further to the case and only cause delay and would not be in the child's best interests. However, if it could be shown that by not requesting a report the judge had deprived him/herself of vital information which would have led to a different outcome in the case, then it could be argued that he/she had failed to make an informed decision and this would be an instance where there would be a ground for appeal.

Chapter 24
Child Support

The Child Support Act 1991 and the Child Support Agency

The intention behind The Child Support Act 1991 was that it would benefit children by ensuring they would receive maintenance from the absent parent, usually their father. The Child Support Agency (CSA) was set up in 1993 and the whole idea was that from then on the agency, rather than the courts, would deal with child maintenance. There were major problems because the formula for calculating maintenance was too complicated and the Agency was unable to deal with the backlog of claims and reviews of claims because the whole process was cumbersome. The result of this was that children did not benefit. In fact, statistics show that only one in five children derived some benefit from the Agency so the Act did not deliver what was intended.

The Child Support Pensions and Social Security Act 2000 was passed to make the whole area of child maintenance easier to understand, more accessible and easier to enforce so that there would be more money for the children. On 3 March 2003 a new way of calculating child maintenance was introduced. Unfortunately, the changes did nothing to improve the collection of child maintenance, the CSA failed to deliver and in December 2006 it was proposed that the CSA be replaced by the Child Maintenance and Enforcement Commission (C-MEC) for England, Wales and Scotland which was to became fully operational by 2010.

The Child Maintenance and Other Payments Act 2008 (CMOPA) and C-MEC

The emphasis of C-MEC was on encouraging parents to make their own arrangements and to take financial responsibility for their children, and was backed up by a tough enforcement regime. Since 2008 C-MEC had the power to withdraw passports from defaulting non-resident parents although it is believed this power was rarely invoked. It also had the ability to deduct money directly out of a non-paying party's bank or building society account where there were child maintenance arrears where that party had failed to co-operate with other collection methods and where deduction from earnings orders could not be used. C-MEC could either apply for a lump sum deduction order for a one off payment or a regular deduction order to collect arrears at regular intervals.

Unfortunately, there were issues with C-MEC and particularly its IT systems. Despite a £107m upgrade of computer systems in 2008, by 2010 C-MEC was being criticised for the sharp rise in the number of cases being dealt with manually. In

January 2011 the government launched a Green Paper *Strengthening families, promoting parental responsibility: the future of child maintenance*[275] which set out its proposals to build a new and streamlined child maintenance scheme and IT system. The new system will be integrated with the tax systems at HM Revenue and Customs. The idea was to launch the scheme in 2012 for new Applicants and close the Child Support Agency to new applications. C-MEC was abolished in July 2012 and the website closed 1 August 2012. The Department for Work and Pensions (DWP) now manages the child maintenance system in GB.

Child maintenance and the DWP

In its January 2011 Green Paper the Government set out detailed views on child maintenance reform. It stated that parents should be encouraged and supported to make their own arrangements for the maintenance of their children before deciding to use the statutory maintenance scheme. The proposals included introducing charges for parents using the statutory child maintenance service although in cases where a party has suffered domestic violence his/her case would be fast-tracked directly onto the statutory services and no payment would be required to enter the system. A 'gateway' process would be set up which would require parents to access advice and support services which would offer them help and information on the range of options available to them (free of charge) before they could apply to the statutory system.

The new statutory child maintenance scheme includes plans to increase the amount of maintenance paid by parents on state benefits and others declaring low incomes. Offered as a fall-back scheme for parents who cannot collaborate, the Government claims the new statutory child maintenance scheme will be fairer, faster and less costly to the taxpayer. It will also be much less dependent on what non-resident parents choose to disclose about their incomes. Parents failing to pay their maintenance would be pursued with the full range of new enforcement tools available and face additional penalty charges.

Existing CSA cases would need to be closed and it was estimated that this would take about two years. At the time of writing to parents with care to inform them that their CSA case would be closing, details of the gateway process would be provided together with details of the options open to them to support them in making a decision about the future, which might include an application to the new scheme.

A new child maintenance system

Following on from the January 2011 Green paper, in July 2012 the Government

---

[275] *Strengthening families, promoting parental responsibility: the future of child maintenance* – public consultation, Cm7990. Start date 13 January 2011 End date 07 April 2011.

published a consultation *Supporting separated families: securing children's futures*[276] with an emphasis on supporting families to make their own arrangements.

- The terminology is changing to the 'parent who pays' and the 'parent who receives child maintenance.'
- There will be a one-off upfront fee of £20 to make an application under the new statutory Child Maintenance Service but this is not applicable if the Applicant is a victim of domestic violence or aged 18 years or under.
- It was made clear that the introduction of a service charge for the use of the statutory scheme will give a financial incentive to parties to make their own arrangements. The Government reduced the application fee which had originally been set at £100.
- The emphasis is on collaborative arrangements and services supporting separated families. This includes a web application, co-ordinated telephone networks, local and face-to-face support and the creation of something called the 'Innovation fund' to encourage the development of interventions that promote collaboration and reduce conflict, and to finance experts to test and evaluate propositions to help parents work together. The gateway process ensures people are aware of those services.
- Once the application to use the statutory scheme is made and the fee paid, there will need to be a calculation of maintenance. The new CMS will use HM Revenue & Customs information provided on taxable income alongside other data to calculate the amount of maintenance that a paying parent is required to pay. It will be sent to the paying parent and the parent in receipt both for information and to check the figures for accuracy. The calculation can be appealed where appropriate.
- By basing the calculation on the latest available tax year data this will provide a fairer but more rigorous service where the paying parent's annual income fluctuates: for example, the self-employed, seasonal workers or those who are in receipt of annual bonuses. The calculation will be updated with fresh income data at no additional cost to the Applicant each year for the life of the case. The expectation is to clear applications where information is received from HM Revenue & Customs within 4 weeks compared to the current system where it is 12 weeks.
- In the vast majority of cases the parent who pays will have the opportunity to pay the parent with care directly and therefore there will be no further charges or fees levied on either parent. This is called Direct Pay and will replace the current Maintenance Direct. Payment could be made by a number of methods including, but not limited to, standing order and direct debit. If a parent needs to protect personal details a referral can be made to a money transfer service.
- If CMS believes a parent will not pay or is unlikely to, or that parent subsequently fails to pay in full and on time, it will move quickly to enforce the

---

[276] *Supporting separated families: securing children's futures* Cm 8399. Start date 19 July 2012. End date 26 October 2012.

payment of maintenance through the collection service. Initially contact will be made by telephone within 72 hours if possible with a request for the paying party to provide evidence that payment has been made. A paying party has 14 days to provide this evidence. If the collection service is used to collect payment it will levy a 20% fee on the paying parent which gives a strong incentive to pay directly in full and on time. Collection fees are necessary to make both parties collaborate or make payments direct. So a 7% fee will be deducted from the maintenance paid to the parent with care.

- A fixed charge for clearly defined enforcement actions that have to be taken will also be introduced, such as setting up a deduction from earnings order, for example. The planned charges are as follows: a liability order – £300; a regular deduction order – £50, a deduction from earnings order – £50, a lump sum deduction order – £200.
- Those parties already in the CSA have the chance to come to their own arrangements or to enter the statutory scheme. The intention is to commence the process in the summer of 2013 of contacting the initial wave of parents affected. And there is also the intention of ending any ongoing maintenance liability in all existing CSA cases over a three year period. It is recognized that it is important to attempt to deal with cases where there are arrears because it is in these cases that the children lose out, so an arrears strategy is being developed to focus on pursuing maintenance owed to children in those cases where it is appropriate to do so. Available powers will be used such as increasing the use made of deductions from paying parents' bank accounts and 'orders for sale' of their property. Accessing wider sources of Government information to locate parents who have tried to avoid paying is also proposed.
- Parents on income related benefits who live apart from their children are to have the amount of child maintenance they must pay increased from £5 to £10 per week. The change will apply to clients of the new statutory maintenance scheme. The new scheme will be introduced slowly from 2012 and the increase in the amount paid by parents on income related benefits will take place when the scheme is opened to all new Applicants.
- In future no maintenance will need to be paid in cases where care is shared on a 50:50 basis.

The following timetable is proposed:
- In 2012 the first elements of the new support services for separated families was launched. From October 2012 CMS was opened to a pathfinder group of new Applicants.
- In 2013 the remaining elements of the new support services for separated families are to be launched and the second phase of statutory CMS which will include charging will not be launched until the service has been shown to be working well. The second phase will consist of the gateway service, the introduction of charging and the beginning of the case closure process. A review will be carried out not more than 30 months after the introduction of

the second phase.
- In 2014-17 the new support services for separated families will be expanded and strengthened to invest in proven effective interventions from the 'Innovation fund' that help parents work together in the best interests of their children. All existing cases will be closed by 2017 except for cases with ongoing arrears action only.

The existing child maintenance system

Since 27 October 2008 it has been possible for a parent with main day to day care to choose to arrange child maintenance through a family based arrangement or (if that is not an option or does not work) through the Child Support Agency (CSA) or the courts. Prior to that date a parent on benefits had no choice but to apply for maintenance through the CSA. Also, since April 2010 parents in receipt of income-related benefits have been allowed to keep all of their child maintenance without it affecting their entitlement to benefit.

DWP is responsible for the statutory child maintenance scheme currently operated through the CSA. Child Maintenance Options is an information service funded by DWP offering newly-separated parents free information and support on arranging child maintenance, but it also deals with issues relating to housing, legal and money concerns.
www.cmoptions.org or 0800 988 0988 or text CALL to 66644.

The existing child support requirement are set out below.

Family Based Arrangement
This is an arrangement the parents make between themselves. If parents have a good relationship, can work together, are committed to making it work, are honest about their respective financial positions and are genuinely acting in the interests of their children this is probably the best option for them. It is free to set up, is a private arrangement and is very flexible. Child Maintenance Options has a child maintenance calculator which will give parents a very good indication of the right level of maintenance and makes a good starting point for an agreement. The parents have complete control of how much is paid, what is being paid for, how the funds are to be paid and when they are to be paid.

The financial arrangements can be changed if circumstances alter provided both parents agree. However child maintenance is paid, it is always advisable to keep a written record of what has been agreed and what has been paid from both parties' point of view in case there are any problems over payment or what has been agreed at a later date. If at some point the family based arrangement breaks down there is the option to apply to the CSA.

Payments through the CSA

An arrangement made through the CSA is legally binding. If there is the danger that a party will not pay or is unlikely to pay then this might be the best option as the CSA has enforcement powers which can ensure the parent without the main day to day care meets their obligations and if a payment is missed the CSA will chase it up. There are several options:

- Maintenance Direct. Once the CSA has calculated a child maintenance amount the parent without day to day care can pay the other parent directly. The CSA will not need to be further involved unless there are problems with payments not being made.
- Direct debit and deduction from earnings orders. If the CSA collects the child support and passes on the payment to the parent with the main day to day care, payments can be made by direct debit so that the payment is taken straight out of the bank or building society account or through a deduction of earnings order where child maintenance is taken directly from earnings and paid into the other parent's account.

The maintenance a non-resident father pays for any relevant children is calculated as a percentage of his net income. There are four rates of pay.

The rates of pay
- Basic rate: This applies to a non-resident father with a net weekly income of between £200 and £2,000. The percentage of net income is 15% for one child, 20% for two children rising to a maximum of 25% for three children or more. The resident parent can apply to the court for a top-up maintenance order in certain circumstances. For example, where there are additional educational expenses or the child is disabled.
- Reduced rate: This applies to a non-resident father with a net weekly income over £100 but under £200. He will pay £5 per week on the first £100 of his net income and a percentage of his net weekly income over £100. The percentages used to calculate the maintenance are different from the basic rate ones.
- Flat rate: This applies to a non-resident father with a net weekly income of £100 or less, or who is on benefits. The flat rate is £5, irrespective of the number of children.
- Nil rate: This applies to a non-resident father who is any of the following: a full time student; aged 16 to 19 and studying full time for A levels or NVQ level 3; a prisoner; living in a residential home or nursing home and receiving assistance for those costs.

Calculation of net income
What is taken into account and what is not?
- Tax, National Insurance and pension contributions will be deducted from a non-resident father's gross income.
- No deduction is made for a non-resident father's housing costs, even if a large

proportion of his income is paid towards those costs!

- If he has investment income that will be included in calculating his net income.
- Deductions are made from the non-resident father's income for relevant 'other' children. A relevant other child includes his natural child from another relationship but the child does not have to be his natural child. A stepchild is included. It is sufficient that the child is a member of his household and that he or his new partner receives child benefit. The percentage deducted depends upon the number of relevant other children the non-resident father has and whether he pays under the basic rate or reduced rate, as this will alter the percentage to be deducted. The CSA maintenance calculation will be a percentage of what is left of his income after all deductions have been made.
- What about those who appear to have no/a limited income? A non-resident father will be given a deemed income if it can be shown that his lifestyle exceeds his professed income and that he ought to pay higher maintenance. An example would be someone who deals a lot in cash and does not declare his true income.
- The mother's income is ignored.
- There are a number of variations that can be made to increase or reduce the maintenance. For example, if a non-resident father pays boarding school fees for the relevant children that would be a ground for a variation.

Shared care

Maintenance is scaled down according to the amount of time the children spend with the non-resident father. The more the children stay with him, the less maintenance he pays as follows:

Number of nights	Fraction to subtract
52 to 103	One-seventh
104 to 155	Two-sevenths
156 to 174	Three-seventh
175 or more	One-half

There might be a situation where the non-resident father has qualifying children to stay for a different number of days. Here he would add up the total number of days for all the children who stay with him and divide by the number of children. For example, if child A stays 104 nights and child B 104 nights the scaling down is 2/7th and 2/7th divided by 2 = 2/14ths.

If the one-half threshold is reached for any given child, that is they stay with him for 175 days or more, then the maintenance is reduced by a further £7.

Payments through the court

If parents are in agreement but feel that they need the security of a legally binding court order they can convert a family arrangement into one. In England and Wales this will be a Consent Order and in Scotland this will be a Minute of Agreement. However, obtaining a court order generally only happens when parties are going to court for other reasons such as sorting our their divorce or dividing up their assets. Parties need to bear in mind that during the first 12 months of a consent order they cannot ask the CSA to put an arrangement in place for them. The court has the power to enforce orders. This is not free as there will be court fees and if you need representation then there will be your legal representative's costs. With a Minute of Agreement this can be registered to make it legally binding and if the paying party fails to pay then the sheriff officer can collect and enforce payments.

Contact & Child Support

It has long been held that contact cannot be made conditional on the payment of maintenance and that contact must be decided and then child support worked out. The fact is where there are outstanding child support issues they do have a bearing on contact and non payment of maintenance has often been a reason for withholding contact. On the other hand there are also many fathers who do pay maintenance and are still refused regular contact with their children. The Family Justice Review made it very clear however that there must be no connection in law between contact and maintenance, and the Government agreed with this although the Government did recognize 'the importance of effective enforcement provision so that court ordered arrangements are not flouted.'[277] We looked at the whole issue of enforcement in Chapter 18.

Maintenance and relocation

A father should ensure that any child support obligations have been put in place before the mother relocates with the child and that these obligations will be binding in the country to which she has moved so that there is no come back on him, otherwise a few years down the line he might find himself facing a claim for child support in the mother's adopted country.

What a father needs to do therefore is to obtain a court order which is made into an order of the court in the country where the child is relocating before the move so that a subsequent order for child support cannot be made there. In the court order it is advisable to set out who will pay the cost of travel for contact throughout the child's minority and from what resources and always include child support in these arrangements.

Enforcing maintenance when the paying parent moves abroad

In June 2011 new EU Rules on maintenance payments came into force assisting in the recovery of child support and other forms of maintenance from someone

---

[277] The Government's Response to the Family Justice Review: *A system with children and families at its heart* – Ministry of Justice & Department for Education, February 2012, Cm 8273, p.80.

in another EU country so, for example, an absent parent who has gone to live abroad and does not pay child support.[278] The Rules have set up an EU-wide system for facilitating the recovery of maintenance payments so that absent parents will no longer be able to evade their obligations. This will speed up procedures and save money. The regulations also sets up rules on co-operation between central authorities to provide assistance in relation to maintenance applications.

---

[278] EU Rules, Regulation No. 4/2009 on Maintenance Regulation.

Chapter 25
The Human Rights Act 1998 &
The Children Act 1989

Throughout the course of this book we have seen the impact of the Human Rights Act and how the courts must give due consideration to the respective parties' human rights and perform a balancing act when making its decisions under the Children Act.

Implications of the Human Rights Act for fathers

The Human Rights Act does not provide more rights for a father, but it should provide easier access to those rights. The Act came into force on 2 October 2000 and incorporates into British law 'most' of the provisions of the European Convention on Human Rights (the Convention). The rights we have implemented are called 'convention rights'. This should not to be confused with the Hague Convention.

If a father makes an application under the Children Act what effect does the Human Rights Act have on the court's decision?

Whenever a UK court is considering the existing law, it has to look at that law and see whether it fits in with Convention rights. The law must be read in a way compatible with Convention rights, so if the court finds that a particular Act of Parliament does not fit with Convention rights what can the court do?

The court can only make what is called a 'declaration of incompatibility' because the Human Rights Act does not allow the courts to overrule an Act of Parliament. It is only the higher courts that will be able to make declarations of incompatibility, so in a family case if a query arises in the family proceedings court or county court, the case should be transferred to the High Court. The Government and Parliament have to decide if the law should be changed.

The Children Act was drafted with the intention that it would be compatible with the Act. The courts must read and give effect to children legislation in a way which is compatible with the Convention rights, so far as it is possible to do so, and it will be necessary for the courts to evaluate the effect of the legislation in particular cases to ensure compatibility.

It is not explicitly stated in the Convention that the children's interests are the paramount consideration, and the European Court, in interpreting the right to family life, has stated that the rights and freedoms of all concerned must be taken into account and a fair balance struck. The European Court has found that the best interests of a child may be the paramount factor in determining custody. The

Commission has also said that the child's interests are dominant if there is conflict between the parent and child, in which event the interests of the child prevail. The European courts have not clearly indicated what factors the domestic courts should take into account in determining what is in the best interests of the child, but have indicated the importance of the continuity of development or consistency in the upbringing of a child.

Bringing a claim

Can a father bring a claim?

The Human Rights Act is like a code of conduct. This is set down in the form of Articles and Protocols. It is not a series of dos and don'ts. If a father wants to take somebody to court under the Act, he needs to show that the code of conduct has been breached. In legal terms this means he is a person who is a 'victim' of a breach of Convention rights.

Who are victims and how does a victim bring a claim?

A victim is a person. This includes an individual or a company, because in law a company is a legal person. The breach could be due to action taken, or failure to take action. The father need not have suffered harm because of the breach, provided there is a risk of him being directly affected. He could bring a claim if his family is at risk of being broken up by a particular policy, even if this has not occurred; for example, against a local authority that has made an application to take his child into care although the application has not yet been heard in court.

Who can a claim be brought against?

Public authorities alone have a duty to comply with the Convention, not individuals. In a contact case it is not possible for the father to complain that the mother is not respecting his right to family life by denying him the contact he desires. Public authorities include local authorities, the Police, and the Courts to ensure a fair hearing.

Which convention rights affect Family law and fathers' rights?

Article 6: the right to a fair trial

Just because a father does not succeed in his case, it does not mean that he did not have a fair trial – but everybody has a right to a fair trial. Each party must have a reasonable opportunity to present his/her case, including evidence, under conditions that do not place either of them at a disadvantage to the other:
- Cases must be brought within a reasonable time. Delays where cases are not listed for lack of court resources will be unacceptable under the Convention

and have been held to be a violation of it, but delays in other European jurisdictions are such that some UK delays may not seem that unreasonable. However, in relation to children, especially where a child has been removed from his/her parents, or contact has been stopped pending the final court hearing, delay is crucial and here there is a very real prospect that Article 6 could be breached.

- There must be an independent judge.
- Everyone is entitled to a public hearing and for the judge's decision to be pronounced in public. However, there are circumstances when a public hearing would not be appropriate, such as cases involving children. The proceedings are in private, that is, behind closed doors, and not open court. We looked at privacy and media access in Chapter 16.
- There is a right to know the judge's reasons for the decision.

Article 6 will be broken if these standards have not been met. Article 6 covers criminal and civil proceedings. Civil proceedings that are covered by Article 6 include disputes about with whom the children of separated parents should live, so Article 6 will be relevant in relation to contact disputes.

Article 8: the right to respect for private and family life.

Respect for private life.

There is no firm definition but it covers:

- The right for a person to get on with his own life without interference.
- The right to his identity and personal development and to form friendships and relationships with other people. A right to identity and personal development is important in the context of paternity and contact. For example, there may be no family life because the child's father is not married to the mother and the child has no contact with him, but the child has a right to know his father and develop a relationship with him and vice versa. This right to an identity and personal development becomes important when considering issues such as paternity, contact and name changes.
- The right to enjoy his sexuality.
- The right to control his body.

Respect for family life.

This does not allow persons to claim a right to establish family life. It is a question of fact, taking into account all the circumstances. Some examples of family life, not exhaustive, are as follows:

- The married father. A child born to married parents will be part of that relationship from the moment he/she is born.
- The unmarried father with parental responsibility. A father with parental responsibility should be able to show that he is a part of family life.
- The unmarried father without parental responsibility will have to show more than just his paternity. An unmarried father who cohabits or has cohabited

with the mother and the children will be able to establish family life as will an unmarried father who does not cohabit with the mother but has regular contact with his children and a strong bond, showing that there are family ties. He should show commitment, although even where an unmarried father had not had regular contact with his child, family life has been found.

- A single mother and child.
- Adoptive parents.
- Family life has been held to exist where there is no blood link or legal link through adoption or marriage.
- Family life goes beyond the traditional family and may be established between children and individuals who are not necessarily their parents to the extended family life.
- When parents divorce or separate their relationship ceases to be family life within the meaning of Article 8, but the relationship between parent and child may survive as family life. Contact is relevant here.
- Step-parents – being a step-parent by virtue of marriage or civil partnership with the child's natural parent goes some way to establishing family life, but if there is a significant period of cohabitation then that would demonstrate a commitment which should be sufficient to establish family life.
- Same-sex partners: where there are children of one or both of them and there is a committed relationship and period of cohabitation. There are a number of scenarios. Put simply, if there is a civil partnership and one of the parties has a child through artificial insemination, the other party as civil partner will be treated in the same way as a father who was married and family life will be established.[279] Where there is no civil partnership and one party is artificially inseminated the other party will be the parent, but only if the party having the treatment agrees at the time of treatment that she will be treated as such. Without a civil partnership, however, the non-biological parent will not automatically have parental responsibility.
- It has been held to include a right for parents to insist measures are taken by public authorities to re-unite them with their children. Local authorities run particular risks in relation to contravention of the Convention with regard to children in care. The right of parents to maintain relationships with their children can be violated by termination of contact and placing for adoption.
- The right to information has been considered to be an aspect of family life protected by Article 8 in relation to records kept by a local authority for a child in their care.

What would be a justifiable interference into family life?

Article 8 is not an absolute right but a qualified one. This means that a public authority can break the right in certain circumstances so that it can intervene, but the public authority will have to show that it had a sound legal reason for doing

---

[279] Human Fertilization & Embryology Act 2008 s 45.

so and that it was reasonable in all the circumstances of the case.

There is a balancing exercise between a court respecting an individual's right to his private life, and welfare of children. In cases where a court declines to make a contact order, particularly in implacable hostility cases, the court will have to justify the decision that in the interests of the child the refusal was justifiable.

Cultural and religious practises have to be considered carefully as failure to respect them could result in the court and local authorities being in breach. An example of this is a case where the parties were Moroccan. When the parties were together, the whole family slept in the same bed. After separation the father continued to sleep with the children on contact visits in the same bed. A Child Welfare Officer reporting on this case felt that there was something 'suspect' about the behaviour and referred to it in an extremely derogatory way.

Care proceedings 'proper' will invite questions over family life and its disruption. Interference cannot be justified just because another family might simply provide a better home for the child. The aim of care proceedings will usually be to reunite the family as soon as possible.

Article 9: freedom of thought, conscience and religion

The right to bring up children in the religion of their parental choice is usually accepted as a parental right, but this is a difficult area and it can be complicated. This is particularly so where both parents are of different religions and when they have separated there is a tug of war over the religion of the child. There may be applications within the Children Act.

Article 14: prohibition of discrimination

Parental responsibility is an area where unmarried fathers have been seen as discriminated against. The discrimination has been deemed justified by the court to protect the interests of the child and mother.

Remedies for breach of rights

Changing a decision

If a party wants to change a decision that has been made by a public authority or for the court to order a public authority to do something, or stop doing something, he can apply for a procedure called a judicial review. A judge will review the case and decide if the public authority has acted unlawfully. He has three months from the decision or action he is challenging in which to take this step.

Compensation

If a party wants compensation as a result of a breach of his rights he can bring a claim for damages. He has one year from the date of breach to bring his case. The Court of Appeal has held that an action for damages should only be brought as a last resort, after all other avenues have been exhausted.

Just because there has been a breach of his rights does not mean that he will receive damages because they are awarded at the discretion of the court when it is 'just and appropriate' and 'necessary'. The level of any award should aim to achieve 'just satisfaction' rather than placing the claimant in the position he would have been in had the basis of the complaint not occurred.

Declarations of incompatibility

If the courts decide that a particular act does not fit with Convention law, all they can do is to declare it incompatible but they cannot overrule it. Only Parliament can do that.

Contact & The Human Rights Act

A number of fathers have relied on Article 8 to argue that they have a right to contact with their children and that a refusal to order contact would amount to a breach of their rights. Equally some mothers have relied on Article 8 to argue that to have direct contact with a man who has been violent to them and/or their children amounts to a failure to respect their right to have a family life, free from the fear of violence. One father even managed to show that there had been a breach of his rights under Article 6, successfully arguing that delays in the court system meant that he had waited over two years for the final hearing of his contact application.

The Human Rights Act has not had a major influence on the decisions made in the majority of contact cases. This is because the Children Act focuses on the welfare of the child, whereas the Human Rights Act requires the court to balance the rights of all those parties concerned. This means that in a contact case, even if the court concludes that the adult person seeking contact has a relationship which comes within Article 8, after weighing up the competing rights of that person and the child, it still has the power to refuse or limit that contact. This is on the basis that on balance interfering with the rights of that person are justified because the rights of the child require it.

Part III: Reform

Chapter 26
Pressure for change

The Final Report of the Family Justice Review and the Government's Response

Throughout the course of this book, where relevant, we have considered recommendations made in the Family Justice Review's Final Report, the Government's Response to them and the proposed changes to be implemented in relation to private law children proceedings as a result. For ease of reference these are as follows:

- An increase in Dispute Resolution Services (DRS) and the promotion of Parenting Agreements – see Chapter 2.
- The establishment of a Family Justice Board and a Young People's Board – see Chapter 3.
- The replacement of a residence and contact order with a child arrangements order – see Chapters 6, 17, 18 and 22. In September 2012 the Department for Education produced draft legislation, which includes new provisions in relation to a child arrangements order. S 8 of the Children Act 1989 is to be amended to omit the definition of both a residence and contact order and insert the definition of a child arrangements order in their place. References in the Act to residence orders and contact orders are to be substituted by a child arrangements order. Having reviewed the draft legislation, which states that a child arrangements order will be an order regulating with whom a child is to live, spend time or otherwise have contact with, I am not convinced that this will make any practical difference for fathers when it is applied by the courts.
- The creation of a single family court for England and Wales – see Chapter 6.
- The introduction of further safeguarding checks at the start of the court process and the allocation of cases to a simple track or complex track system – see Chapter 12.
- Judicial continuity and case management – Chapter 12.
- Transfer of the sponsorship of CAFCASS from the Department for Education to the Ministry of Justice – see Chapter 6.
- Legal Aid cuts and the Legal Aid, Sentencing and Punishment of Offenders Act 2012 – see Chapter 7.
- Plans to raise parties' awareness of parental responsibility – see Chapter 9.
- Public law reforms in relation to delay, case management, timetabling, expert reports, role of the court and local authority, and DRS – see Chapter 13.
- Introducing a shared parenting legal presumption – see Chapter 17 and below.
- Introducing reforms to the make enforcement of court orders more stringent – see Chapter 18.

Judicial proposals for the modernization of family justice

Mr Justice Ryder was appointed as Judge in Charge of the Modernization of Family Justice following the publication of the final recommendations of the Family Justice Review panel in November 2011. The appointment lasted until July 2012 when he produced his Judicial proposals for the modernization of family justice. In the report he recommends, inter alia, introducing a single Family court in the form of a network of Local Family Court Centres judicially led and managed by Designated Family Judges, where all levels of judge and magistrates will sit as Judges of the Family Court. The High Court will remain separate but High Court judges will sit in the Family Court.

His report also recommends developing new methods of assisting litigants in person in private law cases. With legal aid funding being withdrawn, those representing themselves will face more difficulties and the courts will need to respond to this. He refers to creating a private law pathway which sets out what the court can and cannot assist with and how any assistance is to be provided.

Proposed legislation on the involvement of both parents in a child's life

Introduction

Over recent years there has been ever increasing pressure from relevant legal bodies, interested organizations – including fathers' rights groups – and individuals for the issue of post-separation co-parenting to be addressed, and for the introduction of effective measures to achieve it. If a father shows a genuine commitment to his children and has the capability and capacity to look after them and there are no safety issues, then his involvement should be encouraged and facilitated. But the sad fact is that there are so many cases where that simply does not happen.

In Chapter 18 we looked at the existing approach to contact and how easy it is for a hostile resident parent to ensure that the child's contact with the non-resident parent does not take place. Enforcement of orders is an ongoing problem and something which the Government recognizes, as we saw from its proposals for reform in relation to enforcement which we considered in the same chapter. We also looked at proposals for reform and pressure to introduce legislation so that when a relationship breaks down there is a presumption that the children's time will be shared between both parents. We now look at the background to, and proposals for, reform in detail.

Background to the current reforms

The 1998 Consultation Paper *Supporting Families* produced by the former

Government (and to which we have referred in Chapter 1) stressed the importance of fathers which was at least a positive start. In 1999 the Children Act Sub-Committee of the Lord Chancellor's Advisory Board on Family Law issued a Consultation Paper on the issue of *Contact between Children and Violent Parents* and produced its report in 2000 setting out recommendations for contact where there has been domestic violence. It is quite clear that the then Government's approach to reform in the area of contact was dictated and driven by reseach into domestic violence, hence amendments introduced by s 120 of the Adoption & Children Act 2002 and concern to promote contact where it is safe. Certainly, it was after the Sub-Committee produced its report on contact and domestic violence that it then decided to consider the wider issue of contact. A further Consultation Paper *Making Contact Work* was published in 2001 followed by *Making Contact Work: a Report to the Lord Chancellor* in 2002.

Making Contact Work highlighted dissatisfaction with the legal system; that contact issues need to be addressed by means other than court proceedings; that the court process would continue to retain a role in intractable cases; that procedures would have to be improved to be more effective; and that new legislation relating to enforcement would be required to provide the court with a range of remedies in intransigent contact cases where the court order is not being obeyed.

The July 2004 Green Paper *Parental Separation: Children's Needs and Parent's Responsibilities* included a raft of proposals supposed to assist the facilitation of the 'meaningful relationship' parents should have with their children post-separation 'where it is safe', and to help divert parties away from the adversarial court process. These included proposals in relation to collaborative law, mediation, protection of children from harm, case management (earlier listing of hearings, reducing delay, judicial continuity etc), post order follow up, use of family assistance orders to facilitate contact and enforcement along the lines of the *Making Contact Work* report.

As part of its aim to divert parties away from the adversarial court process the then Government proposed the Family Resolution Pilot Project (FRPP). The plan was to provide information to parents at the start of proceedings about, inter alia, the negative impact of parental conflict on children, workshops on conflict management and a planning session where they would be given examples of parenting sessions that work. FRPP did not proceed beyond the Pilot stage but, in my view, it was flawed from the outset because it started from the premise that the welfare of the child is best promoted by quality of contact between the child and the non-resident parent rather than quantum. Contact is about time and for a child to maintain and/or build a quality relationship with the non-resident parent he/she needs time to do that.

In the 2004 *Green Paper* the then Government stated that it did not believe 'that an automatic 50:50 division of the child's time between two parents would be in the best interests of most children' and that the 'best arrangements for them will depend on a variety of issues particular to their circumstances: a one size formula will not work.' For these reasons it rejected a legal presumption of equal contact. When the Government produced its report *Next Steps* in January 2005 setting out its agenda for reform it stated that it would not legislate to introduce a legal presumption of reasonable contact or shared care on the basis that it was not persuaded that any legislative change would benefit children. Since the Children Act states that the welfare of the child shall be the paramount consideration the Government confirmed that no change was necessary; the intention of the Children Act is to encourage both parents to continue to share in their children's upbringing, even after separation and divorce so this must mean by the children spending time with each parent, that is having contact with them.

While all of that may be correct, the problem is how much time should that be? Or more particularly, how much time is necessary to establish the child/father relationship? What apportionment of the child's time with each parent represents the child's best interest? By infrequent visits lasting a couple of hours? By a 50/50 split or a 30/70 split of the child's time? By overnight stays? By alternate weekends and holidays with around 100 nights contact per year or more or less?

When I made my supplemental submissions to the Constitutional Affairs Committee *Family Justice: the operation of the Family Courts* in 2005 I submitted that at the beginning of a case when an application is made to the court, to offer the best possible chance of settlement, it is crucial that firm guidance is given to the parties on how much contact the court is likely to order if they cannot agree, that frequent and continuous contact is in the child's interests and that there should be a clear presumption that the child is going to have parenting time with both parents. The judiciary gave evidence to the Constitutional Affairs Committee *Family Justice: the operation of the family courts* that the only legal presumption we can have is that the child's welfare is the paramount consideration and that any other presumption would conflict with it. Ultimately, the Committee only recommended the insertion of a statement into the welfare checklist indicating that courts should have regard to the importance of sustaining a relationship between the children and a non-residential parent.

Following on from this, in the 2009 *Policy Report by the Family Law Review: Breakthrough Britain, Every Family Matters – An In-depth review of family law in Britain (the Centre for Social Justice)* it was recommended (section 5.1) that 'the Children Act 1989 needs to be amended to include principles for contact and residence that are clearer and more explicit but nevertheless leave room for flexibility and judgment in particular cases.' And that, 'All those with parental responsibility should be presumed to have an equal status in their children's lives following separation.' And further that, 'Legislation should acknowledge that children are most likely to benefit from *substantial involvement* of both parents in their lives.' I was asked to submit my comments on 'Conflict over contact' and one of the points I raised was in relation to the status of a mother or father in the eyes of the law, because the fact is when parents are together they generally have equal status so why should that diminish just because they separate and/or divorce?

In 2010 the Family Justice Review was set up by the Government to consider some areas of family law reform and we have looked at their recommendations in relation to co-parenting, post-separation and divorce. In its Interim Report published in March 2011 statutory reference to a child having a meaningful relationship with both parents was recommended, but ultimately in the Final Report it was recommended that no legislative change was necessary. The Government disagreed.

The current reforms

The Government Consultation Paper *Co-operative Parenting Following Family Separation: Proposed Legislation on the Involvement of Both Parents in a Child's Life*[280] set out four legislative options for the Respondents to the consultation to consider. These were amending the Children Act 1989 to include a presumption in law or principle or starting point or addition to the welfare checklist emphasising the importance of both parents' involvement in their children's lives. The presumption approach was the Government's preferred option. I was surprised to note that there were only 214 responses to the Consultation, one of which was mine, with the greatest percentage of responses from fathers, which is no surprise.

In *Co-operative parenting following family separation: proposed legislation on the involvement of parents in a child's life – Summary of consultation responses and the Government's response*[281] the Government has concluded that the best option is to introduce a presumption in law that a child's welfare is furthered by the involvement of both parents, where that is safe and in the child's best interests. It is believed that both mothers and fathers will have more confidence in the legal process knowing that the court has to consider fully the benefits of their involvement in their children's lives. The Government has made it very clear that the 'proposed legislative amendment to promote 'shared parenting' is part of a wider package of measures to help parents resolve disputes about their children following family separation.'[282]

The Government has been very careful to emphasize that what it is doing is giving legal recognition to the importance of both parents to their children post-separation and/or divorce. A presumption of shared care is not the same as a presumption of equal care and there is no intention to introduce a legal presumption for children's time to be shared between the parents *equally*. It is intended to insert a new clause into the Children Act so that:

- Whenever a court is considering whether to make, vary or discharge an order under s 8 or an order in relation to parental responsibility, the court's default position will be for both parents to be involved in the child's upbringing.
- If however, there is any evidence before the court to suggest that the

---

[280] Department for Education (DFE) 13 June 2012.
[281] Department for Education (DFE) 5 November 2012.
[282] Ibid, p.4.

involvement of the child's parent would put the child at risk of suffering harm and that cannot be overcome by involving the parent in the child's life in a way that will not put the child at risk of harm, then the presumption will not apply.

- If there is no evidence before the court to suggest that the involvement of the child's parent would put the child at risk of suffering harm, then the next question is whether the involvement of that parent furthers the welfare of the child. If Yes the presumption stands. If Not the presumption is rebutted.
- The court will make its decision in accordance with section 1 (welfare of the child) of the Children Act.

Chapter 27
A way forward?

Shared care for 'fit' parents

What practical difference will this legislation make? Edward Timpson MP has stated that, 'The proposed legislative change does not give or imply the creation of any rights of equal time, or that there is any prescribed notion of how much time is appropriate. Courts will continue to make decisions based on children's best interests.'[283]

Currently, when the court is faced with a decision as to what arrangements are to be made for a child where the parties cannot agree between themselves, the starting point will be that a continuing relationship with both parents is in the interests of the child unless that continuing relationship will put the child at risk of harm. The assumption that a child will benefit from an order being made under the Children Act can always be displaced if the child's interests dictate otherwise, thus covering safety issues such as domestic violence and abuse. The welfare of the child will be the paramount consideration even though the court will have to weigh up the rights of the parents because of the right to family life under Article 8 of the European Convention on Human Rights.

There are arguments against making any legislative changes on the basis that it is unnecessary because the Children Act does not require amendment; it is only the system that needs improving. And then there are the concerns of the Family Justice Review, particularly in light of the experience in Australia over the problems with shared parenting and the increase in litigation there, that despite what is said to the contrary, parents will regard shared care as equal care. And what about the argument that with the increased emphasis now on diverting parties away from the court process by forms of ADR (or Dispute Resolution Services as proposed in the Family Justice Review (FLR) November 2011) and in encouraging and directing parents to work out their own agreements for the children more cases will settle, so why the need for change when only a very small proportion of cases will proceed to court anyway?

Because, despite what we are told, too many fit parents are still denied contact/parenting time with their children. The knock on effect is that grandparents and members of the extended family are also denied contact with these children. That cannot be right. Also, it is likely with these latest DRS reforms that more of the cases that do proceed to court will be ones where there are high levels of conflict and will be the hardest cases to settle. Whether this legislative

---

[xx] Edward Timpson MP, Parliamentary Under Secretary of State for Children and Families. Letter to the Rt. Hon Alan Beith MP – 1 November 2012.

reform makes any difference either in practice or for the better remains to be seen, but the Government's position is very clear – it is trying to convey a strong message about a parent's ongoing involvement with the children post-separation and divorce hence the following statement, 'It is vital that both mothers and fathers feel confident that the court will consider fully the benefits of their involvement. We believe that the absence of an explicit reference to this consideration in the Children Act 1989 has contributed to a perception that the law does not fully recognise the important role that both parents can play in a child's life. We remain convinced that a change to the law is needed to help restore confidence in the family court system.'[284]

It may well be that in the future directing a recalcitrant parent to the new legislation may have a positive effect and encourage settlement, but so much is down to the parties themselves and their 'mindset'. Forms of early intervention to keep parties out of the court system are recommended, but much depends upon resources, and again the parties themselves.

A look at what happens in another jurisdiction...

Across various States of the USA there are schemes to ensure that parents and children remain in contact post-separation and these were implemented years ago. In Florida, for example, there is an early intervention model which works on a three stage non-court process:

- Court issued information is given to the parties at the moment proceedings are issued. They are provided with a video focusing on what is best for the child and a leaflet setting out the court's expectations and guidelines on proper parenting after separation. Early Interventions hinges upon giving parents guidance before the case, on how much contact there should be and leads to the development of parenting plans which would set out norms of contact as a framework for negotiation.
- Parent education. A parent orientation class for potential litigants is the next stage.
- Contact-focused mediation. One-off mediation for those still struggling to agree which is compulsory. The compulsory mediation requirement has a direct bearing on cases settling.

So what happens to ensure that the safety of the child is addressed? When an application is made the case is immediately assessed to ascertain whether there are any concerns. If there are it will be taken out of the non-court process and placed into the court process. Because many more cases are kept out of court, the court's time is freed up and valuable judicial input can be given to the more urgent cases. In Florida they have trained court managers to assess the cases when they come in to recognize a case that needs to be fast-tracked in this way.

---

[284] Ibid.

Without knowing what contact arrangement is likely to be in the child's interests for various categories of case, it is not possible to advise parents in advance how much contact they should allow. Parenting plans are open to infinite variation depending upon the facts of the case and deal with the problem that 'every case is different.' By reviewing the information given to them, attending the parent education and resorting to mediation if necessary, parents can design a parenting plan which is in the best interests of the child.

If the court's expectations can be conveyed in advance that creates predictability. Under our current legal process parties do not have a clear indication of what level of contact the court expects them to agree until they are well entrenched in the proceedings. I have dealt with cases where no amount of pleading from one party to the other to reach an agreement has worked, but where the judge has intervened and clearly directed that he will make a certain order if the parties do not agree, and by that direction he has promoted agreement. It is unfortunate that his intervention could not be earlier but that is down to the current process, not the judge. If we had judicially led/backed time-linked guidelines setting out what sort of outcome is appropriate if the parties were to litigate, and which are communicated to the parties at the time the application to the court is made, that would focus the parents' minds.

Final thoughts

In the course of writing this third edition I have been struck by the number of Consultation papers produced, and the number of proposed reforms to family law, since the second edition was published in 2007. The cost of these Consultations is demanding on the already pressured public purse so it is to be hoped that there really is enough money left actually to implement those reforms which will be beneficial to parties with children who are going through a separation and/or divorce. The whole emphasis of the recommendations made by the Family Justice Review in its Final Report in November 2011 and the Government in its Response to the Final Report in February 2012, is that reforms must be introduced that enable people to resolve their disputes safely outside court wherever possible.

I am all in favour of putting a system in place which keeps as many cases out of court as possible because a court order imposed upon the parties can never be a substitute for a fair and agreed arrangement between two parents genuinely acting in their child's interests. Parties need to remember that when they proceed to court they surrender their parental powers to the court when they ask the court to decide what is in the best interest of their child. But this means that any 'out of court' system must deliver a solution acceptable to both parents and in the best interests of the children otherwise it simply will not work.

The problem with introducing any form of reform is that it is unrealistic to expect that it will wipe away completely all the problems and this is only too true when it comes to family law. There are just too many 'what ifs?' and 'buts' and nuances to every case to be able to achieve that. It would be naïve and unreasonable to expect that everything will be resolved simply by reforming the family justice system. This is a highly emotive and contentious area and I do not believe that any Government would be able to introduce legislation which will deal with every single contentious point that could possibly arise. The fact is that although cases have similar scenarios and characteristics, ultimately every case is different and although much can be achieved by way of reform, a good deal depends upon the parties themselves, their mindset and the circumstances of the case. How much do they want to resolve the issue? How far are they prepared to compromise their wishes for the sake of the children? What are the issues in the case? Has there been domestic violence or abuse? What is the background of the parties and the framework against which the case is set? And sadly there will always be those parents who, despite what measures are introduced, will do their utmost to flout court orders and attempts to enforce them.

Moreover there might be proposed reform which will please one sector of society and displease another. This is no more apparent than with the Government's plans to legislate for a legal presumption in favour of shared parenting. It simply is not possible to please all of the people all of the time, but that does not mean we should stop trying. Healthy debate is necessary to make progress and a fear of being criticized for speaking out, as many of us have been, is not a reason for keeping silent. It is a shame that some worthy organizations are so entrenched in their 'father versus mother' positions. They should be working together for the common good not trying to score points off one another.

For fathers it is not a question of taking the children away from their mothers, but about giving loving, caring and responsible fathers a proper chance to be as involved as possible with their children where they are genuinely devoted and committed to them. In Chapter 1 I referred to the case of the father who committed suicide by setting fire to himself. He had not seen his daughter for nearly two years and she had not even reached the age of three. According to his mother the legal system let him down and he lost all hope. Essentially, of course, it was his ex-partner who prevented contact taking place but the legal system allowed that to happen.

A short while ago somebody asked me, 'You've written a book called *Fathers Matter*, so does that mean you think mothers don't?' An interesting question I thought bearing in mind I am female. My response was, 'Yes, of course they do. Only *I* believe that children matter more, and fathers matter *too*.'

Appendix
Some useful contacts and addresses

ADR Group
Head Office
ADR Group
Grove House
Grove Road
Redland, Bristol
BS6 6UN
Tel: (+44) (0) 117 946 7180
Fax: (+44) (0) 117 946 7181

London Office
ADR Group
180 Fleet Street
London
EC4A 2HG
Tel: (+44) (0) 845 539 38 37
Email: info@adrgroup.co.uk
www.adrgroup.co.uk

Catholic Marriage Advisory Council
Clitheroe House
1 Blythe Mews
Blythe Road
London
W14 0NW
Tel: (+44) (0) 20 7371 1341
Email: info@marriagecare.org.uk

Child Abduction Unit
81 Chancery Lane
London
WC2A 1DD
Tel enquiries: (+44) (0) 20 7911 7127
Fax: (+44) (0) 20 7911 7105
E-mail: enquiries@offsol.gsi.gov.uk

Children & Family Court Advisory & Support Service (CAFCASS)
CAFCASS Headquarters
8th Floor
Wyndham House
189 Marsh Wall
London
E14 9SH
Tel: (+44) 20 7510 7000
Fax: (+44) 20 7510 7001
Email: webenquiries@cafcass.gov.uk
www.cafcass.gov.uk
www.cafcass.gov.uk/cafcasscymru

CAFCASS legal
Details as above.

Child Maintenance Options
www.cmoptions.org

The Collaborative Family Law Group (part of Resolution)
PO Box 302
Orpington
Kent
BR8 QX
Tel: (+44) (0) 1689 820 272
www.collablaw.org.uk

The College of Mediators
3rd Floor, Alexander House
Telephone Avenue, Bristol
BS1 4BS
Tel: (+44) (0) 845 65 85 258
Email: admin@collegeofmediators.co.uk
www.collegeofmediators.co.uk

The Department for Education
Castle View House
East Lane
Runcorn
Cheshire
WA7 2GJ
Tel: (+44) (0) 370 000 2288
Fax: (+44) (0) 1928 738248
www.education.gov.uk

Family Matters Scotland
Provides information booklets on family
law and young people in Scotland
Tel: (+44) (0) 131 244 3581
www.scotland.gov.uk/familylaw

Family Mediation Association
Glenfinnan Suite
Braeview House
9/11 Braeview Place
East Kilbride
G74 3XH
Tel: (+44) (0) 1355 244 594
Email: info@thefma.co.uk
www.thefma.co.uk

Family Mediation Council
PO Box 593
Exeter
EX1 9HG
Email:
info@familymediationcouncil.org.uk
www.familymediationcouncil.org.uk

Foreign & Commonwealth Office
King Charles Street
London
SW1A 2AH
Tel: (+44) (0) 20 7008 1500
http://www.fco.gov.uk/en/

Institute of Family Law Arbitrators
www.ifla.org.uk

Institute of Family Therapy
24-32 Stephenson Way
London
NW1 2HX
Tel: (+44) (0) 207 391 9150
Fax: (+44) (0) 207 391 9169
www.ift.org.uk

International Social Services
Cranmer House
39 Brixton Road
London
SW9 6DD
Tel: (+44) (0) 20 7735 8941
(if the child is abducted abroad they can
make enquiries about his/her
whereabouts)

Jewish Marriage Council
Head Office
23 Ravenshurst Avenue
London
NW4 4EE
Tel: (+44) (0) 20 8203 6311
Fax: (+44) (0) 20 8203 8727
Email: info@jmc-uk.org
www.jmc-uk.org

The Law Society
Law Society Hall
113 Chancery Lane
London
WC2A 1PL
Tel: (+44) (0) 20 7242 1222
Fax: (+44) (0) 20 7831 0344
Email: info.services@lawsociety.org.uk
www.lawsociety.org.uk

Office for the Supervision of Solicitors
Victoria Court
8 Dormer Place
Royal Leamington Spa
Warwickshire
CV32 5AE
Tel (+44) (0) 845 608 6565
www.oss.lawsociety.org.uk

Law Society Mediation
www.lawsociety.approved.com/Family_
Mediation.aspx

Legal Assistance
National Association of Citizens Advice
Bureau (CAB)s
www.nacab.org.uk
www.adviceguide.org.uk

Law Centres Federation
www.lawcentres.org.uk
Federation of Independent Advice
Centres
www.fiac.org.uk

Legal Services Commission
Children & Family Services Division
4th Floor, 12 Roger Street
London
WC1N 2JL
Tel: (+44) (0) 20 77591132
Email family@legalservices.gov.uk
(Community legal service direct
(+44) (0) 845 345 4345)

Ministry of Justice
102 Petty France
London
SW1H 9AJ
United Kingdom
Tel: +44 (0) 20 3334 3555
Fax: +44 (0)870 761 7753
www.justice.gov.uk

**The National Association of Child
Contact Centres (NACC)**
Minerva House
Spaniel Row
Nottingham
NG1 6EP
Tel: (+44) (0) 845 4500 280
(Information line Mon-Fri 9.30am-
4.30pm)
Email: contact@naccc.org.uk
www.naccc.org.uk

National Family Mediation
Margaret Jackson Centre
4 Barnfield Hill
Exeter
Devon
EX1 1SR
Tel: (+44) (0) 300 4000 636
Fax: (+44) (0) 1392 271945
Email: enquiries@nfm.org.uk
www.nfm.org.uk

**The National Family and Parenting
Institute**
430 Highgate Studios
53-57 Highgate Road
London
NW5 1TL
Tel: (+44) (0) 20 7424 3460
Fax: (+44) (0) 20 7485 3590
Email: info@nfpi.org
www.nfpi.org

The National Youth Advocacy Service (NYAS)
99-105 Argyle Street
Birkenhead
Wirral
Merseyside
CH41 6AD
Tel: (+44) 151 649 8700
Fax: (+44) 151 649 8701
Email: help@nyas.net
www.nyas.net

Online Mediation Directory
www.civilmediation.justice.gov.uk

Principal Registry of the Family Division
The Divorce Registry
First Avenue House
42-49 High Holborn
London
WC1V 6NP
Tel: (+44) (0) 20 79476000
http://www.justice.gov.uk/courts/rcj-rolls-building/principal-registry

Relate
Tel: (+44) (0) 300 100 1234
www.relate.org.uk

Resolution (formerly SFLA)
PO Box 302
Orpington
Kent
BR6 8QX
Tel: (+44) (0) 1689 820 272
Fax: (+44) (0) 1689 896 972
Email: info@resolution.org.uk
www.resolution.org.uk
www.resolution.org.uk/advice_centre

Reunite
National Council for Abducted Children
PO Box 7124
Leicester
LE1 7XX
Tel: (+44) (0) 116 2556 234
Email: reunite@dircon.co.uk

Royal Courts of Justice (High Court)
Strand
London
WC2A 2LL
Tel: (+44) (0) 20 79476000

Notes

Fathers Matter: The essential guide to contact on separation and divorce

Notes

Fathers Matter: The essential guide to contact on separation and divorce